HOW TO PLAN, DEVELOP & USE INFORMATION SYSTEMS

A Guide to Human Qualities and Productivity

Hein van Steenis

DH

DORSET HOUSE PUBLISHING
353 West 12th St., New York, NY 10014

Library of Congress Cataloging-in-Publication Data

Steenis, Hein van.
How to plan, develop & use information systems : a guide to human qualities and productivity / by Hein van Steenis.
p. cm.
Includes bibliographical references.
ISBN 0-932633-12-9 : $23.50
1. System design. 2. Electronic data processing. I. Title.
II. Title: How to plan, develop, and use information systems.
QA76.9.S88S74 1990
004.2'1—dc20 89-83373
CIP

Cover Design and Illustrations: Jeff Faville, Faville Graphics
Art in {2.14}: Ted Goff

 Published by Dorset House Publishing Co., Inc., 353 West 12th Street, New York, NY 10014.

Distributed in the United Kingdom, Ireland, Europe, and Africa by John Wiley & Sons Ltd., Chichester, Sussex, England.

Printed in the United States of America

Library of Congress Catalog Card Number 89-83373
ISBN: 0-932633-12-9

This book is dedicated to all those persons,
including my wife, Hans,
who have made IBM what it has been for me.

Perhaps nothing is entirely true, and not even that.
—Multatuli, *Ideeën* [167]

Imagination is more important than knowledge.
—A. Einstein

Our risk is not the advent of superintelligent
computers, but of subintelligent human beings.
—H.L. Dreyfus, *What Computers Can't Do* [49]

For the real question is whether a "brighter future"
is really always so distant.
What if, on the contrary, it has been here
for a long time already, and only our own blindness
and weakness has prevented us from seeing it
around us and within us,
and kept us from developing it.
—V. Havel [87]

Disclaimer

Acknowledgments

This book could be written only with the work of many others. I have built on their work rather than reinvent wheels, referencing my source in all cases. I offer my sincere apologies to authors if I have unintentionally lost track of the source or have not referenced the original source. I have tried to preserve the wisdom of many authors by including quotations, and I have tried to stimulate readers to pursue additional sources through quotations and references to other writings.

Special thanks to Mieke de Ridder and other librarians for their assistance in finding books. Many thanks also to Piet Patings for programs used to write this book.

This book would never have been written without my first having been taught. I look back with great pleasure to courses by Gene Ciliberti, Dave Marshall, Gerry Reid, Jeff Salzman, Tom Woods, and very many others. I thank IBM for making their courses available to me.

My interest in human factors was whetted twenty-five years ago by Dick Hirsch and his co-workers, and I continue to treasure our contact. A paper by Morris Dean was the starting point for my interest in psychology. Both Dick and Morris have been instrumental in turning my interest from engineering to the human being at work.

This book could not have been completed without friends and colleagues who reviewed versions of the manuscript. With pleasure I acknowledge the contributions of Otto Boelens, Walter Croes, Freddie Lange, Rolf Moerman, Cees van der Oord, Zus Perelaër-Parfumeur, and Ton Snaterse. Otto Boelens, Len Brown, Jan de Lint, Rolf Moerman, Adri van Praag, and Jeanette Quast reviewed the first complete draft. Many indispensable contributions were made by Dave le Fort who edited the entire text from the beginning. Extensive further editing by Harriet Serenkin and Janice Wormington (Dorset House) has produced the text that you can now read.

Last, but not least, I want to acknowledge the contributions of my wife, Hans Perelaër, during the writing of this book. Studying and writing often occupied my mind. She endured it all with good humor, being a candid friend and wife.

Thanks to all of you!

Preface

After working for almost thirty years with IBM International Operations in Holland, I took the opportunity for early retirement to write this book. During those years, it became increasingly clear that technically we can produce almost any computer system, and we are solving the problem of doing it economically on a large scale. The remaining problem is adapting computers to people—this requires a new attitude toward people and special insights into their needs and capabilities.

This book is the deposit of my experiences, the books I've read, the discussions I've had, and the courses I've followed and taught during the last fifteen years. Its purpose is to share the insights I've gained, to create a better awareness of the person in automation land. I have tried to make it practical and useful on a general level.

This is not a theoretical book: It is a practical guide to how to make computers work for people, rather than make people adapt to computers. To adapt computers to all people is much more than designing a human-machine interface, only one of the many human tasks in planning, developing, and using computers.

My purpose here is to describe all the tasks that are involved in making computers more people-friendly. I want to make you aware of how people react to computers and the inevitable changes that accompany them, and how you can apply this awareness to plan, design, and use information systems in a better way. Because information processing is the work of people with people for other people, you need to understand people to make computerization a success.

The book covers a wide range of subjects, so specialists in one area may find useful material from other areas; it is intended to supplement more technical books on specific computer topics.

I have tried to concentrate on general matters and to provide a framework, rather than present specific recipes or today's fashion. In certain cases, I've provided a historical context to show trends. References throughout the text point to the writings of others for additional reading. Review questions and exercises at the end of each chapter will stimulate you to form your own opinion.

I wish I knew the secret and the recipes to make your automation projects a success, but human situations are just not that simple. All I can do is to increase your awareness and appreciation of human qualities. This will help you to achieve better quality when planning, developing, and using information systems.

Amstelveen, The Netherlands H.vS.
November 1989

Contents

Introduction

...we have developed a sense of the value of technology
and of a scientific approach to it,
but we have meanwhile taken people for granted.
—W. Ouchi, *Theory Z* [155]

This book is a practical guide to best utilizing the human element in planning, developing, and using information systems. It is a guided tour of the human areas in computer land, focusing on the importance of adapting computers to people and of resolving computer problems at the human, rather than the technological, level.

The book introduces the ISVIC procedure (Investigating, Structuring, Verifying, Implementing, Checking) as a means to analyze and synthesize complex subjects, and it examines human qualities so we can better understand how to adapt computers to people. A central theme is how to achieve a high level of quality by providing service to customers.

Intended Audience

The topics and general level of discussion are intended for both developers and users, managers and workers, and novices and experts alike, for they all must work together to make information processing a success.

The book is also designed as a textbook for students at all levels, who want to learn about the important social and psychological aspects of information processing.

Readers can select what they need from the wealth of material presented, and can continue to select topics as their jobs or interests change.

Viewpoint, Scope, and Content

No matter how it looks at first, it's always a people problem.
—G. Weinberg, *The Secrets of Consulting* [206]

While writing this book, I was asked by some people whether there is a human side to computers. This book is my attempt to answer that question. It takes the viewpoint that there are indeed many sides because information processing is the work of people for people.

Computers are what the developers and users make of them. In order to achieve their maximum potential, we must adapt computers to people and to our society. To do this requires an understanding of people and their situation. Any problems associated with computers must be solved at the human, rather than the technological, level. To cure causes instead of treating symptoms, everyone must be motivated to orient his or her work toward people. That's what this book is about.

The book is divided into this introduction, four parts, appendices, glossary, and bibliography. Part I introduces the topic of people and computers and describes an invaluable procedure used throughout the book for analyzing and synthesizing complex subjects. The next chapter deals with human qualities and mind mechanisms that influence people's behavior so we can devise solutions that will remove human bottlenecks in information processing. Suggestions for making best use of these mechanisms are in the appendices. This discussion is followed by considering the differences between humans and machines so that tasks will be apportioned in information systems in the best way.

Part II consists of two chapters, which detail the plans, procedures, and communication necessary to develop and use information systems.

Part III focuses on that perhaps most vital human need: communication. Each of the four chapters in this part deals with different aspects of people's communication, first between themselves (specifically how to say what you intend to do, and to do what you said), and then with the computer (examining the demands for the human-machine interface). A chapter on documentation explains its importance in planning, developing, and using computers, followed by a discussion of the need for training people so they have the proper knowledge, skills, and attitudes to work effectively with computers.

Part IV returns to consideration of people, in how to organize and manage them to assure high-quality products and systems. I stress the need to provide service to customers and how to set up an organization for people to provide that service. This part concludes with a discussion of managing and being managed, of how people function in an organization, and of the personal attitudes needed to achieve the goals for successful introduction of information systems into an organization. Included is an extensive list of some two hundred books and articles, as well as a glossary of terms used. Throughout the text, numbers in brackets refer to references in the Bibliography, and numbers in braces refer to a particular section of the book.

Using This Book

> A classification is a repertory of weapons for attack upon the future and the unknown.
>
> —J. Dewey, *Reconstruction in Philosophy,* quoted in [65]

To get the most out of this book, first become familiar with its structure, by browsing through the table of contents and the text. Then consider how the book can be useful to you:

- Why do you want to read a chapter?
- What specifically do you want to get out of it?
- Whom does the topic apply to?
- Where can you apply the topic?
- When can you apply the topic?
- How can you apply the topic?

After reading a chapter, think about the review questions and exercises at the end. This will help you to increase your understanding and stimulate you to form your own opinions, even if you don't understand all the details. Your answers will often depend upon the context of your particular situation.

This book is structured so you can read it from front to back. A first-pass reading strategy can be to read Part I first, glance through Parts II and III to get an overview of the material, read all of Part IV, and skim the Appendices.

Three Quality Goals for Computerization

> It is always better to say right out what you think without trying to prove anything much: for all our proofs are only variations of our opinions, and the contrary-minded listen neither to one nor the other.
>
> —J. von Goethe, quoted in [65]

Computers are an economic means for mankind. To optimize their usefulness, we must adapt them to people by realizing the following three quality goals:

1. Make information systems attractive by optimizing the effectiveness, efficiency, and well-being of people at the physical, psychological, and social levels. Use computers to help people do a better job, not to displace them.
2. Design information systems to do their work at minimum cost, keeping in mind two factors:
   - Efficiency and effectiveness are goals for both people and machines.
   - Flexibility is needed to maintain efficiency and effectiveness.
3. Discuss the financial and social implications of introducing computers with all people affected, or their representatives, before making final decisions.

We need much human communication to realize these three quality goals. What actions and interactions are needed, and how to accomplish them, is what this book is about.

Review Questions

1. Do you basically agree with the need for all three goals?
   - What would you add, change, or omit?
   - How realistic are the goals?
   - How strong is the need for the goals?
2. Computers often replace some people. What is your view of the quantity and quality of jobs lost and jobs created by automation? Argue why you think that
   - Computerization itself is good, bad, or neither
   - Spread of computers can or cannot be stopped
   - Computerization is desirable or undesirable
3. Neither zero percent nor one hundred percent automation is desirable.
   - What do you consider a desirable intermediate range? Why?
   - What factors influence an actual percentage? Why?

Part 1

INTRODUCING PEOPLE AND COMPUTERS

Chapter 1. Planning Information Systems

Argues why information systems need planning • Explains how to plan such systems with models and how to analyze the associated complex subjects with the ISVIC procedure.

Chapter 2. Understanding Human Behavior and the Mind

Discusses options in and uncertainties of the human environment • Describes mechanisms of the mind important to automation, divided into individual and interpersonal mechanisms.

Chapter 3. Human-Machine Considerations

Elaborates on differences between people and machines • Discusses how to split tasks between people and computers • Illustrates practical problems in doing so with an example involving hospital patients' files.

1

PLANNING INFORMATION SYSTEMS

Take care of the sense,
and the sounds will take care of themselves.
—L. Carroll, *Alice's Adventures in Wonderland* [32]

As computers become faster and drop in price by about fifty percent every three years, their popularity continues to increase. Their basic cost is so low and their power so great that their use will undoubtedly continue to spread even faster. From originally serving as number crunchers only for the technical few, computers have grown into an information and communication facility for almost everyone. Whatever we do and wherever we go, we find computers checking our work, helping us shop, and organizing our lives. We are rapidly changing from an industrial society to an information society, in which information is a prime resource.

Computers can save time, increase efficiency, and give valuable information about organizations and their customers. But they can also prove disastrous when they fail. "Computer error" is often mentioned as the reason for a minor disaster, but in all instances of computer failure, people are the victims as well as the culprits. People, perhaps unknowingly, have made wrong decisions at some stage in the system's development, often at an early stage.

The design and introduction of computer systems is a complex task, with many pitfalls. Because computers are being used in more and more critical ways, planning them right from the beginning is more important than ever. And that's what this book is about.

Specifically, this book is intended as a practical guide to the human element in planning, designing, and using computer information systems. It covers all activities involved in their development—from modeling, managing, and programming to documenting, training, and communicating. Its focus is on *people* and how they can work together to make computerization a success. In that sense, this book presents a psychology of automation.

In this chapter, I define what I mean by information systems: I discuss their complexities, and describe how we can use models to plan them. I then introduce a procedure for structuring a complex system or subject into its components in order to improve our understanding of it.

1.1 What Is an Information System?

In this book, I am concerned with computerization and information systems, which are comprised of computers and people for the purpose of providing information. Contrast this with automation and automated systems, which consist of computers only to perform physical actions (such as assembling parts on an assembly line or controlling a refinery).

Simply stated, *computerization* means that we have a computer carry out some tasks previously done by people. It can also mean the addition of computer tasks as new opportunities are revealed, as well as new human tasks (for example, a clerk must now enter the data that is processed by the computer).

Data are simply facts from the real world, such as a person's name, address, credit card number, and details about that person's order. A *transaction* (short for "transmit action") stores the data in a database along with similar data about many other people. The more data a database contains, the more useful it is.

The computer, by means of an information system, associates meaning to the digits and letters entered and converts the data into information about the customer and the order. In short, an information system processes information for people—users, customers, and others—and so the information system must structure and arrange the data to fit the information needs of them all. Some typical examples of people and their information needs are these:

- Telephone order takers who must verify the availability of items
- Customers who need an invoice with their order
- Tax inspectors who must have a summary of taxes paid and received
- Warehouse managers who want an inventory report
- Store owners who must know what stock needs replenishing
- Marketing people who desire customer profiles for a new campaign
- Planners who want historical information for developing projections

As shown in Figure 1-1, an information system consists of *hardware, software,* and *otherware.*

Hardware includes the physical computer, terminals, printers, and other parts that you can feel and see. Development of hardware is not discussed in this book; refer to Kidder [109] for a description of computer development. The computer that I'll use in my examples in this book can handle several users at a time, each of whom can work with the computer as if it were his or her own using a video display terminal (VDT). Most VDT and other hardware functions are controlled by software.

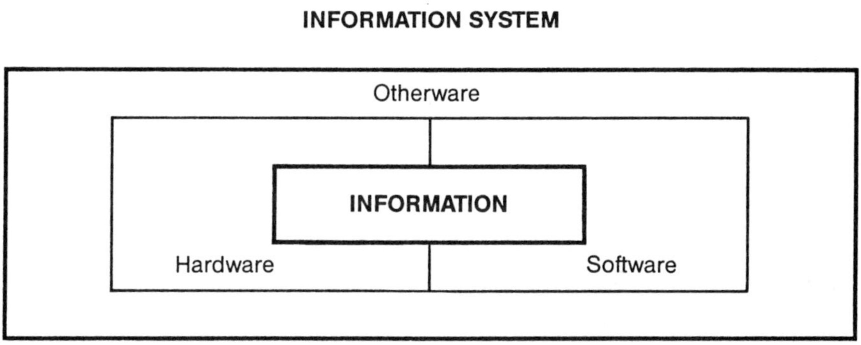

Figure 1-1. Information system = hardware + software + otherware.

Software is the computer programs, the instructions that control the hardware. Software today consists of thousands of programs, each containing several hundred instructions. Special software, called the *operating system,* is the house master of the computer. It maintains law and order among programs and provides services to other programs. An operating system may well contain ten million instructions and require several thousands of man-years to develop. Another form of software is *system programs,* used by professionals to develop application programs for inventory control, word processing, reporting, and so on. *Application programs* are user procedures cast in software.

The basic design of an information system is done through software. Software is the essence of an information system and information its subject. (Chapter 4 deals with software development in detail.)

Otherware is everything and everyone else needed in an information system. Otherware includes the important human organization working with the hardware and software, specifically:

- Objectives, the system's goals
- Owner, the person responsible for the system's use
- Official users, people authorized to work with the system
- Organization, the tasks and responsibilities of the people involved with the information system
- Operational procedures, the instructions for working with the system

- Operations and support, the groups that run the computer system and help its users
- Offices, the work areas and facilities
- Objects, the materials and supplies needed for working with the system
- Operation, all actions needed to initiate and use the system

The design of the otherware must properly complement that of the hardware and software. Because it involves the important human organization, otherware, by my estimation, typically accounts for about two-thirds of an information system's life cycle cost. (Chapter 5 is devoted to otherware development.)

To understand the basics of an information system, consider the six types of information that the system can provide:

- Operational information, for people to perform the routine work in an organization
- Control information, for key users to verify that the operational information is correct
- Management information, for managers to understand how the information system operates
- Decision support information, for the user staff to propose changes to the organization and the information system
- External information, about transactions of the information system, for customers and others outside the organization
- Informal information, for any additional communication between people inside the organization

Information processing is the act of selecting and arranging information in a form that can be used by people. There are four basic types of information processing:

1. Transaction processing, to bring data and their changed values into the system for updating computer data (for example, details about your order or a change to your flight reservation)

2. Output processing, to provide information to people both inside and outside the organization (for example, your invoice or your airline ticket)

3. Decision information processing, to gather statistical information about what is going on inside the information system itself (for example, order details or flight statistics)
4. Informal information processing, to help people do their work (for instance, an electronic message for someone traveling)

1.2 Why Must We Plan Information Systems?

Computers are unique in that we can use them for almost anything. However, we must plan them properly to assure they do the right things. If we can make a model of what we want computers to do, we can implement that model in software and otherware, using appropriate hardware. The basis for success of an information system is careful *planning,* through design of the overall model of what we want the information system to do.

The software builds a representation of the real world in the computer, which uses this representation of facts and events to simulate part of a real-world process. Users work with this simulation as if it were the real thing. In this way, hardware and software can, for example, replace ledger, order, and inventory books.

In only a few decades, software has grown into an amazing collection of work. In all practicality, software has now reached a level of complexity that is impossible for users to comprehend in every detail. Its complexity is sometimes overwhelming even for programmers because programs and their values play hide-and-seek in complicated structures and superstructures. As a general rule, software complexity is roughly proportional to the square of the number of component elements. This is called the *combinatorial explosion.* Complexity in a specific model also depends upon how well interdependencies are contained in each component element. The better we can isolate relations within an element, the better we succeed in reducing the complexity of a model; refer to Aron [7, 8] and Yourdon and Constantine [217].

The purpose of modeling is to structure a subject into elements that can be considered separately. Structured analysis is a set of guidelines for breaking down a complex activity or subject into a structure of less complex steps or parts, as shown in Figure 1-2. Its goal is to contain dependencies within each element so we can treat it in isolation. A simpler structure improves understanding, as well as simplifies design, implementation, and testing. If done properly, structuring also eases the process of making changes later.

Figure 1-2(A) illustrates a *sequential model* of three steps to update a customer record, and Figure 1-2(B) illustrates a *parallel model* of how purchase order information consists of four information units.

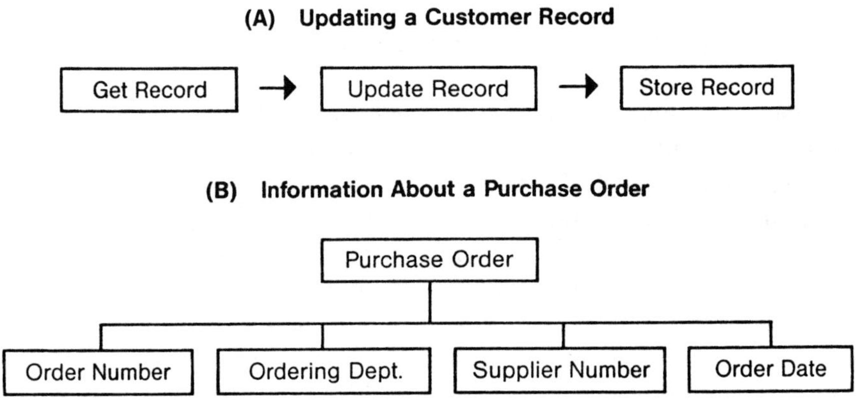

Figure 1-2. Examples of structuring a subject to break down its complexity.

In the real world, of course, activities and subjects are much more complex than are these examples, making it difficult to analyze and verify the designs. Nevertheless, developers must analyze all procedures to the smallest detail before programming can start.* And they must consider all of the related problems, including the following:

- When designing a system, developers are often not made aware of all relevant conditions because people who perform the task often do it intuitively. How, then, can developers make all conditions of an organizational process explicit?

  To model a real-world process, we must make visible or explicit much of what we consider as being self-evident or implicit. Because a computer can only work from explicit instruc-

*Structured programming, which is a valuable set of techniques and guidelines for writing programs in a standardized, organized way, can make programs easier for technical people to understand, check, and change. However, this method does not prevent errors or inconsistencies in the model analysis that precedes programming.

tions, we must completely detail a process before we can automate it.

- Making an apparently small change in one program is expensive because of the many interactions with other programs. How can the programs be designed to be independent from the beginning?
- Change is a dominant characteristic of the course of business in organizations today. How can developers design software to simplify later modifications?

The only answer to all these questions is, by extensive and careful planning. Developers must start every project from a sound master plan. But that is easier said than done. The rule in computerization is that nothing is ever right automatically and nothing ever happens of itself. Consider the simple task of handling a date by computers. Many programs use only the last two digits of the year, for example, 89 for 1989. This will cause many problems in the year 2000 because 00 wasn't planned for. We must plan everything because otherwise we will experience Murphy's Law: If something can go wrong, it will, and at the most inconvenient time.

To simplify planning, we work with many models that each give a partial view of the system. We can make general high-level and detailed low-level models and models for specific parts of the system. There are, however, at least three problems associated with designing a complex system by "translating" it into models:

1. We cannot comprehend both the general framework and the details of a complex system at the same time. We can only understand views that deal with a specific aspect at a certain level of detail.

2. Because so many views are possible, we have difficulty selecting the proper ones for a particular situation. To select the right view, we must understand what is important for that situation and what is irrelevant. The view we select must also facilitate the discussion with users and the implementation in software.

3. Each developer has only a partial view. How, then, can we be certain that all views work in harmony and cover everything? Moreover, if technical people can barely comprehend software, how can users? It is not enough to say that we must plan information sys-

tems right from the beginning. Developers must also consider how to plan software so users can understand its design.

The solution to these three problems is modeling from human points of view, using elements that are familiar to all people involved—developers, users, and others—as I'll discuss below.

1.3 Working With Models

> If one picture is worth a thousand words, then one model is worth a thousand pictures.
>
> —D. Hunt and E. Sullivan,
> *Between Psychology and Education* [94]

Writers of books try to deal with complexity within each chapter, section, and paragraph by selecting material and presenting it in a logical order. Otherwise, if the book has a poor structure, you will have difficulty understanding and using it. Similarly, the elements of information systems must be organized in a natural way, with familiar relationships.

A model indicates relationships by exposing the nature and the structure of what is being modeled. We use many different models for an information system. *Process models* describe activities like those in Figure 1-2(A), and *data models* describe information like that in Figure 1-2(B). A description with diagrams is a *conceptual model,* used to communicate between people. An organization chart is an *organizational model.* A spreadsheet is an *arithmetic model* used to make a *financial model.* A plan is a model of the future. Such models can be combined into a supermodel. (See {1.4} for examples of some simple models.)

To have a successful model, first we must define the boundaries of what is going to be structured. Everything cannot be included. Because of the combinatorial explosion, a simpler structure will result when we restrict the view or the domain of the model. We must also restrict certain aspects based on their importance to the understanding of the problem. For example, we may consider only the monetary value of things, not their color or size. Making and keeping it simple for users, customers, and others is the key to successful computerization.

There are many ways to structure real-world processes and things. Indeed, analysts often intuitively select a view for structuring. Criteria for choosing a view are different for different purposes: clarity and meaningfulness for developers and users in one case, for instance, or ease of implementation and modification for the computer in another. Top-down structuring is often a preferred modeling method, because it establishes relationships before determining the elements. In top-down structuring, you focus on the overall view before worrying about the details. By contrast, bottom-up structuring is preferred when different structures share common elements. Both top-down and bottom-up structuring lead to hierarchical structures.

1.4 Modeling Examples

This section presents some simple examples of modeling a process, text, data, and knowledge, to illustrate model structures.

STRUCTURING A PROCESS

A process consists of actions that belong together. In a process model, major actions are broken down into simpler actions. For example, take the process of someone's buying a theater ticket, illustrated as hierarchical levels in Figure 1-3. In this model, note that only the first-level item "Pay for ticket" is broken down into five second-level items and that the first of these, "Reach for money," is further decomposed into three third-level items.

Go to the box office
Decide on type of ticket
Pay for ticket
  —Reach for money
    —Put hand in pocket
    —Grab money
    —Take hand out of pocket
  —Select money
  —Hand the money selected
  —Get the change, if any
  —Put money back in pocket
Take ticket
Return

Figure 1-3. Process model of buying a theater ticket.

A problem exists in designing such explicit models. Even the simple task of buying a theater ticket involves many options and uncertainties. Money in "Grab money" can be in the form of loose coins in a pocket, paper bills, a check, a voucher, a discount coupon, and so on. What happens if the ticket buyer has no money, if the correct change is not available, or if he changes his mind? People handle such complexity and options intuitively, but computers need to be told every minute detail, including all such options and exceptions.

STRUCTURING TEXT

Text can be structured in various ways. Figure 1-4 shows a generic book model, with only the first-level "Body of the book" expanded. Although there can be many chapters in the book, I include only one element for this item; an asterisk indicates that the element may occur several times. Each chapter has only one title but it can have many sections, each with one or more paragraphs. A sentence can contain many words but only one sentence ending. (Note that a sentence ending may consist of more than one character!!)

Title page
Table of contents
Body of the book
  —Chapter (*)
    —Chapter title
    —Section (*)
        Paragraph (*)
        —Paragraph beginning
        —Sentence (*)
          —Sentence beginning
          —Word (*)
          —Sentence ending
        —Paragraph ending
    —Summary
    —Review questions and exercises
Appendix
Index   (*) indicates multiple occurrences

Figure 1-4. Text example of a generic book structure.

Another, specific book model could list all chapters and sections, such as the table of contents for this book. An index is a model by subject, arranged in alphabetic sequence. The choice of model depends on what you want to use the model for and how you want to implement it in a computer.

STRUCTURING DATA

A data model is usually not a simple hierarchy like the book model. To illustrate this, consider the following example of data for a school, with these four basic ingredients: course, teacher, student, and classroom. These are very different ingredients, and their relationship is not linear. For example, a teacher has different students, and a student has different teachers.

To arrange these data in a single hierarchical structure, we must find a key element to put on top. As shown in Figure 1-5, I put "Course" at the top because it is an essential ingredient of a school. It consists of six second-level items. As before, the asterisk indicates that many students can register for a particular course.

```
Course
  —Course#
  —Title
  —Prerequisites
  —Teacher
    —Teacher#
    —Name
  —Student (*)
    —Student#
    —Name
    —Address
    —Grade
  —Classroom
    —Room#
    —Day of the week
    —Time                    (*) indicates multiple occurrences
```

Figure 1-5. Data example of school data in a single structure.

There are problems with this structure. Although you could store all of the school information in a single file, like cards in a filing box with one card for each course, the cards would have to be very big to contain all the information about the students for the course. Also, every time a student changed his or her address, you would have to check every card since the address could be on any card. Changing cards whenever a student moves may lead to inconsistencies between cards. In general, it is good practice to store data just once to avoid inconsistencies and to simplify revision.

The structure is also not clear because the elements are too different to be a single structure. Figure 1-6 shows the same data arranged this time in a fourfold structure, with four key elements and Course# as the joining element. Such a data structure would require four filing boxes, with one set of cards each.

Course —Course# —Title —Prerequisites	Teacher —Teacher# —Name —Course# (*)

Student
—Student#
—Name
—Address
—Course# (*)
	Classroom
	—Room#
	—Course# (*)
	  —Day of the week
	  —Time

Figure 1-6. Example of school data in a fourfold structure.

Intuitively, this looks better: The structures are smaller and easier to understand. This is important in situations when you must deal with hundreds of elements. If a student changes his or her address, you have to change it in one place only. But this structure also has its problems. If the course number changes, you must update many records in all four files.

What the school example illustrates is that structuring data for practical situations is extremely complex, making it very important to model all information elements before computerizing them. Such models are your plan for the future. When you plan the computerization of a warehouse, for example, you will need to consider in advance how it will connect to other warehouses, to a central distribution point, and to the head office. Since the information elements used in every location must match, you need to plan the entire system in models to avoid costly modifications later on. And you must include all computers in the organization, even personal computers. Otherwise you may not be able to connect them in the future.

There are many dilemmas in structuring data and few ideal solutions. Resolve some problems and you create others; that is the Law on Conservation of Problems. Structuring data for a data model and a physical database is a technical subject that is primarily relevant to those concerned with computer internals. For detailed examples, refer to Gane and Sarson

[68], Jackson [100, 101], Martin [122], Miller and Starr [134], Shneiderman [193], and Yourdon and Constantine [217].

STRUCTURING KNOWLEDGE

Knowledge, as used in the context of computers, comes in two major forms. *Declarative knowledge* describes the assertions you have about a situation: definitions, relations, and facts that you will use. *Procedural knowledge* describes the rules you will use with those assertions. A knowledge system uses reasoning, called inferencing, on assertions and rules to draw conclusions from a specific situation.

There are many ways to describe knowledge, one of which is to put it into the form of a model using rules. In the example of a rule below, the assertions concern a task that is explicit (that is, can be formally expressed) or not, and that is understood by people or not.

```
IF <Task = explicit> AND <Task = understood>
        THEN <Computerization = possible
ELSE <Computerization = not possible>
```

Figure 1-7. Example of a rule in a knowledge model.

You can use this knowledge model to infer whether you can automate a certain task (though as we'll see in {3.3}, this decision is much more involved).

The knowledge model can be structured in frames that contain components of knowledge. One frame can be used to determine whether a task is explicit or not, for example, and another to determine whether a task is understood or not. This way, one can develop a knowledge base that is comparable to a database. The advantage of knowledge systems over information systems is the ease of modifying assertions and rules instantly.

Besides process, text, data, and knowledge models, we can make models of virtually any subject. This book focuses on models that express the way people view things. We have many such models, ranging from global to very detailed. All scientific theories, for example, are a model of reality; refer to Knight's *Ordering the World* [111] for a history of classifying man.

1.5 Physical and Logical Aspects of Information Models

> And thus we distinguish on the one hand what is thought, and on the other what is seen. . .
>
> —Plato, *The Republic,* Book VII [164]

I repeat: The purpose of structuring a complex model is to understand it, to simplify its implementation, and to ease its revision. In order to computerize successfully, you must plan the structure of the models of your information system beforehand, so you can make future modifications in an orderly manner.

An information entity is an element of an information model. Examples of entities include a customer name, an invoice, and a signature. An entity has physical and logical aspects as well as relationships to other entities, as shown in Figure 1-8.

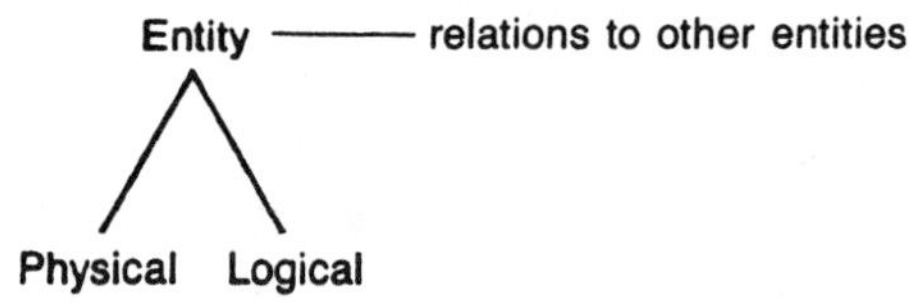

Figure 1-8. Physical and logical aspects of an entity.

In the examples in {1.4}, I have already touched on the two aspects of an entity: a physical aspect and a logical aspect. *Physical* denotes a material existence, and *logical* denotes the idea or meaning of the entity. A period "." is a physical, material example of a sentence ending, and "Sentence ending" is a logical meaning. A data record written on a disk is physical, and a data model is logical. *Context* is the relation of an entity to other entities. A word in Figure 1-4 relates to a sentence beginning, a sentence ending, or another word.

The advantages of the logical form of an entity are that it is generic, simpler, and less subject to change. The many possible physical embodiments have been removed. Concentrating on the logical view leaves you free to choose a physical implementation afterward. You can separate architectural analysis from implementation synthesis, worrying about only one thing at a time.

When you make a logical model, you must be careful not to include any physical elements. McMenamin and Palmer [129] explain the danger of leaving something physical in a logical model. This causes serious problems in implementation because a physical embodiment disguises true meaning and prevents another, perhaps better, implementation.

The logical form is best for developers making an analysis and for users verifying its correctness. Structuring something is only part of the problem. The major problem for developers is to make computers conform to user expectations. This requires an investigation of the user situation and verification by typical users of the resulting models.

1.6 ISVIC Procedure

> Don't bother about the apparent variety and richness of life: get down to the simple truth.
>
> —H. Kitto, *The Greeks* [110]

As I've said, modeling is a universal technique to break down a complex subject into elements that we can better understand. It is used not only in developing software but also in analyzing tasks and communications *before* expressing them in a physical form. Here are key requirements for an analysis procedure:

- Find the essence of things—their logical composition—so you can verify the model before putting it into a physical form.
- Develop a complete minimal model, so you can use it as an architectural foundation for developing a proper implementation. Forgetting essential elements will hinder making changes later. Adding nonessential elements, if nothing else, will cause unnecessary work.
- Find the optimal solution from among many technically good ones. (Of course, to do this, we must find out what users regard as important because they are the measure of all things in computerization.)

Most analysis methods offer a procedure to define a problem and to determine a corrective action; see, for example, Kepner and Tregoe [108]. What we need is a method to analyze an activity or subject for later implementation. The procedure that I will often use in this book is very general, and it can be used to develop software, to prepare a course, and to prepare a speech. I call it ISVIC, after the initials of its five steps:

- *Investigating:* to understand a subject and its human context completely and clearly. An architect, for example, analyzes what sort of house you want.
- *Structuring:* to structure the subject from a human point of view. The architect makes drawings of your desired house.
- *Verifying:* to assure that the structure is correct. The architect verifies that the design will deliver what you really want.
- *Implementing:* to build the structure. The builder erects your house from the drawings.
- *Checking:* to verify the implemented structure. You make a final inspection before accepting the house.

The first three steps constitute the *analysis* needed to design and verify the architecture as represented by a logical conceptual model. The last two steps form the *synthesis* to realize the model physically. ISVIC follows the problem solving plan described by Perkins [159]: finding relevant facts, defining the problem, considering solutions, selecting a solution, and getting it accepted. The five ISVIC steps are illustrated in Figure 1-9 and are discussed further below.

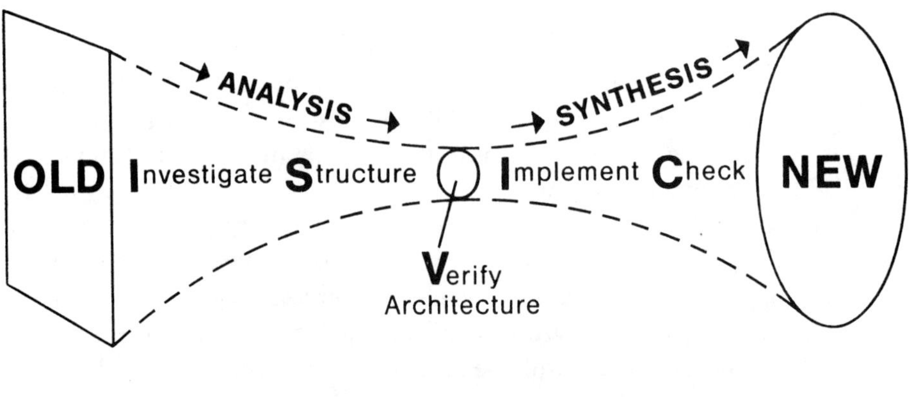

Figure 1-9. The five steps of the ISVIC procedure.

INVESTIGATING

When you structure a subject, the first step involves asking yourself seven questions (seven W's) to help you understand the subject and its human context:

- *Why* do you want to use the ISVIC procedure? Clarify the true goals that you want to achieve.
- *What* exactly do you want to analyze? What is the subject you are investigating? What are its elements? Concentrate on the real problem and ignore unrelated issues.
- *Who* are you planning for? Who are involved in decisions? Define clearly for whom you are conducting the investigation.
- *Whence* are you analyzing? Clarify your role and authority and the organizational context.
- *Where* will the implementation have to fit? Describe the organizational environment and possible roadblocks to its computerization.
- *When* will the implementation take place? Determine when you can start and when you must be ready.
- *HoW* will the implementation take place? After you have assessed the first six questions, you are ready to make some basic decisions about how to realize your structure. Consider what level of detail you require for verification, what alternatives you can use to implement it, and what roadblocks you may expect. These will affect how you will design the structure.

STRUCTURING

After the first step, you will have a clear picture of your purpose and the important human considerations. In this second step, you must analyze and structure or model your subject, working toward an essential architecture. The reason, as you'll recall, is to understand the complex subject, to simplify its implementation, and to ease the making of changes later. The details of how to structure are outside the scope of this book; intuitive notions about structuring are sufficient only for simple cases, so for more information, refer to Gane and Sarson [68] and Yourdon and Constantine [217].

VERIFYING

To close the analysis, you and others concerned must verify that the structure is complete and does not contain physical elements that may obscure true meaning. The result of this step—the logical model—is most easily verified by you and by others. You must correct any shortcomings in the model's structure before starting implementation.

IMPLEMENTING

You have already made some basic implementation decisions in step 1 in answering the "HoW" question. Depending upon the answers to that question, you can now implement the logical structure in a physical form. A proper structure and purpose will allow you to work rapidly.

CHECKING

Finally, you must check the implementation for five characteristics (five C's):

- *Clarity,* assuring the implementation is clear to everyone involved
- *Conciseness,* omitting all nonessential items in the implementation
- *Completeness,* including all essential items in a natural way
- *Courtesy,* showing respect for all people
- *Correctness,* being correct both in content and detail

I repeat that ISVIC is only a general procedure to help you think about the right things in the right sequence; it's not magic. Its goal is to investigate the human context and to develop a logical structure before you start to implement a solution. Verifying and checking will cause many iterations while using ISVIC. The structure must use elements and relationships between elements that are familiar to you and to people who must deal with it later. This makes it easy to verify for yourself and the others concerned. Implementation should start from an architecture that people can easily understand. Besides such human considerations, you must also consider

- Risks—one solution may be better understood than another

- Costs—of development and use
- Timing—when is the solution needed and how much time is available
- Resources—matching what is needed to what is available

ISVIC is a general procedure to develop a solution that is easily understood and used by people. It can be used to ask a question, make a speech, or write a book. In team efforts, different people may carry out its five steps. In planning, for instance, different team members cooperate to describe computerization plans and information models in an information plan. In development, planners investigate, analysts structure, key users verify, programmers implement, and test groups check software. In using the system, implementation teams carry out each activity following the same five ISVIC steps. I will give examples of its specific use in Chapters 7 through 9.

However, there are two difficulties in using the ISVIC procedure. The first lies in the challenge of structuring, a creative process that requires much skill and a keen mind to do it right. The second difficulty is making sure you approach a human situation with an open mind. This requires much knowledge of the world and insight; things are often not what they seem to be (Weinberg [206]). For ideas, refer to books on creative problem analysis, such as Ackoff [1], Adams [2], Halpern [81], von Oech [153], and Perkins [159].

1.7 Summary

1. This chapter presented concepts from information processing and argued that software must match the complexities of the world.
2. An information system consists of hardware plus software plus otherware. Otherware is the important human organization that includes everyone and everything other than hardware and software.
3. Computers process information to fit the needs of people. We can distinguish six basic types of information:

   - Operational information to perform routine work
   - Control information to verify operational information
   - Management information to understand a system's operation
   - Decision support information to propose changes

- External information to communicate with customers and others outside the organization
- Informal information to communicate with people inside the organization

4. A system is a complex structure of elements, which may be smaller systems themselves, that we can consider individually. The elements and their relations must be familiar to people, simplifying their verification and use.

5. The complexity of a system is roughly proportional to the square of the number of its elements, known as the combinatorial explosion.

6. The more restricted the domain and the more limited your view of it, the simpler a model it will be. Making and keeping models simple is key to successful computerization.

7. Processes and information need to be analyzed and structured in detailed models before they can be implemented in software. Models are made to plan information systems and to verify their planning.

8. There are many ways to analyze and structure processes and information. Important criteria are clarity and meaningfulness for people, and ease of implementation and change for the computer. Additional considerations are risks, costs, timing, and resources.

9. Use top-down structuring to establish relationships before deciding what the elements are, working from an overall view to the details. Use bottom-up structuring when several processes share elements.

10. Building a model is our way to break down complex problems into manageable elements that people can understand. The ISVIC procedure is a systematic way to analyze and develop models from a human point of view. It involves five steps (excluding iterations):

    - *Investigating* a subject and its human context
    - *Structuring* from a human point of view
    - *Verifying* if the structure is correct
    - *Implementing* the structure
    - *Checking* if the structure is clear, concise, complete, courteous, and correct

11. We can develop almost any complex system. The problem remaining is to design it for people. Meeting user expectations requires an understanding of people and their work environment as the first step in a project.

1.8 Review Questions and Exercises

1. More than two thousand years ago Plato said, "Knowledge is the strongest of all powers." Some people believe this is rapidly changing to "Information is power," considering information to be a production factor like people, capital, and raw materials. Others believe that knowledge systems will become more important than information systems.
   - What is the difference, if any, between knowledge and information? How is information distributed to people? How is knowledge?
   - Give ten examples in which information is crucial to the activities of an organization. How is knowledge used in each example?
   - What is the time constraint in each of your examples? If the information and knowledge is stored, how quickly must you update it to reflect changes in the real world?
2. A Boeing 747 aircraft engine contains about 1,500,000 parts. Discuss differences in complexity between this engine and a software system consisting of 100 programs with 100 instructions each? Discuss whether you would have more difficulty in understanding the engine or the software system, assuming equal training time.
3. To get a better feeling for what is logical and what is physical, list ten different objects in your environment on a sheet of paper and do the following:
   - For each object, describe physical aspects and logical aspects.
   - Ask someone else to do the same for each object.
   - Compare the two descriptions and consider the differences.
   - Discuss what may have caused the difference. Were there more differences in the physical or in the logical descriptions? Explain.

- Discuss why the logical meaning of your ten objects is easier to understand than their physical embodiment.
- Structure your object entities and their relations by drawing lines between them and describing the relation that each line represents.

4. List ten models that you use regularly in your work. Are these models intuitive or are they explicitly structured? Would you benefit if they were more explicitly structured? What would be the drawbacks of structuring them more explicitly?

5. The ISVIC procedure helps you think about the right things in the right sequence. Prove this to yourself by interchanging steps in different ways and by leaving out a step, describing what could go wrong each time.

6. You can structure a complex system from many points of view, resulting in different structures; there is no one good solution. Rank the following considerations for modeling in your own situation:

   - To increase the independence of elements in the structure
   - To increase the unity of each element
   - To simplify understanding of the resulting structure
   - To ease the implementation of the structure
   - To make the resulting implementation efficient
   - To make the resulting implementation adaptable to changes
   - To make the resulting implementation easy to use
   - To make the resulting implementation economical
   - To make use of the resulting implementation economical

   Add any other consideration that applies in your situation.

7. Structuring can be a complex process that is difficult to describe, but people often have a good intuitive feeling for it. Look at some examples of graphical methods to show structure, for instance, in Blokdijk and Blokdijk [17], Gane and Sarson [68], Shneiderman [193], and Yourdon and Constantine [217]. Summarize your findings.

8. Apply the Investigating (seven W's) and Structuring steps of the ISVIC procedure to analyze a process with which you are famil-

iar. Then verify the resulting structure. Did the procedure help you to arrive at a meaningful structure? Why?

9. Answer the above question, but this time work on the information used in the process. Then verify the resulting structure. Did the procedure help you to arrive at a meaningful structure? Why? Would an information structure or a process structure be more stable against future changes? Why?

10. Besides process and information (Questions 8 and 9), what else must you understand before you can implement your process in an information system?

11. A current topic to increase programmer productivity is "reusable" software, defining single programs so they can be used for different applications. Argue why this idea does, or does not, make sense only when you standardize processes or parts of processes in the real world. Discuss to what extent the structuring philosophy used (top-down or bottom-up) will increase the chance of finding reusable parts in existing software. What are the similarities and differences (if any) between reusable software modules and reusable mechanical parts? Describe the mechanical part that you select for the comparison.

12. Read "Case Study 2: An Urban School Attendance System" in Boehm's *Software Engineering Economics* ([18] Chapter 2), and answer the questions. This case explains why directors vetoed part of a computer system because people were not properly considered in the analysis. It discusses how the classical material-economics approach fails when user needs are not considered in computerization, and argues the case for a human-economics approach.

13. An airline information system handles reservations, ticketing, and passenger check-in. List five requirements that each of the following groups of people have for this system:

    - Passengers calling from their home
    - Telephone operators handling reservations
    - Passengers standing in line for check-in
    - Airline representatives at check-in
    - Airline flight attendants just before takeoff
    - Airline station managers

- Airline administrative personnel
- Analysts and programmers who develop the software
- Airline staff who develop the procedures and organization
- People who service the computer hardware
- People from an international ticket exchange agency
- People from the tax office
- Ten additional groups of people connected with or affected by the airline information system

What is your conclusion about how different people view the same information system?

2

UNDERSTANDING HUMAN BEHAVIOR AND THE MIND

Men are not machines, not even ghost-ridden machines.
They are men—a tautology
which is sometimes worth remembering.
—G. Ryle, *The Concept of Mind* [185]

To adapt computers to people, we must first understand people. In this chapter, I want to discuss some human qualities and characteristics of the mind that are important to information processing. In considering the mind, I will deal both with individual and interpersonal mechanisms.

To set the stage, though, I'll first discuss the need to consider uncertainty in the environment, its effects on people, and the consequences on social actions.

2.1 Uncertainty in Our Environment

> In this world nothing is certain but death and taxes.
>
> —B. Franklin, Letter, 1789, quoted in [205]

Your environment is the setting in which you live and work. This environment, and indeed the entire world, is full of uncertainty. Let me explain how this uncertainty is caused by changes, options, and subjective impressions, and I'll discuss some of the effects of uncertainty on people and their interactions.

CHANGES

"Nothing is permanent except change," said the Greek philosopher Heraclitus more than two thousand years ago. Change is today's hallmark: As I drove from my garage a month ago, I ran into another car; the bushes had grown so high that I didn't notice the other car coming. My child came home unexpectedly because the teacher fell ill. I got a telephone call from an old friend, last spoken to ten years ago. The sun came through my window after a heavy thundershower, blinding my eyes. Television showed a local armed robbery, one person killed. You name it, and it can happen today, any moment, anywhere.

Your circumstances are different from mine. What we share is that neither one of us knows beforehand what is going to happen next. With the advent of new technology, our environment is changing at an increasing rate. Dyer [53, 54] stresses the necessity of doing it today because change will give you many excuses not to do it tomorrow. We look for excuses because we adapt more or less automatically to static conditions, and we resist changes and contrast. We have more certainties today about life and death than did the cave dwellers, but we have many more uncertainties as well. One reason is the man-made environment we have created for ourselves in the twentieth century; refer to Peters' *Thriving on Chaos* [161] for examples. Toffler [202] described the profound effects on people when they are overwhelmed by change. One reason is that we notice deviations from our expectations more strongly than their fulfillment.

OPTIONS

So many options are available that we just don't realize how many there are. As a result, we often do not really know what we want, even when we say we do. As I am typing this, instead of my fingers pressing the keys, I could be doing a hundred other things at home or a thousand other things if I took my car. And so could you if you weren't reading this book. Having so many alternatives is unique to modern times. People once thought that the so-called electronic office would do away with paper, because computers would store all information and transport it via networks. But that same electronic office offers new printing options, so people consume more paper than ever before.

Since the 1950s, there has been a trend for more and more options to be available. Naisbitt in *Megatrends* [145] made "Either/Or → Multiple Option" his tenth megatrend; from this or that way, we can now have it a range of ways. Toffler [202] speaks of "overchoice," also limiting himself to the options for purchasing goods and services. In the context of this book, however, even more important are the many options in what we feel, say, and do. When we exercise any of these options, that likely means an effect on, a change to, other people. In almost all cases, more options lead to more interactions and thus to more uncertainty.

SUBJECTIVE IMPRESSIONS

Almost nothing is the same to everybody. Every person has a unique mind with his or her own views, opinions, and misconceptions. We share much common knowledge with others but have different views on most things. As Weinberg [206] notes, "Each person sees a part of the whole and identifies the whole with that part." As a result, things are subjective; they are not what we thought them to be.

What is debit to one person, is credit to another. Witnesses recall the same accident differently. Even under normal circumstances, people see things differently. An interesting experiment is to have a group of people each describe a simple object, say, a pencil. The variety of answers is amazing because even a pencil has many more different aspects than we usually think of. That variety of answers increases for more abstract concepts, such as "wall" and "money." The word "wall," for example, can have a very different meaning for a Chinese, a Jew, or a prisoner.

Even the same person can see things in a different way. If you look into the winter wind, you see snowflakes coming straight down. If you look to your left, though, you see them coming down at an angle to the left, and if you look to your right, they are coming down at an angle to the right. Which way are they really falling? These examples help you understand one definition of "reality," that is, a shared perception.

The fact that people see things differently has far-reaching consequences for social actions. Because you cannot assume that people see things your way, you have to find out their views before pushing your own. Every view is an interpretation. Sometimes you are proved wrong; often you don't even get to know you are wrong. If there can be so many different views of a simple thing like a wall or a pencil, clearly views of a new information system can be worlds apart (see Figure 2-1). Subjective impressions are one of the major roadblocks to designing good information systems; see, for example, Weinberg's *Rethinking Systems Analysis & Design,* Parts III and IV [208]. Much communication is needed to bring the views of planners and developers in line with users' expectations about an information system. Good communication is crucial to make people part of its planning, development, and use.

To summarize, uncertainty arises from changes, options, and subjective impressions. It may also result from the need for uniqueness (Snyder and Fromkin [197]) or from irrationality (St. Aubyn [187]). Whatever the origin, uncertainty is a key factor to consider when dealing with people, and you will find it mentioned often in this book.

Uncertainty, or the state of not knowing, is reduced when people get information (such as from an information system) and can use their intelligence. Intelligence is an elusive topic with many different facets, for example, the ability to learn from experience, to reason with abstractions, and to adapt to changes. We may have developed our intelligence as a result of an unpredictable environment, needing intelligence to survive. (Gardner [69] discusses the many kinds of human intelligence and human potential. Sternberg and Detterman [198] introduce articles that give different views on human intelligence.)

We use our intelligence to devise solutions to new situations. People once thought that cars were not suitable for mass production because there weren't enough chauffeurs. They thought that telephones would not be viable because too many switchboard operators would be needed. But technical solutions can be found to almost any problem. The difficulty is to find the best solution for a specific human environment and all of its uncertainties. This requires an understanding of people and their working environment.

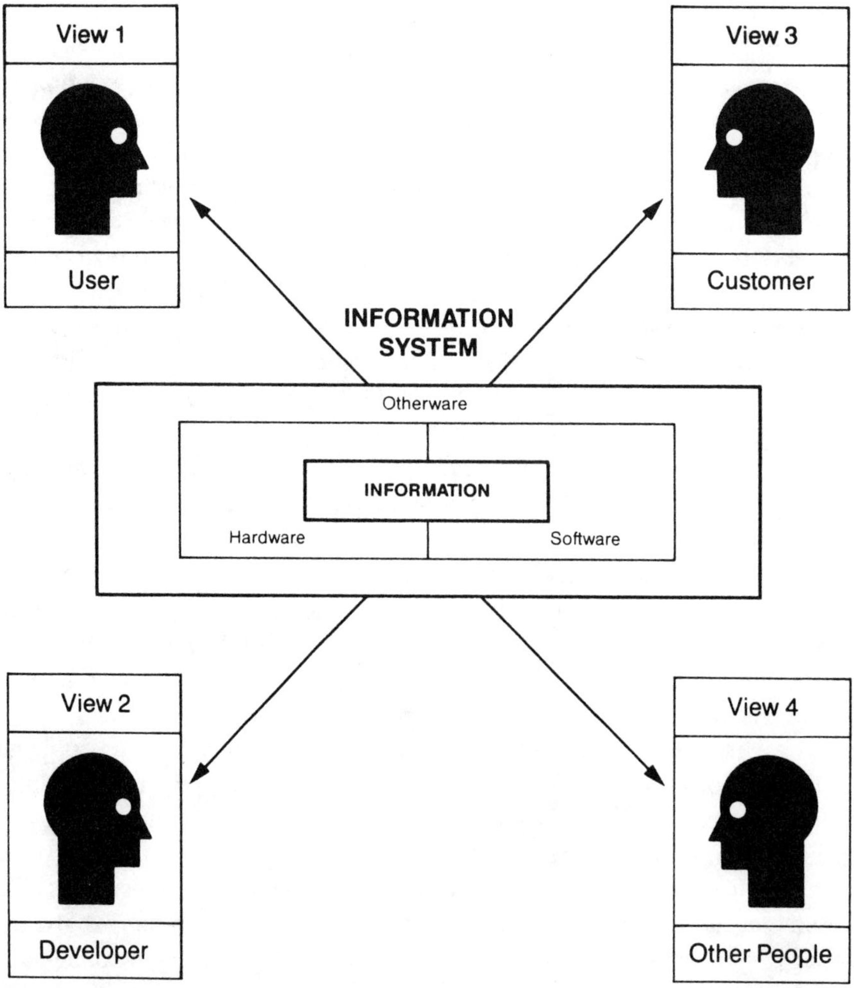

Figure 2-1. Differing views of developers, users, customers, and others.

2.2 Mechanisms of the Mind

The mind's the standard of the man.

—I. Watts, *False Greatness,* quoted in [205]

Mind, like intelligence, is an elusive concept because we cannot objectively define it. The word "mind" is even missing in some languages, for example, in French and Russian (Smith [195]). As used in everyday English, "mind" stands for the mental power of the human being; see Ryle [185] and the *Oxford Companion of the Mind* [77]. I will use the term to describe both the brain as well as its activity, including memory (Furst [66]).

The body and the mind are closely linked; the body informs the mind of the human environment, and the mind enables the body to function within it. They complement one another and they cannot exist without the other. The mind controls the human body (Smith [194]), including everything we do or say. "It's all in the mind," as they say [147]. In 1970, for example, there were only a few people who could run the marathon. Today there are tens of thousands who can because they set their mind on doing it.

The mind is what makes every person unique, in spite of its exhibiting some common mechanisms (Snyder and Fromkin [197]). Common rules of chess do not prevent every game of chess from being unique, and common rules of grammar do not prevent every book from being unique (Ryle [185]).

Although the capabilities of the mind are boundless, people's performance is often limited. People don't learn how the mind works and consequently cannot use it optimally (Buzan [27, 28]).

This may not change soon. Despite much research, we may never be able to understand the inner workings of the mind. Understanding is more than having all the facts and rules. We can put a description of the computer into the computer, but that does not enable the computer to understand itself. Is it necessary to understand the mind to control it? Who knows? Is the model of the mind presented in this book correct? Again, who knows? We have got this far without having an answer to these questions! (Remember that Columbus traversed the Atlantic using the erroneous model of Ptolemaic astronomy!)

Psychology offers different approaches to understanding the mind, notably the *behavioristic* approach (how people behave), the *cognitive* approach (how people think, plan, and decide—Lindsay and Norman [115]), and the *humanistic* approach (how people are responsible for their actions); for an introduction to psychology, refer to Hilgard et al. [92].

I will primarily follow the humanistic approach because in my book anything we do is always the *choice* of the mind. We are what we think, believe, and anticipate because we act accordingly.

For convenience, we can think of the mind having three main parts:

- Conscious mind, where we knowingly make decisions
- Subconscious mind, from where we can recall information and make it conscious
- Unconscious mind, where actions start that we are not aware of

In reality there are many levels of the mind, ranging from very conscious to very unconscious and maybe even superconscious. I am consciously writing and at the same time I know that I am writing—showing that even the conscious mind has at least two levels.

Whatever the structure of the mind, more important in the context of this book is the way the mind behaves—its mechanisms. This chapter distinguishes two different types:

- Individual mechanisms, which operate when you act alone
- Interpersonal mechanisms, which operate when you act in a group

My list of mechanisms presents an extension of Dean's papers [42, 43] on the use of psychology in technical writing and computer communication. I have changed the order of what he calls principles and altered the term "principles" to "mechanisms." My list contains the following *individual mind mechanisms* important to human relations in computerization:

Perception .... the way the mind sees patterns
Conception and cognition..... the way the mind makes mental models
Short-term memory.......... the capacity of immediate memory
Mind set .... a frame of reference
Reinforcement .... feedback to correct actions
Selection .... choosing meaningful options

Learning	acquiring knowledge, skills, or attitudes
Fatigue and confidence	the overall state of mind

The following sections describe each of these mechanisms in more detail.

2.3 Perception

Through our five senses, the mind receives a constant stream of changing impressions from the environment, and we become conscious of anything that we perceive. Vision is our strongest sense. Seeing truly is believing! Loosely speaking, we retain ten percent of what we read, twenty percent of what we hear, and thirty percent of what we see. Senses strengthen each other: Retention may be fifty percent when we see and hear something at the same time.

The windmill of our mind searches for patterns in the stream of impressions, grouping related elements, but it *perceives* only one pattern at a time. Gestalt psychology calls this pattern the *figure;* all else in the view is background, called *ground.*

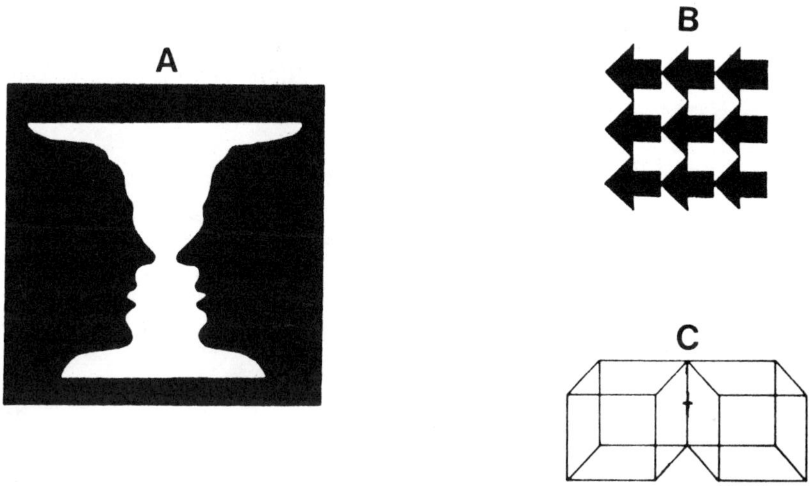

Figure 2-2. Examples to illustrate perception.

In Figure 2-2(A), you can see a white vase as the figure against a black ground, or you can see two opposing black faces as the figure against a white ground. You can switch from the white figure to the black figure, but you cannot see both figures at the same time. One figure is always ground to the other figure.

In Figure 2-2(B), you can see nine black arrows pointing to the left or four white arrows pointing to the right. Again, one figure is ground to the other figure and you can see only one figure at a time.

Figure and ground need not be complementary. If you stare at the little mark between the two cubes in Figure 2-2(C), you can change from one view to the other.

We constantly search for patterns not only in our environment but also in our thoughts, behavior, feelings, and almost anything else. We are continually trying to find sense in what we perceive. In fact, it is difficult to reduce the activity of the mind, even in our sleep.

How can we take advantage of the perception mechanism to improve other people's perceptions of our intentions? For one thing, we can follow the trusted 3T formula, which uses "telling" three times to assist perception by others:

- Tell them what you are going to tell them and why: the framework.
- Tell them your story.
- Tell them what you told them: the summary to reinforce your story.

Explaining the framework first is important because people's anticipated future needs influence their perceptions. People perceive ideas better when they know what is coming and why it is important. The summary at the end allows them to check their perceptions of your story.

2.4 Conception and Cognition

Conception is the mechanism by which we interpret the elements perceived, determine their relationships, and draw conclusions about them. It thus operates on the results of perception, and it may even support perception. *Cognition* is the knowledge accumulated from our interpretations, the mechanism for developing the mental models that we use to conceive of all of our ideas.

Mental models are one of two types of models discussed in this book. The other type is conceptual models (discussed in Chapter 1), which are visualizations of a physical system used for communication between people; they must be complete and stable. Mental models are what we have in our head; they are often incomplete and unstable.

Making models seems characteristic of the human mind. Our views and stereotypes are models that govern our expectations and perceptions (Lindsay and Norman [115] and Hunt [95]).

We continually try to match patterns with patterns, constructing a meaningful model of the world in our mind out of a stream of perceived ideas, notions, and feelings. We also continually check our models against the real world, and update them as required. The first time you heard about a computer, for example, you formed a mental model of what it looks like, what it can do, and so on; you then checked that model against the real thing.

Incomplete things bother us because we don't understand them. Examples are illogical situations and drawings that leave out important details. Ambiguous things also bother us; it took some time before people appreciated Escher's etchings.

The mind seeks to complete anything that is incomplete. Gestalt psychology calls such completion a "closure." You may not even realize that the IBM trademark logo consists of horizontal bars because your mind automatically closes the gaps between them. We enjoy closing our models; closing is the way to get things off our mind.

To decide whether something is complete, we use similarities, analogies, and associations to apply our cognition. The mind is trained to work with parallel constructions and it expects them. If I use the present tense in a sentence, for example, you will expect me to continue using the present tense in the rest of the paragraph. "Open" models stay in the mind, possibly causing too many things to be in the mind at one time. If we know that we can deal with something later, we can always temporarily "close" it by writing it down.

Most of what we learn is in the form of mental models: rules of arithmetic, language syntax, behavior, and so on. Image models include a writer describing a scene, a musical tone poem, and the smell of lilac blossoms on a warm spring evening. We can experience an image model as if it were real.

To understand how we can use models, consider the following problem:

> On Monday, starting at 9:00 A.M., I walk from Nice to Monte Carlo along the Mediterranean coast. On the way, I stop to have a snack and to enjoy the spectacular views. That night, I sleep in Monte Carlo and walk back to Nice on Tuesday, along the same route. I also leave at 9:00 A.M. but stop at different places.

QUESTION: Is there a point along the route where I will be at exactly the same time on both days?

ANSWER: To find the answer, let's make a simple conceptual model. Suppose you walk from Nice, and I walk from Monte Carlo on the same day. We must meet each other at some place, obviously at the same time. As it does not really matter whether you or I walk, and what day it is, the answer must be yes.

Once you understand this model, you can apply it to similar problems—it becomes your mental model.

We learn to perform an activity by "visualizing" it in our mind, seeing the example and making the model our plan of action. A good coach puts the vision of victory in the minds of players. To perform something, we must first imagine it. The better we can imagine something, the better we perform it.

Cognitive psychology proposes the following analytical steps in making a mental model:

1. Recognize that you must solve a problem.
2. Recognize the conditions of the problem.
3. Apply suitable analytical strategies.
4. Decide which one gives the best solution.

When we try to understand a communication from someone else, it is very helpful to have the context and overview first—the first T of the 3T formula. We can then relate details of a story to it, placing them where they belong in the framework without having to worry about them any longer. After the story, we can use the summary to check our mental model (the last T of the 3T formula).

If we get details without having a context or overview, two problems arise. First, our mind tries to deduce a model structure, causing an overload and interfering with our understanding. Second, we may come up with an incorrect model that will be difficult to correct later. (Gentner and Stevens [72] and Newell and Simon [146] discuss human model making.

2.5 Short-Term Memory

We have three major types of memory (Baddeley [10, 11]):

- Sensory memory, where we automatically store for a few tenths of a second what our senses perceive, until we store it in short-term memory.
- Short-term memory, which we use for immediate interpretation and action. If we think the information is important, we appear to rehearse it in short-term memory (Hilgard et al. [92]). We lose it after some time, when it is "overwritten" by new information unless we consciously decide to store it in long-term memory.
- Long-term memory, where we can store information and retrieve it by conscious effort. We store all of what we learn in long-term memory.

Short-term, or *immediate, memory* is where we store information from the senses for immediate use. The information stays there until we lose our concentration and our mind wanders off to something else. Obviously, short-term memory is important to our immediate functioning.

It is short-term memory that creates the requirement of meeting a critical response time for efficient on-line communication (Miller [136] and Shneiderman [193]). For example, consider these requirements:

- Entering data must show a result within a second.
- Updating a large file must take only five to ten seconds.
- Processing an end-of-month report must take no longer than a few minutes.

Meeting these requirements through a faster computer or a network will easily pay off, since having to wait too long makes us lose our concentration on the job at hand.

A property of short-term memory is that it has a maximum capacity of 7 ± 2 similar items. Miller [135] has shown that this capacity is about the same for all five senses. This physiological limitation has several consequences.

To avoid overloading, we must try to limit the number of words, concepts, or constructs in a sentence. The sentence "Short words are often better understood" is simpler to understand than "The shorter the word, the better it is often understood." The second sentence uses more words and more constructs. Word and letter reduction, however, should not be carried out at the expense of clarity; sentences must be complete, enabling the mind to close them.

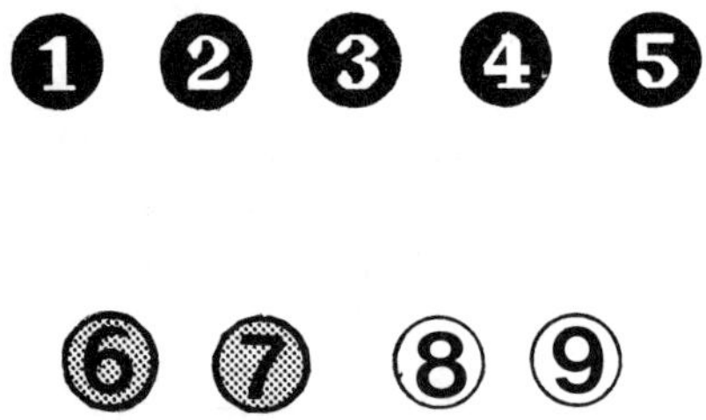

The 7 ± 2 capacity applies equally to visual information. Examples are choices on a menu, items in an illustration or graph, and entries on an overhead projection slide. Use fewer than five items if it is vital to get the idea across or if the items themselves are complex. If there are many choices, structure items in two or more levels with 7 ± 2 items or fewer each. In a restaurant, for example, I will first decide whether I want fish or meat and then decide within that group.

Finally, I must point out that the 7 ± 2 capacity refers to similar items only. We can simultaneously keep 7 colors and 7 objects and 7 words in short-term memory. Presumably, we need this capability to make associations.

2.6 Mind Set

Mind set, also called *frame of reference,* is the tendency of a person to think or act in a particular way, depending upon his or her prior experience and future need. Mind set can be considered as a kind of superstructure of mental models.

To experience mind set, look at the drawings in Figure 2-3. In Figure 2-3(A), which line is longer? You, like everyone else, will judge the vertical line to be longer than the horizontal line. In Figure 2-3(B), are the vertical lines parallel? If they don't seem to be, it is because you cannot properly judge whether lines are parallel if they are in a background of radial lines. Similarly, in Figure 2-3(C), a line that intersects other lines at an acute angle seems tilted. In Figure 2-3(D), a circle surrounded by smaller circles appears to be larger than the same circle surrounded by large circles. These illusions are almost universally experienced; they are evidence of how the mind works, proof that what we see is subjective (Coren and Girgus [34]).

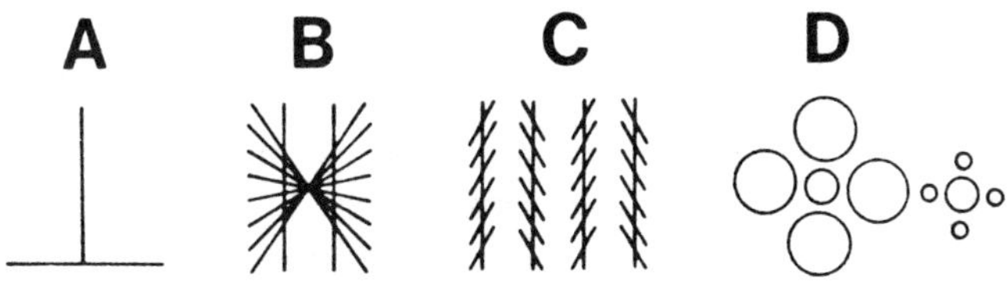

Figure 2-3. Examples of optical illusion.

In 1943, Craik [35] proposed that the brain symbolically parallels the structure and logic of the human environment in mental models. He suggested that thought consists first of translating a problem into symbolic terms, then of manipulating those symbols within the mental models to determine applicability, and finally of translating the derived symbols into actions.

If something fits in our mind set, we can make the transition and accept it easily. If it doesn't, there is a clash, causing dissonance and ultimately conflict in our mind; we cannot make the translation. Because we cannot live with conflict in our own mind for long, we rationalize one way or another. Making the wrong choice could create subjective impressions. What I have written, I hope, has prepared your mind set for the phrase "short-term memory." If I were to now use the phrase "short-*time* memory," you would experience dissonance and wonder what the difference is. Using different words for the same thing burdens the mind unnecessarily because we don't know whether they mean the same.

It is not just terminology that creates mind sets. If I start with an -ing verb, it will disturb you if I switch to a -tion noun. Similarly, you will get annoyed if the heading of a section does not correspond to its content. For me, the writer, it may well be the same thing, but what is important is how you, the reader, see it.

Physical objects can also create mind sets. My workstation keyboard used to have function keys on the right-hand side, arranged three by four. My old PC had them on the left, arranged two by five. My new PC has them on the top, arranged ten by one. I have been lucky to work with three types only, having had to change my keyboard mind set only twice.

Because of mind set, any standard is often better than no standard. Why is the numeric keypad on the telephone different from that of a calculator? It escapes me why keyboards that we need to use automatically are changed. The keys in the typewriter area are at least standardized, although their placement is not optimal. The letter keys were laid out actually to *reduce* typing speed, a necessity at the time due to technical limitations of the first mechanical typewriter [153].

There is much more to mind set. Mind set determines what you can and cannot do. Until I was 53, I simply couldn't do push-ups, no matter how hard I tried. It took someone else to convince me that I could. When my children were young, they wanted to eat only Dutch food. Now they love foreign food; their mind set has changed. The Roman poet Virgil said, "They can because they think they can." Similarly, you cannot because you think you cannot.

How can you match the mind sets of others, and avoid interference? You need to know the type of people they are. If you have met and talked to them, you will have a mental image to which you can tell your story. Without such a mental image, unknowingly, *your* mind set will get in the way of good communication and meeting the expectations of others.

Preparatory set, or *expectancy,* is an important kind of mind set; it is your plan for the immediate future. It exists when you are expecting something to happen after you are conditioned for it. You can try to make use of your expectations, but it is not possible to avoid interference from other mind sets.

2.7 Reinforcement

"Feedback" literally means feeding back the intermediary effect of an action for its control. We speak of *reinforcement* when the feedback serves to achieve the goal more accurately or to adapt to changes faster. When I speak about feedback in this book, I mean reinforcing feedback.

Simple and direct feedback systems are most effective because we easily understand the mechanism. An amusement park in Holland, for example, employs statues with a vacuum mouth to help keep the park clean. The statue repeats, "Paper here" until you insert a piece of rubbish; then it says, "Thank you." The feedback is simple, direct, and very effective.

Feedback is an essential part of all human interaction. Imagine how a conversation would go if you couldn't hear or see the other person; there would be no possibility to react. Would you be able to walk in a shopping center without visual feedback? One can only admire deaf and blind people for how they have learned to live with their physical handicap!

Feedback tells us how close we are to being on the right track. It enables us to check and correct our course of action and to adapt ourself to changes. We listen to our own speech, and get disoriented if we hear our voice distorted by a delay of a quarter second.

Feedback is essential to achieve quality in everything we do. "Success breeds success," as they say. The feeling of being successful reinforces us to have more success. With fear of failure, we reinforce ourselves to have failure after failure. Positive reinforcement of achievements is more effective than sanctions. Feedback can use all our senses, of which sight, hearing, and touch are most commonly used in automation. When I type a character, I can see the cursor move to the next position, showing that the typed character is accepted. When I press a key, I hear a click. The key's spring is such that I can feel when the key is pressed sufficiently. It is therefore disconcerting to use a silent, motionless keyboard, because without tactile and auditory feedback, I must check the screen all the time.

An effective learning process uses extreme reinforcement. A teacher poses questions in class to verify learning and to inform students of their progress. Students check their models of understanding and ask questions when they don't understand a point.

When listeners check their mental models against observations, that is the feedback by which they reinforce their viewpoint or eliminate possibilities. By exposing a subject from different viewpoints, we can help listeners to achieve a more accurate verification. Similarly, by telling what a user should do and what the result is, a writer of a technical manual helps a user to learn an action. Without feedback, we will never get and stay involved.

Without reinforcement, we have the feeling that we are doing something for nothing. A common form of feedback is our weekly or monthly paycheck. But payment is not the only feedback; the reinforcement from colleagues or a manager is at least as important in our affluent society. A deserved "Well done" comment can make one's day.

2.8 Selection

There is no simple formula that can predict what the mind chooses to *select* from the stream of ever changing impressions, ideas, and feelings it receives. Our frame of reference is no doubt involved. People tend to select options that are meaningful now or in the future; they may also select options to reduce uncertainty.

Selection is present in other mechanisms as well, for example, selective perception and selective memory. The selection may depend on our interest, irritation, frustration, familiarity, and need at a certain moment. Some examples of the selection mechanism are these:

- You are preoccupied with a fascinating book and cannot wait to continue reading it. Your attention to other items is low.
- You get bored with a book you are supposed to read. Your mind wanders off on other subjects, and the book's contents do not register.
- You are reading a difficult book, and you only retain what is meaningful. You put aside the things you do not understand.
- A program that you use has many more functions than you need. You don't bother to find out what they are because you get along well with the few simple ones.
- You will likely "forget" to do things you don't really want to do.
- Given a choice of actions, you select one that gives you the greatest reward or pleasure for the least effort.

Selection is an act of self-preservation and efficiency. Since you cannot properly store things that you do not understand, they would keep troubling you and interfering with all that you do. We use self-deception, a form of selection, to close off our awareness of such things (Goleman [75]). Meaningfulness, on the other hand, improves our involvement with something, and increases the chance of selection. If we retain ten percent of what we read, twenty percent of what we hear, thirty percent of what we see, and fifty percent of what we both see and hear, we retain ninety percent if we also find it meaningful.

Efficiency motivates, probably because we experience it as meaningful. If we bring automation to someone's workplace, it must make the work more efficient for that person. If automation means more work, the person will be demotivated. Thus, inefficiency demotivates.

We select a daily routine, a meaningful pattern that we follow during work days, to avoid having to choose among too many options. I noticed this when I retired. It took me weeks to settle down to a new pattern. A daily routine is a matter of efficiency. A fixed pattern enables us to focus on all important routine matters, without having to worry constantly about all possible options. But in the extreme, a completely fixed daily routine may get in the way of our functioning as a human being.

2.9 Learning

Learning is the act of acquiring knowledge, skills, and attitudes.* It is the conscious effort to store a model or facts permanently in long-term memory, with enough associations for later retrieval. Reinforcement and selection are the primary mechanisms used to learn and retrieve what we need in the future.

Pavlov and his dog have shown us that we use associations to retrieve information; the association is the relationship between things. There must be some transformation process active to store the words, the relationship between the words, and the meaning of the words. Often we use visual relationships, employing imagery to associate ideas and concepts: A picture is worth a thousand words, and a model is worth a thousand pictures (Hunt and Sullivan [94]). Or you may use verbal information, including symbols, analogies, and comparisons (Buzan [27–29]).

Retention allows us to recall and use what we have learned. But even with using associations, our memory capacity for easy recall is limited. Since the power of recall depends on its frequency of use, we try to keep the things in the foreground that we expect to need the most, and put unimportant things in the background. There is doubt whether we can ever truly forget. But the mind has many dark corners, from where it is almost impossible to recall.

The *primacy effect* causes first impressions to be more lasting than all later ones except the last one, the *recency effect.* It is as if we form a model in our mind the first time something happens and cannot easily change that model afterward. Instead, our mind tries to fit new perceptions into the mental model, rejecting something if it does not fit. Thus we learn more efficiently when we develop a correct model straight away.

Learning is important for people in information processing; it is a way of life for most of them. I estimate that computer professionals spend at least fifty percent of their working time learning about applications, software, hardware, and so on. Part of that is formal learning in courses (ten to thirty percent); the rest is informal learning from write-ups, documentation, discussions, thinking, and doing.

---

*I will discuss the mechanism of learning in this section and deal with the related subject of training and courses in Chapter 9.

How can we improve learning so that all our time is spent productively? One way is to work by using more than one sense. By reading out loud, for instance, you can improve your learning of words and understanding of sentences. Through the use of pictures and schematics, you can improve your understanding of the text of a chapter. By making a *mind map**—a visual summary of what you have read or seen—you can verify and improve your understanding of that chapter. The mind map links key words to the central theme by means of visual cues (shape, color, emphasis, and pointers) to show the chapter's structure. Making the mind map forces you to summarize what you have read and reinforces your mental model. Figure 2-4 shows a sample mind map of this section on learning.

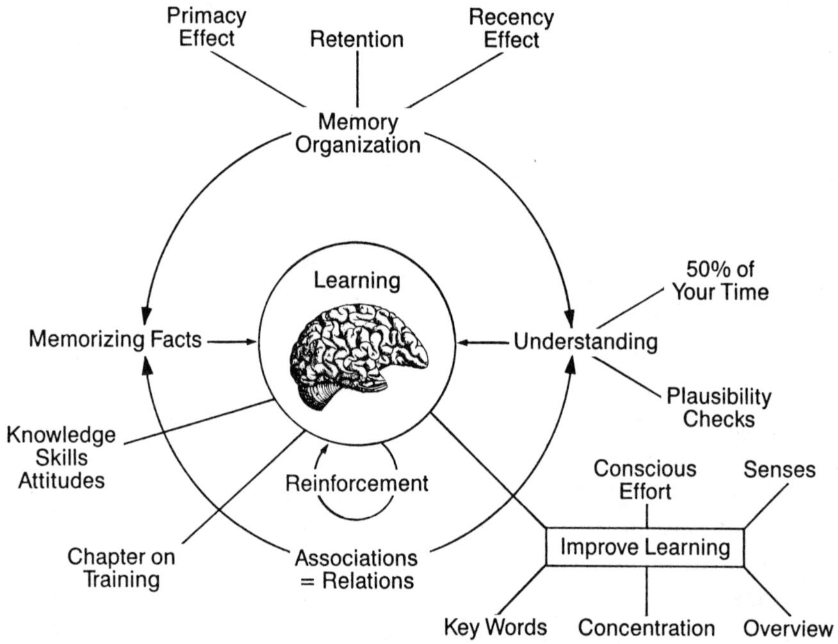

Figure 2-4. A mind map of this section on learning.

Concentration—that is, doing one thing at a time and not being distracted—also improves your learning efficiency. How well you concentrate depends on how meaningful you find a subject and how strongly you are involved in it.

---

*Like Russell [184], I am using the term "mind map" to indicate what Buzan [27] calls "brain pattern." Mind maps are conceptual models that can help establish mental models.

Another technique is to begin with an overview, which enables you to relate the general concepts to the details and thereby reinforce a model and again improve learning. Without having an overview first, you would have to keep all the details in your mind until you finally got to the overview; that is not efficient.

These techniques can be combined. If I read something, I first try to get a general impression of what the text is about. I look at the introduction, the table of contents, and the chapter summaries. Then I consider the way in which the material can be important to me. Next, I read out loud selected parts, relating the heading to the content and marking key terms. I review these key words and the chapter summary before starting a new chapter to further enhance retention of concepts. In this way, I follow the 3T formula: Establish an overview and determine meaningfulness, read, and review. (Chapter 9, which discusses the important subject of training, again shows the usefulness of the 3T formula.)

2.10 Fatigue and Confidence

Fatigue results when your mind is overloaded, when there are too many things going on in your mind. That produces dissonance because you don't get to do what you feel you should do. Then you get annoyed at yourself for not achieving goals, and that makes the situation even worse, possibly leading to burnout. Such frustration can also cause stress since it causes you to dislike or even hate what you are doing.

Uncertainty in the environment, as well as in yourself, is a cause of fatigue and stress. That's because things you are uncertain about are hard to do. We all seek security from achievement and recognition (Dyer [53, 54]).

Stress means that the mind is overloaded, not the person. Stress is not necessarily all bad, though, for short-term stress can make you more sensitive and alert. But long-term stress causes mental fatigue; it impairs functioning of the mind and your general well-being. You may need to step outside yourself once in a while to consider which type of stress you are experiencing. Is it short term and can you get through it? Or is it long term and something needs to change? Yates [214] offers several general stress-reduction insights and techniques to restore peace of mind.

Confidence (that is, trusting yourself) enables you to do things better and easier because your mind is free from fear. Being confident means that you are at ease with yourself and can concentrate on performing a task. Achieving that task increases your confidence. When you do things with confidence, little fatigue results.

Remember that your expectations shape how you feel about something via the mind set mechanism. If you think something is difficult, it will be difficult. If you are confident that something will be easy, it will be easy. (Almost as important as confidence in reducing fatigue in job performance is a good ergonomic design, as I discuss in Appendix A.)

Hambly has written a concise book [82] on how you can improve your confidence, and I borrow the following advice from that book:

- Become more aware of yourself and your special qualities.
- Relax and control your tensions.
- Improve your social skills.
- Fulfill your expectations.

Understanding and trusting yourself are the keys to being confident. Confidence comes from proper training and human support at work. We establish a human network for things that we cannot handle ourselves; we use colleagues, a support group, or a manager to help us when we are in trouble. And confidence grows on confidence.

I described these individual mind mechanisms separately, but of course in reality they are not separate. They are all part of the mind and they all interact with each other, making us who we are.

Other mind mechanisms that I'll discuss below are primarily interpersonal, and play a role when people communicate with one another. They also affect how you work with a computer. (This does not imply that the computer reacts, or even should react, in a human way, but only that certain mechanisms are at work.) I will discuss the following *interpersonal mechanisms* because of their importance to the human context in computerization:

Appearance	the outward aspect
Role	the acting part selected or imposed
Environment and time	the location and occasion
Suggestion and the self-fulfilling prophecy	a way to influence the mind
Groupthink and a hidden agenda	ways of communicating and deciding

Conformity and assertiveness	methods of acting and communicating
Integrity	honesty

2.11 Appearance

We not only listen to the content of a communication, we also perceive its *appearance.* Content appeals to our rational side, and appearance to our emotional side. In order for communication to be effective, content and appearance should support each other. If they don't, the listener or reader cannot make up his or her mind about the communication and confusion will result.

When forced to make a choice between a conflicting appearance and content, many people will unconsciously choose the appearance. Some politicians are very clever in saying nothing, but their appearance is so reassuring that people accept what their appearance expresses. Thus body language (that is, body movements and dress) can support or distract from what we are saying. Similarly, a person's body language may be so uncertain that we will not listen to the words spoken, even if they are meaningful.

But appearance is more than body language. In offices, it is also the look of a receptionist's desk, the arrangement of the furniture, the size of the room, and so on. In presentations, it is the writing quality and the organization of the material. In books, it is the paper quality, layout, and spelling. Although perhaps these things shouldn't matter, unconsciously most people do interpret them and draw conclusions based on them. (Appendix N elaborates on nonverbal communication, including body language.)

2.12 Role

The coordination and control of activities within an organization take place through the mechanism of a *role.* We expect certain behavior of a person occupying a specific position; that is, there is an expected role associated with that position. Role conflicts arise between people when their roles are not clear or when a person occupies two positions with opposing roles.

You assume a role, willingly or unwillingly, when you communicate with another. That role is how you appear to the other person, and vice versa. The role you assume, which depends on your mind sets and expectations and the mind sets and expectations of your counterpart, has a major impact on the course and efficiency of a communication.

Here are some basic elements making up a role in an interaction:

Power ..... your ability to influence others
Opening.... how you start
Approach .. how you introduce a subject
Style ...... how you perform the interaction
Tone....... the voice you use
Pace....... the speed with which you perform the interaction
Emphasis... where you place emphasis and how much

An important ingredient of power is *position power.* To understand this concept, consider an experiment conducted by Zimbardo (reported in [9] and [173]) in which some students were made prisoners and others guards. After six days, the experiment had to be stopped because hostilities between the two groups became too strong; the students ceased role playing and actually became prisoners and guards. Also consider how different we appear when we talk to a baby, a colleague, our boss, or someone beneath us in an organization. In all cases, we adapt our approach to the assumed position of the person we are talking to, presumably to make our communication more effective.

Besides position power, people also have *expert power,* derived from their skills and knowledge, and *personal power,* derived from their character; see Handy [83], Korda [112], and Robbins [173]. All power, like muscle, gets stronger by use, and deteriorates by disuse. You must properly exercise your role, for example in the development process, to be effective; this may imply behaving differently to different people.

The *opening* sets the stage for all remaining communication. Due to the primacy effect {2.9}, the opening can either clear or block a communication channel. Recovery from an improper opening is difficult because you're forced to continue at a disadvantage, in view of the counter role assumed by the other person.

After the opening, your *approach* to the subject is important. Depending on what is customary, you may state your purpose directly, or carefully explain the conditions leading to your purpose first. In some countries, you must wait until tea or coffee is served before stating your purpose or even wait until you're asked. In other countries, you must start with an apology.

Style, tone, pace, and *emphasis* are other aspects of the role mechanism. Their influence becomes noticeable when roles are not clear and you try to deduce from them what the role of the other person is.

The role mechanism extends beyond person-to-person communication. It also affects thing-to-person communication:

- A pleasant and efficient style makes a book easy to read.
- A powerful and convincing style can cause a book to influence you.
- A difficult opening procedure of a computer program can be detrimental to its subsequent use.
- An erroneous description and dull beginning of a computer-assisted course can completely ruin a learner's efficiency.

How can you select a role that supports your purpose? First, you must realize there are two roles: your role and the role of the other person. Then you must understand that the reason why the opening is so important is that when it's successful, the other person must choose a counter role. In other words, your offense is frequently the best defense. If roles do not complement each other, a conflict can result. An effective role leads to the desired goal in a short time and with a minimum of effort. Intuition alone is not always sufficient to find such an effective role. Analysis can help you achieve better results, for example, in a negotiation (refer to Appendix J). In any case, reject a role that seems effective but is disagreeable to you personally; only professional actors can act roles other than their own. (Handy [83] devotes Chapter 4 to roles and interactions and Chapter 5 to power and influence.)

2.13 Environment and Time

Consider the many factors discussed so far that lead to effective communication. Then, all other things being equal, you can select the most appropriate *environment* and *time* to communicate most effectively. Choose a proper occasion, day, method, medium, location, and facilities to give a communication the best chance of registering.

A person should attend a course when the occasion is appropriate; otherwise the course material will not be meaningful, and the whole experience very frustrating. Obviously, communicating to many people is best done on a day that most people are available. Don't plan meetings on Monday mornings at 8:30 or Friday afternoons at 3:00. Communicating to a person whose mind is occupied with problems will likely not be effective either. The communication method and medium must fit the occasion and the person who is communicating. The president of a major company, for example, may well choose to record a message on video for showing it to an entire department, but a first-line manager speaking to his team shouldn't try to use that approach.

Location and facilities should accommodate the communication method and medium and the size of the audience. Don't have a sales meeting in a shed unless there is a very good reason!

In addition to affecting your interpersonal functioning, the environment and time mechanism affects your personal functioning. In one environment, you can easily do things you find difficult to do in another environment. For example, tropical heat may paralyze you, while a quiet room helps your concentration, and bright light makes you uncertain. Even more important is your psychological environment. Are you being motivated or demotivated by your manager? Do others encourage or discourage you? These topics are discussed in Chapter 12.

Similarly, time affects you. The sooner you complete or close something, the easier it seems to be and the more you enjoy it. The longer you wait, however, the bigger it gets in your mind and the more difficult you find it. Some people can only work under time pressure, whereas others cannot. In either case, you must choose a proper time; not too early so that you cannot prepare sufficiently and not too late so it occupies your mind unnecessarily.

2.14 Suggestion and the Self-Fulfilling Prophecy

We don't like it if people tell us to do something. We prefer that they suggest we do it. *Suggestion* is a powerful way to make something happen, either in ourselves or in others. The *self-fulfilling prophecy* uses the suggestion mechanism to cause a statement, expression, or thought to happen, presumably by means of the mind set mechanism.

A synonym for the self-fulfilling prophecy is the *Pygmalion effect.* Pygmalion was a mythological sculptor who carved a statue, believing it would come to life—which it did. Most events in our life clearly are self-fulfilling prophecies, but what isn't so clear is who started the suggestion or even what the suggestion was.

A common example of the power of suggestion is advertisements, for example, beauty fluid ABC will revitalize your skin or after-shave lotion PQR will give you that masculine quality. Advertisers often associate their product with a desirable person to strengthen the suggestion.

An example of the self-fulfilling prophecy is the popular Wall Street guru who predicts that the stock market will go up or down, and his many followers act on that prediction, causing the market to follow his prediction. I remember a French movie in which the mailman went around the village telling everybody what was going to happen the next day—which of course it did because all the villagers accepted his suggestions. Politicians suggest things all the time. They say, "Mark my words, XYZ is going to happen" and it will if people believe them.

You can also make things happen in yourself through your own expectations, your plan for the future. Convince yourself that you are going to win a match, and you will be certain to win. Convince yourself that you will fail and you will. That so many people run the marathon can be attributed to this mechanism of the mind; people decide that they can do it. The centuries-old *Book of Changes,* called I Ching, works similarly. You ask a specific question and throw three coins six times, to get an answer (believed to be influenced by the subconscious mind [144]). If nothing else, it will at least convince the believer.

In goal setting, we are practicing the self-fulfilling prophecy; we estimate our level of achievement and we suggest a plan to ourselves, which we then fulfill. The performance of our group also influences our goal setting; and being part of the group often suggests to us that we should conform to its norm. Parkinson's Law states that work expands to fill the time available for its completion; that time is suggested by ourself or by others.

Important uses of the self-fulfilling prophecy in information processing are in planning and in management. Something will happen if we plan it properly and make people part of the plan. Conversely, things will not happen if they are not properly discussed beforehand; this is the inverse of the self-fulfilling prophecy. Moreover, since plans change regularly, it should always be clear who suggests a plan and who is responsible for it.

Managers can best motivate their people by convincing them. Some people have an intuitive feel for that and can strike the proper chord; others fail. Someone with a persuasive personality has more chance to be successful than someone who is timid, since the former is able to project more conviction. The projection of conviction and confidence, of power, is what the positive self-fulfilling prophecy is all about.

2.15 Groupthink and a Hidden Agenda

According to Nietzsche, madness is the exception in individuals, but the rule in groups. In an analysis of six U.S. government group decisions from a psychological point of view, Janis [102] introduced the word "groupthink." In his words, "Groupthink refers to a deterioration of mental efficiency, reality testing, and moral judgment that results from in-group pressures."

I add to this definition of groupthink that pressures are often assumed and assumptions insufficiently discussed, thereby creating a *hidden agenda* of unverified assumptions. Because people are not aware of the real issues, they make and realize their own plans and work without coordination. With either groupthink or a hidden agenda, the result is not what is desired.

Two examples of a hidden agenda from information processing are the following:

- A division director must cut next year's budget. Since he does not want to upset his development people unnecessarily, he suggests leaving a function out of some software under development. The company budget is revised three months later, and a planner works out details of the cut. She finds that leaving out the function necessitates changes to other software functions. When the working-level managers find out, they object, saying it is the wrong thing to do. But then the director believes they always say that when things change. The director decides to make the cut.

  At the end of the next year, it turns out that the changes to the other functions have many unforeseen repercussions and the new software does not meet the true requirement. The software product cannot be shipped, and a crash program must begin. The additional cost is ten times the original cut, the delay is a year, and many people are unhappy. Making the right people part of the plan could have avoided such problems.
- A brilliant programmer develops an idea for a software tool that will revolutionize programming. To sell the idea, his manager estimates a small development cost. The idea is accepted because the sophisticated tool fills a strategic need, while seeming to require little expense.

  A chief executive grumbles about duplication with a similar but simpler tool developed by another division, but then the effort is small and the need is great. The simpler tool is announced six months later, at the same time the division needs the features of the sophisticated tool. Meanwhile, the tool's development cost estimate has increased ten times.

  A year later, thirty times the originally estimated effort has been expended, and the sophisticated tool is tested. It turns out to require too big a computer and too much support. We can only wonder what would have happened if the real assumptions had been properly discussed at the beginning.

A hidden agenda happens more often than we realize. It is usually not detected and, if detected, people at the working level often consider it history. A characteristic of the hidden agenda is that the real issue is insufficiently considered, causing assumptions to remain hidden. The truth is that the impact of the decision should have warranted a wider or repeated discussion. More examples of hidden agendas are these:

- To speed up an inquiry to the database, a programmer uses a nonstandard search routine that works only on the old product line, not on the new line.
- A programmer spends six man-months optimizing a program used only one night a month because it contains an interesting optimization problem.
- Fields on a data entry screen are in the same sequence as in the database, but in a different sequence from how they appear on the form because the programmer did not bother to find out their sequence on the form. As a result, people have a hard time entering data and make many errors.
- A small detail in a specification came up at 6:30 P.M.; the group leader said, "We'll worry about that tomorrow," and everyone forgot about it. The same small detail comes up during pilot test, causing ten times more work and weeks of delay than if it were fixed originally.

Groupthink and a hidden agenda are always easy to diagnose afterward, when things have gone wrong. Janis [102] gives six major causes of failure because of groupthink:

1. Only a few alternatives are considered, often only two.
2. The original plan of action is not reexamined.
3. Initially rejected possibilities are neglected afterward.
4. There is little or no attempt to get information from experts.
5. Attention is paid to facts and opinions that support the preferred course of action, while other information is disregarded.
6. There is little or no discussion of obstacles to the preferred course of action, and there is no contingency plan.

From Janis's analysis, it is clear how to combat groupthink: The person above the groupthinking people must demand more alternatives, a reexamination, working-level opinions, expert information, and a contingency plan. To combat a hidden agenda, you must make people part of the plan as well as part of the activity.

The extremely complex world of information processing requires much planning and communication, so that all important details are discussed. Unwarranted assumptions give the illusion of evidence (Perkins [159]), but experience shows that planning things correctly from the beginning and making people part of the plan will repay itself many times over later. To do things right, you must do them consciously and understand their assumptions. The next section discusses conformity and assertiveness, internal aspects of groupthink and the hidden agenda, and what you can do about it.

2.16 Conformity and Assertiveness

> . . .don't assent to what you don't believe in.
>
> —Plato, *The Republic,* Book I [164]

Conformity is the change in a person's behavior or opinions as a result of real or imagined pressure from others. In order to work successfully in groups, a certain degree of conformity is desirable. But forbidding all deviant behavior leads to total conformity, which is undesirable. Today's world of change requires that people conform to general policies, but consciously use their own initiative in specific matters; this is explained in Chapters 12 and 13.

Assertiveness is the act of individuals who pursue their own rights and views without infringing on the rights of others. Its purpose must be the improved functioning of individuals and groups, that is to get something done in the best way, overcoming formalities, implicit assumptions, and in-group pressures.

Assertiveness serves to uncover the unclear assumptions in groupthink and a hidden agenda and can ensure good and open communication. But for people at the working level to be able to refuse wrong decisions requires an environment in which managers accept such behavior and do not penalize it. Assertiveness requires a certain discipline; it needs to be allowed from one side and pursued from the other.

Smith [196] presents a Bill of Ten Assertive Human Rights as a framework for human relations. In the context of this book, the following six are relevant:

1. You have the right to judge your own behavior, thoughts, and emotions, and to take the responsibility for their initiation and consequences upon yourself.

4. You have the right to change your mind.

5. You have the right to make mistakes, and be responsible for them.
6. You have the right to say, "I don't know."
9. You have the right to say, "I don't understand."
10. You have the right to say, "I don't care."

To this list, I would add an Assertive Human Duty: Say and repeat things that you really believe in. Smith recommends the best tactic is repeating, like a broken record, without getting angry. There's nothing new here, as the Roman censor Cato Maior around 150 B.C. allegedly ended all his speeches with, "But I think that Carthage must be destroyed." Repeating, however, must not result in long discussions or filibustering. Its purpose is merely to express strong feelings.

Dyer has many more recommendations on being assertive [53, 54]. His theme is to take charge of yourself and to avoid being victimized by others. His words differ from those of Smith, but his ideas to master your own life are similar.

2.17 Integrity

Integrity is behavior in line with sound moral values. There are three important aspects of integrity:

- Integrity toward others, to establish a basis of trust, which is necessary for communication
- Integrity toward oneself, which is necessary for self-respect
- Integrity toward others and oneself as a guarantee against manipulation

The first aspect simply states that good communication between people requires trust to achieve credibility and be successful. We cannot continually test every alternative every time. We must, therefore, trust that other people's intentions are honorable and that we will resolve problems as they inevitably arise. Similarly, the human user must trust the computer to do only predictable things. Otherwise, a feeling of distrust will dominate the user's mind and will interfere with doing useful work.

Integrity toward oneself involves personal honesty, responsibility, and accountability, and is necessary for self-respect. Self-respect is precious; it is an important part of your self-image (Bradshaw [23]). If you have a conscience, maintaining self-respect keeps it clear of guilt, enabling the mind to function optimally. Mowrer [142] suggests that when in doubt, try to get by with the truth.

Once you understand the effects of the various mind mechanisms, it becomes possible to manipulate people, to operate on them using unfair methods. In Europe, we have seen disastrous forms of manipulation that led to World Wars I and II. For that reason alone, many people fear manipulation.

Manipulation of people can also aim to reach a desirable goal in an effective manner, but there must obviously be rules to make certain that the goal is desirable. A question therefore is, How can you make certain that a goal is desirable? It is not good enough to let money alone decide that; there are enough cases in which the gains for the payer are greater than the costs. How then can we make certain that motives are honest? I certainly have no complete answer, but we can seek the following:

- Have maximum openness toward and discussions with all involved.
- Have a formal statement of objectives and goals, allowing and supporting verification by all involved.
- Stimulate codes of ethics for people involved in essential activities.
- Make individuals—not groups—responsible and accountable.
- Strive for an environment that supports assertiveness.

These precautions should maximize confidence that the goals are desirable. In any case, we must allot time for discussions instead of trying to hide issues under the table.

Mind mechanisms can be used to optimize the process of planning, developing, and using information systems so as to achieve laudable goals for computerization. Understand, however, that the mind has many more mechanisms than were discussed here and that there is more to people than a few mind mechanisms. For example, I have not discussed instinct, intuition, and emotions; refer to Ellis and Harper [56].

2.18 Summary

The following individual and interpersonal mind mechanisms were selected because of their importance to human relations in information system development:

Individual Mind Mechanisms

Perception	the way the mind sees patterns
Conception and cognition	the way the mind makes mental models
Short-term memory	the capacity of immediate memory
Mind set	a frame of reference
Reinforcement	feedback to correct actions
Selection	choosing meaningful options
Learning	acquiring knowledge, skills, or attitudes
Fatigue and confidence	the overall state of mind

Interpersonal Mind Mechanisms

Appearance	the outward aspect
Role	the acting part selected or imposed
Environment and time	the location and occasion
Suggestion and the self-fulfilling prophecy	a way to influence the mind
Groupthink and a hidden agenda	ways of communicating and deciding
Conformity and assertiveness	methods of acting and communicating
Integrity	honesty

This has been a long chapter, covering a difficult and interesting subject—the behavior of the human being and the underlying mind mechanisms. You need to understand this behavior so that you can adapt computers to people and achieve the goals of computerization.

If our mind were a machine, it would certainly be a very complicated one, operating simultaneously at a very large number of levels. From a human point of view, however, we are certainly not a rational machine (St. Aubyn [187]). We consider many points when we select an option and our selection is often not rational. The next chapter therefore discusses differences between humans and machines.

2.19 Review Questions and Exercises

1. Why is it so difficult to put yourself in someone else's position?

2. Few people will question that the mind controls the body, but there is no consensus to what degree the body can influence the mind. Discuss your opinion and give examples that prove and disprove how the body influences the mind.

3. A relaxed mind will more readily accept new ideas, but relaxing the mind is not so simple. As Hambly [82] indicates, you cannot mentally relax if you are physically tense.
   - What methods do you use to relax your body?
   - What methods do you use to relax your mind?
   - How can you relax the mind of others?

4. List and visualize the following processes in which feedback is essential for achieving quality or adapting to change.
   - Five processes in your bodily functioning
   - Five processes in your mental functioning
   - Five processes in the organization in which you work

   Describe how these processes reinforce or regulate quality.

5. Some people feel that the body and mind are comparable to hardware and software. Others disagree, arguing that the body and mind are completely interwoven and inseparable entities? Investigate this point by doing the following:
   - List ten properties of the human body and mind. How do these properties apply to hardware and software?
   - List ten properties of computer hardware and software. How do these properties apply to the human body and mind?

   What is your opinion?

6. Think of another person whom you know well and reflect:
   - In what respect could this person function or perform better?
   - To what degree is this due to mind set?
   - What would it take to change the mind sets of this person?

   Is your functioning and performance limited by your own mind set? Use Exercise 7 to convince yourself that you can change one of your mind sets.

7. The French pharmacist Emil Coué is known for his successful autosuggestion method whereby his patients had to repeat, "Every day in every way, I am feeling better and better." Select an activity that you know you cannot do very well. Tell yourself repeatedly, aloud or in your mind, that you *can* do it well. Visualize yourself doing it well and then do it. Did you improve?

8. Laing [113] poses this problem: "Seeing, we say, is believing. To what extent do we both believe what we see and see what we believe? How far does it go?" Answer his questions, giving examples from your own personal experience.

9. Section 2.1 states that the environment is uncertain because of changes, options, and subjective impressions. Give five examples each of changes, of options, and of subjective impressions from your experiences during the past week.

10. Name some recurring activities in which you perform two nontrivial tasks simultaneously. Try to do them separately. What difference does that make to you and to the result?

11. Consider a presentation that you attended recently:
    - In what respect did appearances support content? How could you turn the situations into conflicting appearances?
    - In what respect did appearances conflict with their content? How could you turn the situation into supporting appearances?

12. Consider some people you deal with regularly:
    - What role(s) do they play relative to you? Relative to others?
    - Are these roles effective or ineffective for their purpose?
    - How could people improve their effectiveness toward you?
    - How could you help them be more effective?

13. Before doing your next activity, reread {2.13} on environment and time and consider all the items mentioned. After you do the activity, ask yourself about the differences, if any, your consideration has made to the result.

14. Recall how some people have influenced you during the past week.
    - What methods did they use: yelling, telling, suggestion, or other?
    - Which way do you prefer that people influence your behavior?

- Is behaving in a specific manner an effective way of suggesting that same behavior to others? Why?

15. Section 2.14 states that most events in your life are self-fulfilling prophecies. Make a list of ten recent events and consider whether they were a result of a plan or suggestion. If you cannot identify people in an event, consider whether and how people were indirectly involved.

16. Find reports of some examples of poor planning in your environment or in public life.
    - Do the examples show any of the six major causes of failure due to groupthink? Are they due to a hidden agenda {2.15}?
    - Which assumptions turned out to be unrealistic?
    - Where and how could assertiveness have helped people plan better?

17. Comment on each of the following lines of reasoning:
    - Uncertainty assumes an important role in human society.
    - Uncertainty is a factor leading you to do things in a specific way.
    - Groupthink and the hidden agenda cause uncertainty when the unverified assumptions are brought into action.
    - Assertiveness can help prevent uncertainty.
    - Conformity can be seen as the act of avoiding confrontation, seeking certainty elsewhere.

    Explain whether and how assertiveness can still serve a useful purpose if everyone uses it to the same high degree.

18. Self-respect is the good opinion of one's self. Why is self-respect so important for people? Considering {2.17}, do you agree or disagree with the following observations:
    - "It is necessary for the happiness of man that he be mentally faithful to himself." —T. Paine, *The Age of Reason,* quoted in [205]
    - "All I am saying is that to lie, and be the victim of a lie, and to be ignorant in the soul concerning reality, to hold and to possess falsehood there, is the last thing any man would desire." —Plato, *The Republic,* Book II [164]

- "...those who deceive themselves generally know at bottom that they are doing so, and live in a state of apprehension lest some untoward event should force unwelcome realizations upon them." —B. Russell, *The Conquest of Happiness* [182]

Illustrate your answer with examples and consider how you can increase your self-respect.

19. Weinberg [206] tells the story of a man who goes to a tailor to get a custom-made suit. When the tailor is finished, the suit doesn't fit. The tailor directs the customer to take a strange posture, making him fit the suit. Later, on the street, another man approaches and asks for the tailor's name, explaining, "That tailor must be a genius to fit such a cripple." Discuss how interpersonal mind mechanisms were at work in the story

    - Between the customer and the tailor
    - Between the customer and the other man

    Describe similar incidents in which people feature something that they cannot properly fix or sell.

3

HUMAN-MACHINE CONSIDERATIONS

The distinctive potential contribution of the human
being in contrast to the machine, at every level of
the organization, stems from his capacity to think,
to plan, to exercise judgement, to be creative,
to direct and control his own behavior.
—D. McGregor, *The Human Side of Enterprise* [127]

An information system is a combination of people and computers working in unison. One of the first questions in computerization is how the tasks can best be split between the people and the computer. The answer involves the first principle of computerization: Organize before you automate. The many considerations underlying this principle are discussed in this chapter.

First, I will explain the reasons for organization and how to divide the tasks between people and computers based on differences in their capabilities. A section on artificial intelligence and expert systems helps to clarify these differences. This leads into an exposition of general human-machine dialogue considerations. The chapter ends with a taste of some practical problems, to illustrate the concepts discussed and to set the stage for Part II on developing and using information systems.

3.1 Analyzing Human and Machine Tasks

To introduce computers successfully into an organization, analysts must proceed with the understanding that their purpose is first and foremost to serve people. As a first step, analysts begin by modeling all of the processes in an organization; processes consist of tasks (both human and computer) that fulfill the goals of the organization.

The result of this analysis is a *business model,* which represents an overall (or top-down) logical view of all organizational processes and their tasks. The model also reveals the many relations and dependencies between processes that are to be integrated into a coherent whole. Only then can analysts determine the division of tasks between people and computers. To complete this top-down analysis, analysts must determine what information is necessary to carry out the tasks. The processes and tasks of an information system are indicated by dotted lines in Figure 3-1.

To develop the business model, analysts must make explicit *all* processes in the organization. This is easier said than done because analysts must describe not only implicit processes but also any new organizational processes.

An alternative approach, which I don't recommend, is to isolate a process in an organization and to automate just that. The result is invariably the creation of "information islands" that can be integrated only at great cost later on. Their later integration is inevitable because computers are much more useful when they can combine the information from more processes.

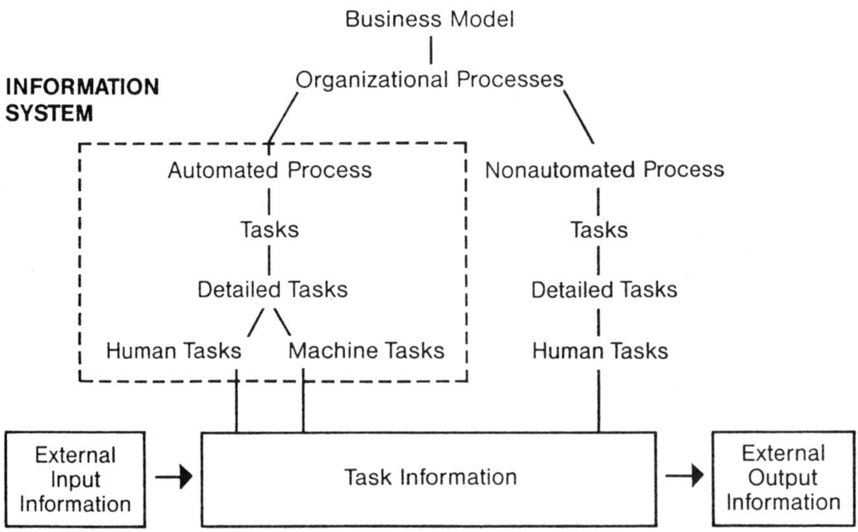

Figure 3-1. Logical structure of processes and tasks.

A process itself does not necessarily change when computers are introduced. Let me explain why this is so. In the process model, analysts focus on the logic of what is to be done, not on how it is to be carried out. For example, an Order Handling process can be structured into Order Entry, Order Dispatching, and Order Reporting tasks. Next, each of these tasks must be analyzed into their detailed tasks. Order Entry consists of Get Order, Verify Order, Enter Order, and Transmit Order, and so on. The structuring continues in this way to make explicit all logical task elements, without regard to the physical details of their implementation.

In addition to defining all processes, analysts must define the information needed to carry out the tasks, as shown at the bottom of Figure 3-1. External input information—for example, a customer order taken over the telephone—often starts a process, by providing customer and order details. External output information in this example could be a customer invoice and information about sales tax charged.

Both components—the definition of processes and information needs—form the architectural foundation for an information system. Like processes, information must be planned; all of the definitions are contained in a document called the *information plan,* which I'll discuss in more detail in Chapter 5.

Once an architecture of processes and tasks is made, detailed tasks can be divided between people and computers. This division must be made at all task levels. In our example above, at the highest level, people enter new records for customer orders and the computer prints a report at the end of the week about all orders for that period. Decisions at the highest level are often relatively simple to understand and make.

At the lower, more detailed levels, developers have more difficulty assigning tasks because their decisions will have a critical effect on how users will work in the future. Must the computer, for example, check whether a certain function code is allowed, or whether a credit limit is exceeded? If yes, there is a better chance that input data will be correct. If no, the system will be simpler to develop and understand, more flexible, and require less maintenance, but users will have to be more skilled and will have to be better trained.

The division of detailed tasks depends, then, upon whom the computer must serve and what they expect and the developers' understanding of these two facts. A common theme in this book is that computer tasks must properly match and interlock with human tasks.

The traditional view is that computers must be adapted to end users. I believe that computers must be adapted to all people: users, their customers, and everyone else. Consider, for example, the person issuing tickets in a skiing resort. It is *not* sufficient that the human-machine interface is superbly designed if the computer cannot prepare tickets in advance and the organization does not accept credit cards, or if the system cannot make proper tax reports and summary reports. Remember, information is always processed for many people and computers must be adapted to the needs of them *all,* not just the person at the terminal or workstation.

One final point is that all aspects of both general and detailed tasks must be allocated to either a person or a machine. There are two categories of considerations: The amount of lead time to implement human tasks is small since you can tell people that something will change tomorrow and they will adapt, but you must plan changes in the computer far in advance. Software as well as any changes to the software require careful planning because years may go by before they are implemented. An additional consideration stems from fundamental differences between people and machines, as discussed in the next section. For more information on task-oriented design, see Mumford's [143] examples that use a socio-technical system design method. Chapter 11 is devoted to organizational structure.

3.2 Differences Between Humans and Machines

When deciding about the division of work, keep in mind some basic differences between humans and machines. Recall from {2.1} that people have learned to live in an environment full of uncertainties caused by changes, options, and subjective impressions. We may not like people telling us what to do, but we will consider suggestions. We can make decisions on the spot, depending on our experiences and future needs. A computer, on the other hand, doesn't have a mind of its own and is preprogrammed to do only certain things. Its software spells out in exact detail what to do when. As a consequence, we must leave decisions about other issues to people, who can make ad hoc decisions.

A computer cannot process all human information. Dreyfus [49] noted that the following types of human information processing have resisted description in formal rules and therefore cannot be programmed in software:

- The ability to assess a situation from many levels and to make an intelligent decision that cannot readily be described in a determinate procedure. Dreyfus's example is chess, in which a person needs to consider only a few strategies whereas a computer must use brute force to explore all possible moves.
- The ability to assess a situation without having all the necessary information, by understanding the global context and the subject. Dreyfus's example is foreign language translation, in which a translator uses his or her understanding of the context and the subject to interpret sentences that would be incomplete or ambiguous for a mechanical translating device.
- Insight, the ability to distinguish what is important and what is not. Dreyfus's example is problem solving, whereby we must understand what the problem is before trying to find a solution and applying it. Understanding the problem is an obvious barrier for any mechanical device.
- The ability to distinguish patterns common to seemingly unrelated objects, conceptions, and thoughts. Dreyfus's example is character recognition, whereby we can recognize letters and numbers in an amazing variety of shapes, sizes, orientation, and quality, even on smudged paper. Another example is classifying people by their features as belonging to one family or another.

To summarize Dreyfus, people use a global understanding of the context as well as insight, discrimination, and pattern recognition to handle alternatives and different conditions. They draw on many years of general training and experiences to perform important tasks. For a computer to perform such tasks, developers must make all elements, structures, alternatives, and conditions explicit. This may not be practical, or even possible, in many real-life situations.

Because of people's subjective impressions, each entity can have many aspects, or views. Which aspect is pertinent depends on the context. In one case it may be weight; in another it may be color, size, cost, or shape. People have learned which aspect is relevant when (that is, to interpret meaning from context), but you must program that in the computer. Clearly, things can get out of hand if you must tell the computer under what condition each aspect is important, especially when circumstances change frequently.

What makes people even more different from machines is that we are often not even aware of the conditions ourselves. We handle many things intuitively on an ad hoc basis and take responsibility for our actions. Even if we could program a computer to make decisions on an ad hoc basis, it could not take responsibility for its decisions. Dreyfus argues that we often deal with open-structured problems, when we must judge whether a decision is reasonable and what its effect is. The computer could not do that.

According to Gestalt psychology, each part that we see gets its meaning from the whole, which may exist only as a concept in a person's mind. The meaning of the word "long," for example, depends entirely upon the context in which it is used and the experiences and expectations of the person using it. (Will a computer ever be able to understand what subject "it" refers to in the previous sentence? This will be necessary for translation from English to other languages!)

Because we remember what was important in a specific context some time ago, we have a predisposition to know what is relevant and not relevant now. We consider meaningfulness all the time {2.8}. Computers, however, just carry out software instructions. The great difficulty to model the nature and use of even simple human knowledge and understanding is clear from Dreyfus and Dreyfus [50], Newell and Simon [146], Schank and Abelson [189], and Goldkind's [74] review of Dreyfus's ideas. To appreciate the richness of human insight and communication, read Boulding's *The Image* [22], Gardner's *Frames of Mind* [69], and Schank's "Explaining Intelligence" in [198].

3.3 Appropriate Tasks for Machines

To my knowledge, Dreyfus [49] is the only author who has classified intelligent activities and described their relation to computers. He distinguishes four areas of increasing complexity:

1. *Associanistic,* an area where meaning and context are irrelevant to the activity. The system can process information without understanding what something means. In this area, program logic can consist of standard logical operations, decision trees, and lookup tables. It is suitable for use on computers.

2. *Simple formal,* an area where meaning is completely explicit and independent of the situation. Program logic can consist of fixed procedures. There is no principal problem to implement this area on computers, but the practicality of doing so depends on the complexity.

3. *Complex formal,* an area where meaning is determined by factors inside the system, and is independent of factors outside the system. In principle, we can also implement this area on computers, but the complexity often makes it impractical. Intelligent decisions are needed to reduce the number of computations.

4. *Nonformal,* an area where meaning and situation are not explicit. This includes all the everyday activities in our society that are not rule-governed and require intuition and insight. This area, which is not suitable for computers, includes our use of language.

The dividing line between the second and third area will shift with the advent of more powerful computers and software and an improved insight into human intelligence. Obviously, the dividing lines also depend upon the degree of perfection with which the activity is done and the effort spent in developing; for example, imperfect or simple language translation can be done on any computer and thousands of man-years in research have resulted in very good chess programs.

A problem in deciding to which area a situation belongs is that we often do not realize what is explicit, and what is not. We may feel that an activity is simple but that does not mean that we can make it explicit, a requirement for implementing it in a computer. The only way to find out is to analyze it, write it down, and let others review it, using a procedure such as the ISVIC procedure {1.6}.

Since an information system consists of both people and computers, Dreyfus's classification has consequences for how we can distribute the work between them. That is, we can only allow computers to perform tasks for which the meaning and the context are simple and explicit. To be useful in a real-world situation, machine tasks must be

- Explicit for specifying them completely
- Verifiable for checking their correct implementation
- Semipermanent to minimize software changes
- Updatable to be maintainable
- Understandable for both developers and users
- Uniformly applicable so there are few exception conditions

In summary, computers can perform certain tasks more precisely and more consistently than people, but tasks that require skill, expertise, and intuitive intelligence to make decisions in a changing environment should be left to people. Side by side, people and computers can perform well in most respects, if the tasks are divided properly. We are closing the period during which people were used as machines and we must now avoid using machines as people.

3.4 Artificial Intelligence and Expert Systems

Although I don't treat specific software technologies in this book, I must discuss artificial intelligence and expert systems because their name may suggest that the border between people and computer capabilities is vanishing. I don't believe this is true—computers remain machines, with all the restrictions and capabilities inherent to a machine, as outlined before. Their new functional possibilities are certainly a useful addition to the arsenal of software development tools, but I'd like to make the following observations:

We should not use the terms "artificial intelligence" (AI) and "expert system" to describe these new systems. There is serious doubt about whether intelligence can be artificial [49, 50], and the notion of a machine being intelligent contradicts the notion that machines can carry out only preprogrammed instructions {3.2}. Expert decision making is often nonformal, raising a barrier to implement it in any machine. The term "knowledge system" is more realistic and differentiates it sufficiently from the conventional information system. We can also use the terms "knowledge base" and "database" to indicate where knowledge and data are stored, respectively. (For an opposing view on AI, read Haugeland [86].)

Because knowledge systems must be implemented on computers, they suffer from the same limitations as conventional systems. There is no magic ghost in a computer and no magic ghost in a knowledge system; all their functions are explicitly programmed by people.

Because knowledge systems are often used in critical places and because their effects are not well understood, we must be cautious about introducing them. Being treated for a wrong medical diagnosis from a knowledge system is worse than receiving a wrong order.

Because we use much knowledge intuitively, we have a hard time describing it in the form needed for knowledge systems. That is, knowledge acquisition is a bottleneck in developing knowledge systems. It is very difficult to make human knowledge explicit and almost impossible to verify that knowledge definition is complete. Consequently, the choice of their application area and its delimitation are important.

There are often no objective criteria for knowledge systems. Developers need explicit criteria to test systems before they are put into operation.

Because our thinking and rules in our environment change all the time, the knowledge base must also change. This creates a maintenance problem at least as great as that of conventional software. How can we know when maintenance of a knowledge system is required?

Because computers cannot take responsibility, a person must always decide about important matters. Computers can only make well-understood and -accepted decisions and provide recommendations.

As I describe in the next section, the human-machine interface of a knowledge system must be very well designed and its users well trained. In order to take responsibility for its use, a user must understand the conclusions of a knowledge system.

Dreyfus discusses eight reasonable conditions for the successful application of a knowledge system, as given by Cook in [50]. In the next section, I consider working with a computer from a human-machine point of view.

3.5 Putting Human Experts in Charge of Computers

Computers and software are mechanical things that must follow their users, not lead them. The art of on-line dialogue design is to make certain that people do indeed feel in charge.

To feel in charge, users must be able to

- Take responsibility for information system operations
- Control hardware and software actions
- Check that the system operates properly
- Make and use ad hoc decisions in exception cases
- Intervene when they see that things go wrong

The objective of dialogue design should be that the machine does what the users want it to do. Developers need follow only one general recipe for designing a proper human-machine dialogue: They must understand the system as well as the end user groups to find a right match for each case. Because developers must make some assumptions on how users will work with their program, they must understand the users.

Users react differently, depending upon the following factors:

- Previous work experience
- Current way of doing the job
- Available alternatives for doing the job
- Expectations
- Conceptual and manual skill level
- Level of job understanding
- Amount of job training needed
- Frequency and duration of jobs and tasks
- Characteristics of the work environment
- Social environment, that is, relationships with other people
- Quality of support available to them
- Job title and description
- Expected performance (speed and errors)

Of these factors, previous work experience and expectations are especially important. People will have fewer problems if they have used a technology before, often when young. Today's youngsters have no problem in using a keyboard and a display, for example.

A proper introduction shapes expectations during training. A knowledge system raises higher expectations for its human-machine dialogue than does a conventional information system. Long tasks with many options will require more training than short and simple tasks.

Job titles are important to people and cost nothing. I remember when it was impossible to hire "card punch operators" but very easy to hire "data entry assistants" to do the same work. Most people have a desire to distinguish themselves in one way or another; the job title is one means to do so.

Users who deal with customers have the additional requirement that the computer must help, not restrict, them in servicing customers. They must be able to handle all matters, without referring the customer to someone else, so that customers also experience the use of computers as a step forward.

People generally assume responsibility for a whole task and do not find it meaningful to share tasks with someone else. As a general rule, make individuals responsible for what they see as a whole task. For example, if someone takes an order over the telephone, have that person also check the stock and enter the order information. Such an approach avoids mistakes caused by poor handwriting and achieves data entry while the customer is still on the telephone. It also illustrates how information tasks must blend naturally with other human tasks, such as a nurse taking care of patients and entering patient information. I want to stress that proper integration of computer tasks and human tasks is more important than the use of specific screen layouts and colors.

Because of different value systems, customs, and views, people in different countries also react differently; for examples, see Pascale and Athos [157] and Payer [158]. Developers of software intended for international use must not automatically assume that a good design for one country is equally good for other countries.

Another important consideration in dialogue design is *ergonomics,* the discipline that tells how to best adapt the work environment to the person. Ergonomics derives from the Greek words "ergon," meaning "work," and "nomos," meaning "laws of." For examples of using ergonomics, see Curtis [38, 57], Schneider and Thomas [190], and Shneiderman [193]. Norman [151] explains how good design makes the operation visible by employing familiar relationships, combining function and control, and using proper physical, semantic, cultural, and logical constraints. Unfortunately, computers are more complex and work at more levels than the everyday things Norman treats.

Ergonomists can analyze tasks theoretically (Card et al. [30]), based on *ease of use,* which is defined as the inverse of the

- Effort needed to learn or relearn the task
- Effort needed to perform the learned task
- Effort needed to recover from errors while doing the task

Ease of use depends upon the entire work context, including both the human interface design and individual job design, and the users.

It is usually better to let ergonomists test alternatives on a mock-up of the proposed product early in development. This allows them to compare alternative solutions, important because specific human reactions cannot be found in books. Testing done by professionals will reduce the chance of designers arriving at a Pygmalion solution that only confirms their misconceptions.

Unfortunately, applications and people differ too much and technology changes too fast for me to give any additional general recommendations for human-machine dialogue design. However, based on the previous discussion, I can offer some practical considerations for putting the human experts in charge of the human-machine dialogue:

Make and keep it simple for all people. This is necessary in order for users to fully understand their system and feel in charge, for their customers to feel happy about using computers, and for other people to use the computer information. Remember, keeping it simple for people is the key to successful computerization.

Provide flexibility in on-line communication. It may be important to provide alternatives for how the end user works with the system, depending on experience level. Equally important is customizing the interface to the organization's standards on color, function keys, terminology, and so on.

Involve end users in the design of human-machine dialogues. Only the users know the practical details of the human environment in which the dialogue will take place. Since you cannot put human insight into words, there is no substitute for their help in development. Involve users to design better dialogues.

Prepare effective user documentation. Users refer to printed manuals to learn about capabilities and limitations of the product and in case of problems. Structure manuals for how people will want to use them. Provide a table of contents and an index in each manual to help users locate commonly needed information items.

Provide proper training and support. Proper training must explain the overall concept of an information system and provide hands-on experience. No matter how well trained users are, unforeseen points will crop up and they will get stuck. A human network must support users to be the human experts on the system. Such a support network is often more important than an ergonomic design and good documentation but you can make some trade-offs between efforts spent on dialogue design, documentation, training, and support.

Finally, two major problems must be addressed in designing a proper human-machine interface. The first problem is that while its cost is in the development budget, the benefits of the interface are not. As a result, a development manager may reduce its development, even though increased expenditure is justified. To avoid this problem, consider the human-machine dialogue as a necessary function of the system, include it in development procedures, and test it under realistic conditions.

The second problem is that the theory of human-computer interaction is elusive because human reactions are difficult to predict. (The theory is also complex, see for example Norman and Draper [152].) A practical alternative to relying on theory is to draw on the insights of actual users during development, as proposed earlier. Another practical alternative is *evolutionary development,* that is, providing evolving versions or prototypes for getting user reactions (Gilb [73]).

Chapter 7 discusses details of the human-machine dialogue and Appendix B lists design principles for human-machine dialogues.

3.6 A Taste of Practical Problems: A Hospital Example

There are of course many practical difficulties in analyzing and assigning human and machine tasks. To get a taste of reality, I offer the following example of some problems facing an analyst investigating the computerization of patients' medical files in a hospital. Reality is never simple, as you'll see by the analyst's questions following the descriptions.

The hospital has a diffuse, non-hierarchical organization that uses a central information system to handle financial data. Hospital management now wants to include patients' medical data on this system.

Consulting physicians, who are either employed by the hospital or self-employed, are the medical experts. They examine patients, order tests, make diagnoses, and treat patients. Each physician has a secretary to handle paperwork and administrative details. The hospital employs nurses and trainees, with the manager of nursing services as their formal manager. A head nurse coordinates the work of nurses and trainees in a unit, following standard procedures and specific instructions given by consulting physicians during their visits. The nursing team changes three times a day. There is a meeting at the end of every shift, to hand over patient care to the new team.

The hospital has three types of files for each patient:

1. Out-patient file for consulting, located in a separate clinic of the hospital. This file is handled by the consulting physician's secretary, who will make appointments for consultations, tests, and treatments.

2. In-patient file for patients admitted to the hospital. This file is handled by the nursing unit and contains temperature and blood pressure readings, test results, X-ray results, and a wide variety of other medical records, all in chronological sequence. For some patients, this file is an inch thick, since old records are kept in case they are needed.

3. Nursing file, containing the nursing plan for the patient, with reports and medication plans. This file is handled and used by the nurses.

Patients usually start as out-patients; after a stay in the hospital as in-patients, they may become out-patients again for further treatment. This means there are usually three files for every patient. The three files are separate because combining them would make them unwieldy and more difficult to use.

The first two files are used for billing purposes and for a national medical registration system, but unfortunately, with different codes for each purpose. The files are physically moved to the billing office and to the medical registration group, thus making them unavailable in case of an emergency. Access to medical files is also a problem when the keeper of the files is not in the archive room.

The duplicate information in these three files is undesirable. Ideally, information should be stored just once to avoid inconsistencies and to simplify changes. That fact plus the need for correct information and timely access are all good arguments for automation of the medical files. Because of the difficult financial situation facing the hospital in the coming years, hospital management has done some strategic planning. They have decided to focus on nursing efficiency, hospital bed planning, and contacts with general practitioners as the areas that would benefit most from automation:

- Nurses are a major expense item for the hospital and they are in short supply. Moreover, they spend much of their time on administrative duties, which automation could reduce.

- Knowledge systems can be used to predict treatment patterns to improve the planning of hospital bed use. This requires medical information from the out-patient and in-patient files to be entered into the computer.
- By automating medical records, the hospital wants to improve the communication with general practitioners who refer their patients to the consulting physicians in the hospital and assume responsibility for the patients again after hospital treatment.

In addition to hospital management's strategic planning, three new types of legislation may affect out- and in-patient files in contradictory ways. Hospital liability legislation requires that all treatment details be recorded in the files, but privacy legislation dictates that only a minimum of personal information be kept and the patient must authorize any disclosure (Rule et al. [180]). Medical treatment legislation may give patients the right to see and control all information in their files. It is obvious that the combination of such contradictory legislation can have a profound impact on national medical registration and trend analysis.

Given this situation in the hospital, the desired changes, and the pending legislation, some of the questions facing an analyst on the automation of these files include

- How can existing files be converted to computer files? What part of the information should be put into the computer database? The files are too large for complete conversion; some information is obsolete while other information is in the form of photographs. Physicians will insist on keeping the two current files for patients because they may need all available information for treating them.
- How can the paper files and the computer files be made to match? If they can't, which one will be the master file? Will a computer file printout need to be added to the paper files for

completeness? If so, how can it be done and how can it be kept current?

- Should the analyst consider automating other hospital processes at the same time as the patient files? For example, can billing and medical registration be combined when their data is in the computer? What about file registration in the archive room and information on patients' diets? Since everything ties into everything else, where does the analyst stop?
- Who are the users? Although the users may seem to be the consulting physicians, right now very few of them want to touch a keyboard. They have no desire to perform what they regard as administrative chores. Their secretaries are more likely to be users, but this may well change. And, of course, almost everyone else in the hospital will add information to or extract information from the out-patient and in-patient files.
- Who will enter data into the computer? People in a hospital are always in a hurry, with patient care as their first duty and administrative details their last. Will nurses have time to enter patient information? What is a good division of tasks between people and computers? How can information processing tasks be integrated in the different jobs? How can whole tasks be defined?
- Who owns and is responsible for what information? Who has authority for data access? What security measures must be considered?
- Should the hospital choose a rigid system with complete checking or a flexible system, relying on human judgment and correction?
- Can a medical knowledge system really serve a purpose for hospital bed planning? If the answer is yes, what type of knowledge system is needed? Must a knowledge system be integrated with the central information system of the hospital? What are the performance implications of such an integration? If the answer is no, what alternative planning methods are available?
- What alternatives are available to computerization of files? Can microfiches or videodiscs be used, if only for part of the information?
- To what extent, and how, must an analyst consider future privacy, medical treatment, and hospital liability legislation?

- How can the analyst discuss proposed solutions and seek agreement from the many hospital groups involved so they will accept a proposed solution, not fight it?

These are all tough questions, but such is life for the analyst and it is getting such-er and such-er. The analyst must plan the tasks of people and computers, replacing the way of doing certain things. To do so successfully, an analyst requires much wisdom, insight, and imagination about technology and the human world, and there must be much discussion. Above all, the hospital needs a sound master plan because even partial solutions will take years to develop.

In real life, as in this example, most things are not straightforward and there are many unknowns. Everything ties into everything else, making it difficult to distinguish cause and effect. Many compromises must be made to arrive at a suitable solution, typically a year before it is installed. Therefore, we require a formal procedure to investigate and develop the many aspects of an information processing solution. Chapter 4 discusses such a procedure for developing information systems, and Chapter 5 discusses one for using information systems. Chapter 7 deals specifically with on-line communication, and Appendix B contains a list of on-line dialogue design principles.

3.7 Summary

1. Much careful analysis and insight are needed to devise an architecture for an information system that properly fits into the human working environment. Specifically, there must be early decisions on tasks to be performed by people and those by the computer. Since people are an integral part of an information system, the computer tasks must blend with their other tasks.
2. People, as opposed to computers, intuitively understand meaning and context, can attach significance, have insight, and can assume responsibility. Tasks that require these capabilities should be allocated to people.
3. Assign tasks only to a machine when they are
   - Explicit so you can specify them completely
   - Verifiable so you can check their correct implementation
   - Semipermanent so they will not change often

- Updatable so you can maintain them
- Understandable so that developers and users can understand them
- Uniformly applicable so there are few exception conditions

4. Especially important is the decision as to how much checking will be done by the system and how much you can or must rely on human judgment.
5. To develop a solution in which human experts feel in charge, you must understand the characteristics of the user groups. Users, customers, and others involved must all feel the solution is a step forward.
6. Professionals must test human-machine dialogues early in development, letting typical users compare alternative solutions.
7. Use a systematic method (such as ISVIC {1.6}) to analyze practical problems.
8. Introduce computers properly by providing adequate training. A human support network can further increase users' confidence about working with them.

3.8 Review Questions and Exercises

1. Consider how information is processed for people. Select an application that you know well and make a list of all users, their customers, and others involved. Then add what information is processed for each group of people. Explain if any processed information is not intended for people.
2. Section 3.6 poses several questions an analyst must try to answer while investigating a new information processing application.
    - How would you arrive at a proper answer for each of those questions?
    - How would you find and analyze pertinent facts, form a preliminary opinion, and verify this opinion with knowledgeable people to make certain that future users agree with your proposal?
    - How would you find alternatives?
3. Consider the application of knowledge systems in the hospital example {3.6}.

- In which of the four areas of intelligent activities described by Dreyfus {3.3} do you think medical diagnosis and the prediction of medical treatment patterns belong?
- Do you think that consulting physicians will welcome a knowledge system for medical diagnosis? If not, why not? What could be done to make it acceptable to them?
- Do you think that bed planners will welcome a knowledge system for bed occupancy planning? If not, why not?
- Describe what you think is the major use of knowledge systems in a hospital.

4. Although no one can predict the future, knowledge systems that are capable of learning may become a reality. Use your imagination to consider how such a learning knowledge system might work side by side with a human expert to learn from the expert's decisions. The expert decides what problems the system can handle and checks its answers. Assuming that it is technically possible to realize such a symbiosis,

   - Describe some problems you would encounter:
     - Technical problems
     - Human-machine dialogue problems
     - Task integration problems
     - Social problems
   - How could such a symbiosis work in detail?
   - What is needed before a knowledge system could start learning?
   - Would it ever be possible to let a knowledge system make decisions that are not checked by a human? If yes, what type of decisions? If no, why not?

   Explain why you think that such a symbiosis would or would not be a good idea.

5. Any organization that wants to use its resources (facilities, people, and tools) in an optimum fashion must make plans and be able to adjust them accordingly when resources change. Describe the general planning process as a self-regulating feedback process. What is the relationship between planning and management control in your description?

6. Scheduling is a complex planning process because of the many interdependencies between items. Discuss similarities and differences

of the following planning processes, as well as how the differences would affect the allocation of human and machine tasks if the planning process were computerized. Name the groups of people involved in each case. If a planning process has no best solution, how would you reach a compromise?

- Planning 250 programmer tasks in an 8 man-year software development project. There will be task definition, content, and sequence changes during development.
- Planning the week's schedule of 1,000 high school courses. The 75 teachers have requirements on specific days of the week they are available. Also, they want to teach at least three courses per day and prefer to have no gaps between them.
- Planning daily bed occupancy in a hospital so as to assign 700 beds to 70 consulting physicians whose incomes depend on how many patients they treat. Treatment patterns are difficult to predict and some beds must be reserved for emergencies.
- Planning for 4 nurses and 2 trainees to work in a nursing unit during each of 3 shifts, 7 days per week. Everyone must get a fair share of regular work, overtime, and being on call for emergencies. There must be flexibility to make changes, to get sick, to go on vacation, and to take a day off.
- Planning airline seat occupancy and fares for a company with 40 airplanes, having 10,000 seats, and making 75 flights every day. Assume that passengers often change reservations and that airline companies often change their fares.

7. Rank the following type of texts according to difficulty of machine translation:

   a. A novel

   b. The *Readers' Digest* abridged version of the same novel

   c. The review of the same novel in a newspaper

   d. A newspaper article discussing a historic event

   e. A technical book on mathematics

   f. A legal document on a subject

   g. The law on the same subject

   h. The functional specification of a new information system

i. An introductory booklet for that information system

Describe the assumptions you made and explain the reasons for your ranking.

8. Imagine that a knowledge system can look up words in a grammar book, a dictionary, a thesaurus, an encyclopedia, and any other book. Why or why not will such a knowledge system be able to understand the meaning of text like you do? Give examples to support your conclusions.

9. "Can computers do more than you tell them to do?" is the title of a section in a book by Flores and Winograd [64]. Answer this question and compare computers to people who can and sometimes will do more than they are told to. Give examples from your personal experience.

10. Imagine you are the commander of a warship equipped with a knowledge system to determine friend or foe and to trigger the ship's defense system. Only the knowledge system can make the quick decision needed to defend the ship against an offensive attack.
    - Describe under what conditions you would enable the knowledge system to trigger the defense system automatically.
    - Describe under what conditions you would disable the knowledge system.

11. Consider to what degree computers are taking over people's jobs:
    - If you think computers are taking over tasks that should be left to people, write a summary of your opinions to convince decision makers that there are plenty of better uses for computers. Give examples.
    - If you think that computers are not taking over enough tasks from people, write a summary of your opinions to convince decisions makers that they should use computers for other tasks. Give examples.

12. To understand the proper division between human and machine tasks, you first must understand who are the future users {3.5}. As an exercise, consider a supermarket check-out station. You have the following options in assigning human and machine tasks:
    - Clerks type a code that the computer translates into a price.
    - Clerks type a code and a price; the computer checks both.

- Clerks type a price checked only for obvious keying errors.
- You choose another option.

Select one of the above options and discuss how your choice will affect each of the following groups of people:

- The clerk entering the data
- The manager of the clerk
- The accountant of the supermarket
- A client of the supermarket
- A planner of the supermarket
- A system programmer of the supermarket's computer
- Anyone else affected

13. Section 3.5 states there is no general recipe for designing a proper human-machine dialogue. Two reasons given are that applications differ too much and that technologies change too fast.
    - Browse through Chapter 3 and make a list of other reasons why the human-machine dialogue is so elusive.
    - Discuss the alternative suggested in {3.5} to use the insight of users, or their representatives, in the development process.

Part II

DEVELOPING AND USING INFORMATION PROCESSING SYSTEMS

Chapter 4. Developing Information Systems

Describes the plans and organization needed to develop information systems • Includes planning, development activities, roles of people, the development phase process, training, and guidelines for creating documentation.

Chapter 5. Using Information Systems

Describes the plans and organization needed to use information systems • Includes planning an application, implementation activities, roles in the user organization, and practical considerations in using computers.

4

DEVELOPING INFORMATION SYSTEMS

Everyone doing any job ultimately
is providing a service for someone else.
—P.W. Metzger, *Managing Programming People* [133]

In this chapter, I will explain what it takes to develop software. I will discuss planning, development activities, roles of people, training, and guidelines for creating phase and development documentation. (Communication, documentation, and training are elaborated on in Part III.)

Whether you are developing a small information system or a large one, you need to follow a certain sequence of actions in order to work efficiently. Only the management control and procedures will vary, depending upon the size of the project and the experience of the developers. This chapter discusses the general procedures for a large-scale software development project. For a smaller project with fewer control requirements, you can then select the appropriate procedures from those presented here.

Determining procedures and plans and keeping to them are not favorite tasks. We don't like to tie ourselves down beforehand to do things a certain way and we feel restricted from reacting to changes and choosing new options. Nevertheless, many procedures and plans are necessary for developing software, to keep many people working in unison to a common goal.

Most computers today use thousands of system programs and many application programs, all developed by trained professionals. The idea of users programming anything more complex than a simple program is unthinkable.

Software is difficult to develop, and requires extra management attention to address the symptoms of what has been called the "software crisis" since the early 1980s (Booch [21]). These symptoms include

- Systems that do not meet user needs and expectations
- Software that often fails in operation
- Unpredictable and excessive cost of software development
- Complex, costly, and error-prone maintenance of software
- Software that is delivered late and incomplete
- Software that is not portable to other computers
- Software that does not optimally use the computer

Curtis et al. [39] have analyzed software developed in the middle 1980s and found three salient problems:

- Developers' lack of knowledge about the particular application area
- Fluctuating and conflicting requirements
- Communication and coordination breakdowns

If nothing else, these symptoms and analysis clearly show the need for good planning when developing information systems—the major topic of this chapter.

4.1 Planning the Development Process

> There is an old saying, "well begun is half done"—'tis a bad one. I would use instead—Not begun at all until half done.
>
> —J. Keats, Letter, 1817, quoted in [78]

As Seneca observed, a mind anxious about the future is miserable. The purpose of planning is to remove anxiety by presenting an image of the future in which people can believe—thus becoming a self-fulfilling prophecy. A good plan states the desired results and provides a rationale. It details how you will overcome expected as well as unforeseen obstacles, how you will monitor progress, and how you will measure the success of the plan itself. It considers costs, values, and benefits.

Much insight and foresight are needed to make good plans. The quality of a result depends upon the quality of its plan. A sound long-range vision is vital for the strategic plans that provide the basis for lower-level plans. Management interest will determine how well people use their plans. And, although a plan is never perfect, having an imperfect one is better than having no plan at all.

For a plan to be good, it must change as your understanding of the future changes. Regular review of all plans is necessary to keep them current or else people will not use them. In addition, reviewing and recording changed assumptions are basic to good planning, as well as necessary to avoid a hidden agenda.

Planning in development begins with the creation of a *development business plan* that contains the long-range objectives and strategy of the development organization; see the planning hierarchy in Figure 4-1, which shows general plans at the top leading to specific plans at the bottom.* Many

*I distinguish between development plans (for the development work) and information system plans (for the use of computers). Because developers use computers to develop software,

strategic points in this business plan will relate to computers because they are vital to the software development business.

Next in the hierarchy is the *development strategic plan,* which addresses the work area (including products, customers, technology, and location) and objectives of the development organization as a whole (Galbraith [67]).

Figure 4-1. Hierarchy of development planning.

Three plans follow from the strategic plan: the tactical, operational, and project plans. The *development tactical plan* translates the strategic plan into specific activities needed during the coming one- to two-year period (like the development of a special software tool needed for a new project). Specific project proposals start during tactical planning.

The *development operational plan* contains the current year's plan for all development projects, consolidated from the individual project plans.

Project plans contain the details for each development project, based upon the activities discussed in {4.2}. These plans describe in essence each project's life cycle and detail how a development manager will control time, costs, quality, and reviews to develop software and supporting materials.

The rest of this chapter will concentrate on software development activities, as contained in a project plan. Like other complex matters, any development project of three or more months in length must be carefully structured so that intermediate results can be reviewed and plans adapted. (Section 4.5 describes a phase process to review each activity upon completion.)

---

they also need information system plans. To avoid any confusion, I will discuss development plans in this chapter and information system plans in Chapter 5.

4.2 Activities for Software Development

The project activities make up a project's life cycle from start to completion. Different authors use different names for the activities, but they all follow the general sequence of planning, design, development, and support. In my preferred life cycle, I have chosen eight activities and used names for each that describe the activity carried out. The output or result of each activity is on the right in Figure 4-2.

Activity	Output
1. Definition and Proposal	Detailed proposal for the project
2. Study and Analysis	Detailed analysis of the requirements
3. External System Design	Design of interfaces to the outside world
4. Human Interface Design	Design of interfaces to the users
5. Internal System Design	Internal design of the software
6. Program Development	Software programs
7. Test	Test results for software acceptance or rejection
8. Support	People and materials to support users and others to install and use the software

Figure 4-2. Eight activities of software development.

Note that Maintenance is not included in these eight activities because it includes *all* of them; as I'll discuss in {4.3}, developers must go through these activities again every time a piece of software is modified, corrected, or enhanced. Installation is considered a user activity and will be discussed in the next chapter {5.3}.

Notice too that External System Design and Human Interface Design precede Internal System Design. The reason is that internal design must follow the design of interfaces to external computers, as it must support, not dictate, the way the system will work with people and other computers. Supporting materials {4.7} are an integral part of the software product; their development takes place throughout the first six activities, and the materials produced are tested along with the software in the seventh activity.

The following sections discuss the eight activities in a project life cycle to develop a new piece of software; for a detailed discussion, see (Aron [8], Blokdijk and Blokdijk [17], and Yourdon [216]).

1: DEFINITION AND PROPOSAL

The first activity generates an overall proposal and statement of objectives in response to a user request or user need. It establishes the fundamental requirements (Gause and Weinberg [70]). It answers the questions, What is it and why should we do it? Included in the overall proposal is a financial section that gives the development business rationale of the project. Other parts address social, administrative, and quality assurance aspects. The review of the proposal is a prerequisite for the decision to start the next activity.

2: STUDY AND ANALYSIS

This activity investigates the requirements of the proposed system in detail, includes a user business rationale, and produces a preliminary project plan. A major part of the activity is used to analyze how the proposed system will function within the user organization. (Recall from Figure 3-1 the user organization is documented in a business model.) This activity consists of process analysis, which produces process models, and data analysis, which produces information models. In addition, event analysis is needed when there are time dependencies, and otherware analysis yields requirements on supporting materials.

In addition to these models, analysts describe the proposed system in language that users can understand and prepare a financial proposal to explain the user business rationale. Analysts also identify every group of people that the computer must serve—users, their customers, and anyone else involved—and their requirements on supporting materials. Finally, the activity yields a preliminary decision on the technology to be used to implement the system (including the possible use of knowledge systems), which is confirmed during the design activity. The output of this activity is the system description, a component of the *functional specification* (see Figure 4-4).

3: EXTERNAL SYSTEM DESIGN

This first design activity concerns the architecture of all external interfaces and the design of the databases. External interfaces for sending data to and from other computers are often already established and cannot be changed. Therefore, this activity is needed to assure consistency with existing systems as well as their future extensions. A basic decision at this stage is also whether to use one central computer or several decentralized computers. This activity also defines the tasks and the information that belongs to each task, allowing a first division of human and machine tasks.

4: HUMAN INTERFACE DESIGN

This second design activity concerns the overall design of the interface with the user. It includes defining system options, procedures, screen designs (including Help facilities), menu options, report layouts, and prototypes. Tests must verify the ease of use of tasks designed and test alternative design approaches {3.5}. Design of such supporting materials as manuals and tutorials follows from the design of the human interface.

5: INTERNAL SYSTEM DESIGN

This third design activity comprises the design of the software, structuring it into subsystems with detailed flow diagrams, internal interface specifications, and design descriptions. Designers concentrate first on frequently used functions (since they are critical to achieving an acceptable performance), followed by other less important functions.

In this activity, developers must also anticipate how information entities like prices, rates, and conditions will change, so that they will be easy to modify in the software.

By the end of Internal System Design, developers will understand all unknowns so they can make a firm commitment to further development. The project group continues to increase during this stage, as key people join the team to complete internal design. The entire design is verified during design inspections and reviews (see, for example, Fagan [58]. As an aside, he received one of the largest bonuses in IBM's history for the savings realized through inspections.).

While the design is being completed and verified, good documentation of the design must be made so that everyone can understand what the system must do. In this activity, developers also consider installation, conversion, and testing, including any special utilities needed, and they specify different hardware configurations for measuring response times. The results of this activity complete the *functional specification,* comprised of the system description, configurations and performance, user environment, process and data models, and the designs.

6: PROGRAM DEVELOPMENT

Program Development is the actual building of the software from the models and the design specifications. Besides programming, other tasks at this time are to

- Develop supporting materials for different user groups
- Develop test cases
- Complete recommendations for installation and conversion

Because the software consists of many programs developed by different people, this activity involves many unit tests of the individual programs in isolation as they are completed, and integration tests on an ensemble of units.

7: TEST

The final activity of software development is Test, whereby developers and users verify that programs work together according to the functional specification. Using the test plans made during the three design activities, the software is thoroughly checked that it indeed meets the criteria specified. The integrity of the system as a whole is verified to make sure that it is complete and that the documentation accurately describes it.

Test is a fairly simple and straightforward activity if the tests are properly prepared. A comprehensive test plan describes what to test and what facilities are needed. Because it is not possible to perform an exhaustive test of every possible situation, the selection of test cases is important. Here are descriptions of various types of tests:

- *System test* is the formal and extensive test of the system according to specified acceptance criteria. Its purpose is for developers themselves to check the system, its documentation, and its interfaces with other systems. This test takes place at the developers' location with made-up data.
- *Pilot test* is an optional test with real data to determine whether users can install the software and tailor it to their needs. This test is often performed under shared responsibility of developers and users at the users' location.
- *Installation and acceptance test* checks whether users can install and use the software without help from developers. It is

mandatory when you will sell many copies of the software. An acceptance test enables users to officially accept a software system.

8: SUPPORT

Support, the final activity, involves assisting the users and generally smoothing the transfer of the product to the users. It involves answering their questions and helping them to solve problems they encounter with the software and its supporting materials, and with training. Support requires a separate group, whose sole purpose is this job.

This sequence of eight activities is independent of the product developed and the tools used because it follows a general approach of analysis followed by synthesis. These activities can follow the ISVIC procedure presented in Chapter 1: Simply replace Investigating by Study and Analysis, Structuring by Design, Implementing by Program Development, and Checking by Test. Verifying would replace reviews conducted throughout the project's life cycle.

The main difficulties in carrying out these activities concern the difficulties of imperfect human qualities and communication. Developers must always talk with users to understand their situation, and they must draw on all their skills and imagination to convert their interpretations of users' needs into a model and then into software. System development is a team effort with changing participants, complicating the communication problems. Figure 4-3 illustrates what can go wrong in this process if communications break down.

4.3 Implications of the Software Product Developed

A development project must deliver both software and supporting materials for training and assisting the end users, but the physical form of that software is only as a magnetic tape or disk.

Software and its related documentation are developed as computer files. As a result, a very short manufacturing cycle of the software product itself is possible, and production of the documentation in quantity requires only slightly more time. Both programs and documentation can be sent as computer files to users and maintained via a network. Because programs are translated into unreadable codes before they can be used on computers, software cannot be checked visually.

The development computer files must be protected since they contain the valuable software developed. This has several implications that are considered next.

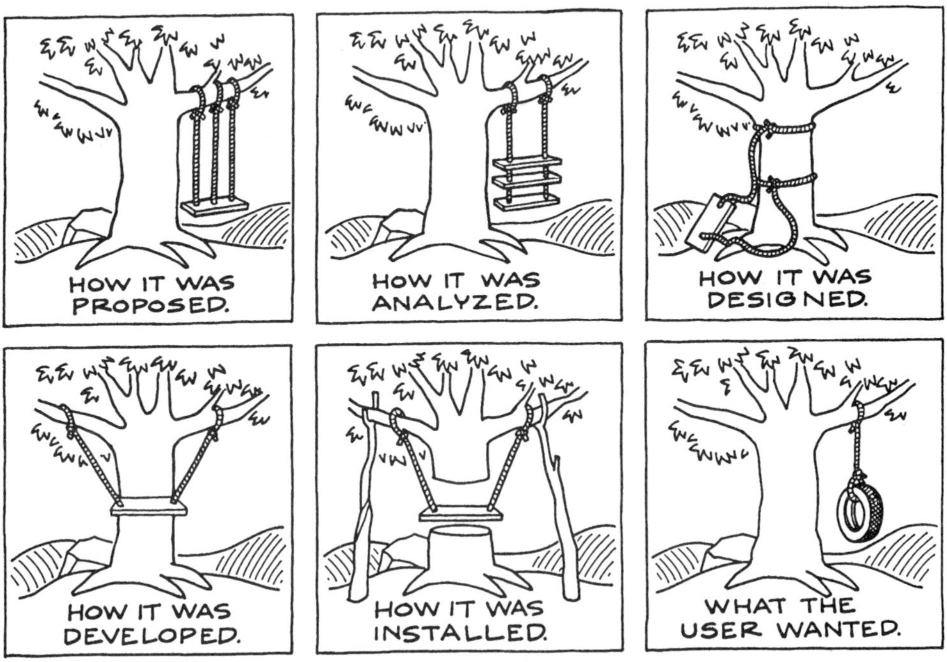

Figure 4-3. Swing analogy of the development process (adapted from unknown author).

CHANGE CONTROL AND CONFIGURATION MANAGEMENT

Change control is common practice in much of product engineering, in which design changes and their control are well established. Once a basic design is available, it is straightforward, say, to extend a bridge by ten feet, to widen a building by four yards, and to reduce a wheel diameter by two inches. But change control is different for software and its documentation. Because of the many interdependencies between elements, changes often necessitate new designs.

What is needed is *configuration management,* which involves setting up a library system and procedures to control how changes are made to the thousands of files and their different versions. A library system is special software to store the different program versions during development. Major projects could not take place without proper configuration management (Metzger [132]).

Support and maintenance may require retrieval of older versions of a system. The loss of an old version of a file, an update not made, or an incorrect change may cause months of delay and even jeopardize an entire project. An approval committee reviews and ranks change proposals according to certain procedures, especially if a system is developed or used at different locations. In addition, conventions are needed for using meaningful file names so that programmers can easily identify them.

SOFTWARE MAINTENANCE

Maintenance is the development of new versions of software, including adding functions and correcting problems. Because change is a constant in our environment, software maintenance is an extremely important consideration. According to Boehm [97], for every dollar spent on development, you will spend two dollars on software maintenance. Indeed, a system that is developed over a period of one or more years may no longer even satisfy the requirement by the time it is installed. At my former company, we often said, "IBM means It's Been Modified."

Sadly, software maintenance is a fact of life, but proper planning and design can reduce the impact of a change in one part on other parts of software. Proper planning also applies to the documentation. Note that software maintenance must go through the same eight activities as the original developers but on a smaller scale because the effort is usually smaller and the project better understood.

Hardware maintenance is relatively simple, involving only the ordering and installation of a new processor model, new networks, or other terminals. (Otherware maintenance is discussed in {5.3}.)

SOFTWARE SECURITY

The idea behind security is that the system and its information should be used only for specific purposes. Security is needed to prevent intruders, computer crime, viruses, and so on, because computers simply carry out program and user instructions. Computers don't know what instructions are good, bad, erroneous, or unintended, which is one reason why security is such an important and difficult problem. As it is not possible to achieve one hundred percent security, we can only prevent most misuse.

The security of an information system depends upon its hardware, software, and otherware. The use of networks especially makes computers less secure and requires additional security measures. Developers must design security facilities into the system that users can employ; security doesn't happen automatically. Examples of hardware security are workstation locks, identification card readers, and a dial-back feature on public networks to verify a telephone number. Examples of software security are access authorization, password control, and coding of data sent over networks. Examples of otherware security are identification cards, physical access control, and individual user authorization.

Some security facilities that appear during actual use, and therefore need to be considered during development, are the following:

- Users commonly accept that they must identify themselves to the system with an identification card and a password. It should be equally well accepted that the system must identify itself to a user so as to prevent use of fake terminals to steal codes and passwords. This is not a trivial problem because it is a chicken-and-egg situation: Who must first reveal identity?
- Security requirements affect how people work with a system in more than one way. For example, people must key in passwords to gain access, and they will have to set up and follow procedures for illness and vacation. Since security measures affect the system's ease of use, users will have to appreciate the importance of security, so they will comply with them and not try to bypass them.

(Section 5.5 discusses user security considerations.)

4.4 Roles of People in the Development Organization

Organizing properly is important to software development. The following is an overview of the principal roles in a project and its supporting groups. Different people may play the same role during the project life cycle; practical considerations often determine just how people participate.

Project manager supervises people on a project to develop software. Large projects have a layered management structure whereby coordinators and team leaders may handle specific technical aspects. Blokdijk and Blokdijk [17] discuss seventeen plans of a development project manager.

Project planner formulates the project's objectives, prepares and handles procedural matters, and pursues all unresolved issues for the project manager.

Development analyst works with the users to investigate their requirements and to develop the application as the solution for user organization. The analyst's role is vital; it provides the architecture for how the eventual product will fit into the user environment.

Development architect specifies the overall structure of the software, detailing the interfaces between components in a large system and with other computers (Mills [137]). This role serves as an intermediary between analysts and designers in medium to large projects. In small projects, this role is split between analysts and designers.

Development designer conceives of the implementation of an information system from the analyzed architecture, and documents it in a design specification.

Development programmers, the worker bees in a project, carry out the actual programming from the functional specification, producing the desired product.

User (or *user representative*) is the client or customer who ultimately must accept or reject the system. The user has the vital function of contributing expertise about the future application and the user environment to the project. Ideally, this key person has sufficient authority to make major decisions and is an effective communicator in explaining how the software will be employed. In the beginning, the user or the user representative works with the analyst to define organizational processes. Then the user helps the development architect and designer to design the human interface. This person coordinates and reviews the documentation for the system as it is prepared and is involved in formulating the criteria by which the system will be accepted. The user also helps to devise test cases, to test the system, and may also serve as a facilitator or an agent of change in the user environment to accompany the introduction of the new system. (London [116] Chapter 6 further discusses user involvement.)

Supporting materials developer creates the manuals and the training materials for end users. Ideally, an excellent communicator and writer, this person must understand both the technical aspects of the product, as well as the users' level of understanding and information needs to address them properly.

Customer support answers users' and others' questions about the system, and is able to correct minor problems. (Major problems are the subject of software maintenance, discussed in {4.3}.)

Development support, a staff group, provides the development project with programming tools and software library facilities. It administers all of the process and information models created during the development activities.

Software quality assurance, also a staff group, collects data on the work of development projects and uses that to estimate new projects and to evaluate continued projects for management {4.8}.

For further information on roles in development, refer to Aron [8] on project management and organization, DeMarco and Lister [46] on productive projects and teams, Lammers [114] on programmers at work, and Metzger [133] on life in a development project.

4.5 Development Phase Process

The goal of any development is to arrive at a solution that the user truly wants. The process for doing that is called the *development phase process.* Each development phase may comprise one or more of the eight activities discussed in {4.2}, with a review concluding each phase.

The purpose of the phase process is to make development issues visible to all concerned, thus avoiding surprises. A kind of self-fulfilling prophecy, it is a vast communication and planning process to establish proper proposals and plans. Specifically, the phase process is

- Self-regulating to ensure that all important issues are considered
- Structured in phases to assure review of progress at the end of every phase
- Documented for review and discussion of issues and progress

There are many ways to structure the phase process. Very large projects often use more phases than the eight activities, and small projects may use fewer phases than activities. It is impossible to give any hard-and-fast rules (Turner et al. [203]). The most important point is to keep the process flexible, adjusting it to the situation. Good software must be the goal, not adherence to procedures. The following are some general considerations in designing the procedural structure for a particular development project:

1. Every project needs a phase process. Adapt the number of phases and the extent of the reviews to the complexity of the project. Use as few phases as possible to reduce the overhead each review causes. The minimum number of phases is three: Proposal/Study (Activities 1 through 4), Development/Testing (Activities 5 through 7), and Support (Activity 8).

2. The purpose of the phase process is to reach consensus on important assumptions and issues *before* they are cast in software. Phase reviews provide an overall check-and-balance function in project management.

3. The minimum gestation period for a project depends upon its complexity and the skills of the available people. Development of a program version (Activities 1 through 7) should not last longer than two years; otherwise, the basic assumptions will certainly have changed.

4. The best phase process follows the logical sequence of work in a project; the procedure must be a supportive tool, not a dictator. Tools and people will determine the content and schedule of development phases.

5. Conclude each phase with a formal review, to determine whether the project is still on target, to discuss plans and issues, to decide on continuation, and to plan for the next review. Phase documentation, as described below, is distributed before each review to give participants time for studying it. The outcome of each review, as well as undecided issues, are documented for later consultation and so that important issues won't be overlooked.

Aron [8] and Metzger [132] present a project documentation plan in case the user reviews development phase documentation. Other documentation plans are necessary when software is developed for general marketing to users who are unknown at the time of development.

4.6 Phase Process and Development Documentation

I estimate that documentation can take as much as one-third of a development budget, and this proportion is not likely to decrease. Although participants often consider paperwork a nuisance, it is needed to verify assumptions and to document requirements and designs. Documentation is of two major types: phase process and development documentation, discussed in this section, and user documentation, discussed briefly in {4.7} and in more detail in Chapter 8.

Phase documentation presents the results of the development phase under review, the project plan, and detailed plans for the next phase. It also contains all basic decisions for the next phase so that reviewers can study and perhaps modify them as a result of the current phase under review.

In many development organizations, a Policies and Procedures Guide contains all the formalities of their phase process. Some of these guides are an inch thick, describing every possible exception and how to handle them; that is an effort doomed to be inefficient and one that can only cause irritation.

A much better way is to "grow" phase documentation. Instead of a guide, provide an outline containing headings and text that explains what will be described and when. This outline can serve as a framework that people add to as the project progresses. It lets everyone see the undecided issues and makes the goal visible. Moreover, such an outline eliminates the need for a detailed, rigid procedures guide and keeps the procedure flexible.

Whatever form you select, there will be much phase documentation produced over the life cycle of a project. Aron [8] draws a useful comparison in the number of words of two texts to illustrate the difference between something general and something specific:

- 56 words in the Lord's Prayer
- 26,911 words in the explanation of the European Common Market export rules for duck eggs

Like the export rules, phase documentation requires many words and diagrams to describe the many aspects and details of an information system and how it will be developed. This requires much writing and review time. However, since absolute precision is impossible and impractical, try to limit phase documentation to items that are essential for the reviewers.

Structure phase documentation for different reviewer groups, so each can easily find what is relevant and of particular interest to them. Financial information, for example, is often restricted to certain people and should be in a separate section. User groups are interested in scenarios and descriptions, not in the technical details. Some reviewers are interested in summaries only.

Phase documentation and development documentation overlap to a degree. The purpose of *development documentation,* as the name implies, is to document all work performed during the project life cycle; this documentation is so important because people come and go in projects. The most important parts of development documentation are described below and pictured in Figure 4-4:

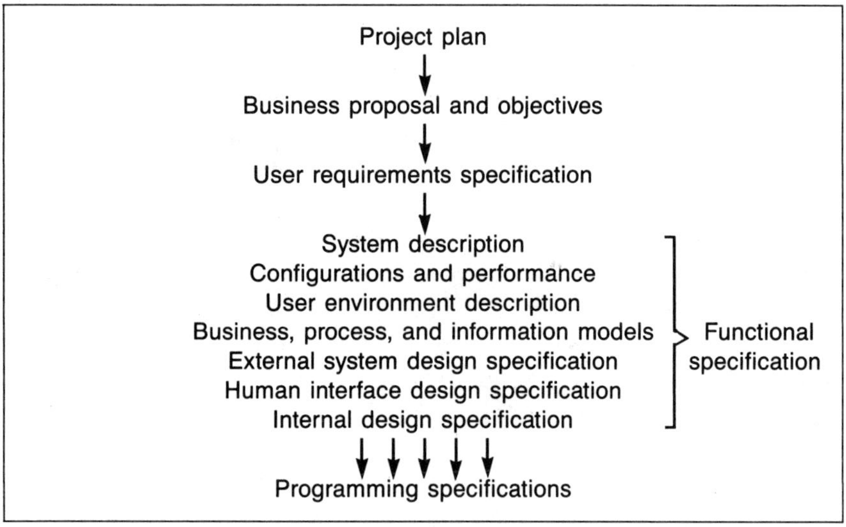

Figure 4-4. Overview of development documentation.

Project plan describes how to carry out the project and contains the following details:

- A phase plan that specifies the number of phases, the type of reviews, the participants in each review, and the project schedule
- Dependencies and assumptions
- Tools to be used and assistance that will be required from other groups
- Alternatives that were considered and rejected (this information can counteract a hidden agenda and will be useful to decide on a change in direction in the case of a catastrophe)
- Quality assurance plan tells how the project will meet certain criteria against which the product can be measured for its quality level
- Supporting materials plan that describes the manuals and training materials to explain the software for different user groups; includes details about conversion and installation

- Test plan that specifies test cases and test criteria
- Customer support plan that tells how the product will be supported
- Maintenance plan that explains the procedure for revising the software later on
- Project estimate and business justification covering the financial analysis of the project

Business proposal and objectives contains the business reasons for the project. In a general manner, it answers these questions: Why should we do it? What are the alternatives? What are the financial costs/benefits of the project? What customers/users does the project serve? How many? Why is the system important to them? Which customers/users are not considered? Why? How will users migrate to the new system?

User requirements specification details the system's capability needed from the user point of view. How does the project fit in with the strategic and tactical plans of users? What are the specific user requirements and information needs? These requirements are the basis for the acceptance criteria for the test plan (for checking conformity in Test). Note, however, that you cannot fully express human requirements in words, which is why it is so important to have real users involved in the project.

Functional specification is the composite of the system descriptions and various specifications; it details the functions of the system, but does not describe their implementation. The functional specification begins during Study and Analysis with an overall system description. Next, specifications for the external design, human interface, and internal design are added, thus completing the functional specification. It is updated during Program Development and Test.

The seven elements of the functional specification, shown in Figure 4-4, are discussed next.

System description is the result of Study and Analysis, stating in everyday language what the project is and how it fits into the work environment of a user organization. This description addresses why the system is needed and what its advantages and possible disadvantages are for each group of users. It explains the system from a human perspective, making it useful as an introduction for new developers and users.

Configurations and performance specify the hardware, software, and otherware needed to run the system, and the expected performance. Performance has many aspects, for example:

- Response times: What are they under typical and extreme conditions?
- Reliability: How often will the system break down and for how long?
- Availability: Over what periods must the system be up and running?
- Operability: What is needed to keep the system in operation? How vulnerable is it? How amenable is it to future changes?

User environment description gives special environmental considerations at the user location, including details of the

- Conversion and migration that must take place and possible roadblocks
- Effects of the information system on the environment and vice versa
- Special safety considerations that may apply to users and equipment
- Security concerns for people working with the system, for the data in the system, and for the system itself
- Privacy considerations for the system, both for users and their customers
- Legal requirements and standards in the countries in which people will use the software
- Exposures from a legal sense and liabilities when using the system
- Auditing considerations that specify the internal and external checking of administrative systems

This description of the user environment can later form the basis for user plans concerning fallback and recovery, liabilities, auditability, and safety, security, and privacy {5.5}.

Business, process, and information models are the results of system analysis and identify the general information system tasks and the data structures.

External system design specification describes data interfaces to other computers. It includes formats for moving data to and from other systems, network interfaces, and the design of system databases. External system design, or architecture, must provide for ways to make future changes and enhancements following implementation.

Human interface design specification springs from the external design, respecting certain technical limitations. Performing the task orientation (Figure 3-1) is critical to designing the human interface and to arriving at a good structure of the system and its documentation.

Internal design specification describes in detail the design of the component programs and how they work together. It completes the functional specification, shown in Figure 4-4.

Programming specifications contain the details for the programmer to write the code. Unlike the functional specification, they are not kept up to date on the latest changes. Therefore, it is good practice to include comments in the program itself. Because of their highly technical nature, these specifications are usually not reviewed in the phase process.

4.7 Supporting Materials

Supporting materials, which include general overviews and reference manuals, must be geared to user tasks; see Figure 3-1. Good supporting materials will enhance ease of use and reduce false error reports.

Because so much effort is put into development, phase, and user documentation, it is a good idea to try to combine the material. But that sounds simpler than it is. User documentation must take the users' view, phase documentation the reviewers' view, and development documentation an opposing system view. Therefore, much planning is necessary to share parts. See Chapters 8 and 9 for general information on how to develop supporting materials, and Appendices K and L on writing a manual and making its index.

4.8 Software Engineering and Software Quality Assurance

Software development has evolved from an individual effort (sometimes called the "garage approach") to a highly organized group effort (sometimes called the "army approach"). From an individual art, it has grown to include the structured techniques and other methods that incorporate proved engineering principles to guide development of practical and reliable software in an organized and predictable manner (see Aron [8], Boehm [18], Booch [21], DeMarco [45], and Jensen and Tonies [103]).

With this evolution, software development has earned the term "software engineering." Boehm cites four goals for software engineering:

modifiability, efficiency, reliability, and understandability. In addition to these techniques and methodologies to develop software, there have been similar developments of supporting tools that use graphic notations to increase programmer understandability (Chapters 1 and 2 explain why this is important to the field).

Now what is needed is a similar evolution to *information system engineering,* which will focus on software and otherware development. Its object should be to jointly design the human organization and the software {3.1}. However, this is only possible when developers and users work together on a one-time basis because user organizations are all different.

Besides the technical approach of software engineering, a management system called *Software Quality Assurance* is needed to guarantee quality (see, for example, Gilb [73] and *IEEE Software* [97]). This system employs software estimating techniques to predict software development and to assure quality of the software developed.

Estimating development work is making a judgment, based on prior experience, of what it takes to develop a product. Good estimates are needed to make realistic plans, and requires that experience is available from previous projects. Brooks [24] quotes a Dutch proverb: "A ship on the beach is a lighthouse to the sea." We must have recorded earlier development experience to understand how program complexity relates to effort required for developing a new project.

Techniques for software estimating and quality assurance are continually evolving. For more information on methods available for estimating software, see for example Aron [8], Blokdijk and Blokdijk [17], Boehm and Papaccio [19], and Shneiderman [193]. All measuring metrics are more or less arbitrary but what's important is to select a metric and learn to use it in your own particular situation. Of course, in order for the metric to be most useful, use the same metric for estimating and measuring.

A word of caution about using measurements: Developers resist them because they feel that no one can measure their work. They argue that every program is different, every metric is arbitrary, and recording job times is a useless exercise. Because of this resistance, measurements must be simple and be supported by management. I recommend that a neutral person or group be responsible for such measurements in an atmosphere of trust; refer to DeMarco [45]. After all, procedures and methods only provide a necessary framework; you need competent and motivated people to use them.

4.9 The Human Element in Software Development

In this final section of the chapter, I have collected some practical points on software development, to touch on a few of its many human sides. Software development requires experience gained by doing, employing much feedback in a learning process. As I've said before, this must be measured and recorded if your organization is ever to profit from the mistakes made.

Boehm [97] points out that in 1987, projects typically spent sixty percent of their effort on analysis and design, fifteen percent on programming, and twenty-five percent on integration and testing. Aron [8], Boehm and Papaccio [19], and Martin [122] stress the importance of making correct early decisions. An error made late during Program Development is usually corrected in hours, but errors made during Study and Analysis may take many months. Errors made during Definition and Proposal may not be correctable at all.

To find human errors, conduct design reviews and inspections at various stages in development. Of course, more checking is required when the scale of use or the impact of errors is large. Most houses in Holland are built on long poles that reach into underground sand layers; the soggier the ground and the larger the house, the more solid a foundation we need.

Development tools are also advancing human effort in the development cycle, because they automate much of the actual programming. Their general term today is computer-aided software engineering (CASE); see for example *IEEE Software* [98]. Always remember that people need to get experience in using even the best of tools and that people ultimately determine the quality of the result. The old saying "Garbage in, garbage out" expresses the notion that a computer result depends upon the quality of its input, which comes from people.

I repeat that software development is a team effort. To be successful, developers must work well together in a team that is properly managed. The programming environment is different from most other working environments and poses special requirements on team members and their manager; refer for examples to books by Weinberg [207, 209] and DeMarco and Lister [46].

Brooks's essays [24, 25] contain useful reflections on the software development process. He describes how in 1958 he felt a jolt on hearing about *building* programs, instead of *writing* them. He now recommends *growing* software, that is, adding functions continuously because that motivates people to see something already working. *Prototyping*—imitating software in a simple fashion—may be the start of growing; it may be sensible in some projects and not in others.

Gilb [73] argues the case for evolutionary system development to maximize visibility and deliver benefits at each stage. I recommended growing phase and user documentation since that makes the goals visible, which you can use whether you build or grow software. People have a natural tendency to fill in gaps; remember from {2.4} the human desire to close open items. Growing adds some overhead in the early phases, but it can save much time later and will improve the understanding of the development process all along.

Many destructive factors are external to software development proper. These are all caused by people making a wrong plan or decision. Examples from McMenamin and Palmer [129] are as follows:

- Politics that emphasize change for nontechnical reasons
- Requirements changing as the environment and needs change
- Staffing changes caused by movement of key people out of the group
- Budget reallocation as a result of the above and other changes
- Technical changes in the hardware and operating systems
- Development management's impatience leading to a desire to move on
- Schedules of long duration making the project vulnerable to all of the above

These factors and many more can have a serious effect on the software development process. They are a good reason to begin with small projects and to try growing them, though that is not always possible. Finally, beware of scheduling based on mythical man-months (Brooks [24] and Boehm [97]). As we say in Holland, it takes nine months to deliver a baby, no matter how many people join the effort. The duration of a project depends on people understanding its complexities and developing an implementation concept. Computer tools can only help to make concepts visible and assist with mechanical tasks; they cannot prevent poor software systems.

This chapter presented a brief overview of the software development process, concentrating on planning, procedures, participants' roles, and the documentation created. For more information, refer to Aron [7, 8], Blokdijk and Blokdijk [17], Boehm [18, 97], DeMarco [45] and DeMarco and Lister [46], Metzger [133], Turner et al. [203], and Yourdon [216]. See Weinberg [209] for tips on understanding the professional programmer.

4.10 Summary

1. Software development must be planned. The usual planning hierarchy consists of business, strategic, tactical, and operational or project plans.

2. Software development requires eight major activities:

Activity	Output
1. Definition and Proposal	Detailed proposal for the project
2. Study and Analysis	Detailed analysis of the requirements
3. External System Design	Design of interfaces to the outside world
4. Human Interface Design	Design of interfaces to the users
5. Internal System Design	Internal design of the software
6. Program Development	Software programs
7. Test	Test results for software acceptance or rejection
8. Support	People and materials to support users and others to install and use the software

3. Maintenance requires the same eight activities be done for each new software version, but on a smaller scale.

4. Every development project needs a controlling structure, called the development phase process. Divide the above activities into phases, depending upon the complexity of the project, and include a review after each phase. Use as few phases as possible to reduce overhead.

5. How to develop a software system is an important early decision, with these factors to consider:
    - What critical human skills are available?
    - Should you build or grow software?
    - What tools are available for development, project management control, and change control?

- What development support is needed?
- How long is the total software development period?
- How can you structure software versions and accommodate changes?
- How can you estimate the effort needed and get software quality assurance?

6. Carefully design and test the human side of an information system. Task-oriented user documentation is an integral part of the system. The prospective user must be well represented in development projects and in the phase process.
7. Paperwork is a significant part of the work in development, so optimize its usefulness and effectiveness.
8. Supporting materials, including user documentation and training, are an essential part of the software product developed.
9. Gather experience from other projects to improve estimating for your own organization, personnel, and type of work. To be successful in software quality assurance, a neutral person must do the estimating across projects, and management must support the effort.

4.11 Review Questions and Exercises

1. Explain why the eight development activities are in the given sequence. Give three examples of what could happen if you interchange the positions of any two activities.
2. Use your imagination to consider confidence levels during development. Assume that you, as a project manager, have agreed to write software for a large system during the next twelve months. You have estimated the project effort at the beginning and the software quality assurance group has agreed that you can do the project with the people at your disposal.
    - Assume that you meet the end date. Make a plot of how your confidence level (from zero to one hundred percent) could vary over the twelve months. Discuss why you think the curve will progress as you drew it.
    - Do the same exercise, but this time assume that you will not meet the end date. Describe the factors that might influence the shape of the curve and discuss their effects in both cases.

3. Weinberg [206] explains how you could incorporate a feedback system into an antipollution law by forcing companies to return their waste water upstream from where they take it out. Consider feedback systems in development. The reviews in a phase process provide reinforcing feedback for development at an overall level. Feedback processes, however, also occur more immediately at lower levels.
   - Describe some lower-level feedback processes mentioned in this chapter.
   - Sketch other lower-level feedback processes that you would expect in development.

4. A new system often surprises end users. It may not do what they expect, thus making them feel insecure. Give some ways this could happen for each of the following systems:
   - An operating system for a personal computer
   - A program to print address labels for envelopes
   - A mainframe office automation system
   - A mainframe accounting system
   - A system to make customer proposals for an engineering company
   - A project planning system for a program development center
   - A library system for program development
   - A program to design and plot engineering drawings

   What is the major reason for the surprise in each instance?

5. What are your recommendations for building or growing each of the programs in Exercise 4. Why?

6. There are four basic ways to make users' requirements visible:
   - Rapid prototyping, whereby you make panels for display on a screen to discuss and develop users' requirements
   - Formal prototyping, whereby you analyze users' requirements in some detail and then show a prototype to check your understanding
   - Writing detailed requirements, whereby you analyze users' requirements in some detail and then let users check the written documentation

- Evolutionary development, whereby you develop and install a system in parts or stages, getting user reactions throughout development (Brooks [25] and Gilb [73])

What are the advantages and disadvantages of each of the four basic approaches? Recommend one approach for each of the systems in Exercise 4 and justify your choice.

7. Imagine that you want to set up a software quality assurance group for a center with a thousand people who are developing various application programs. You must present your plans to the development business director who is more interested in starting the development of a new application program instead. Discuss what you will propose and how you will justify your proposal on the following issues:
   - Profitability in the long run of a software quality assurance group
   - The number of people you need and their qualifications
   - Organization of the quality assurance group
   - Reporting line in the organization
   - Selection process of a metric to measure program complexity
   - Estimating experience obtained
   - Confirmation of your methodology
   - Procedure for fostering goodwill from the people whose assistance you will need in order to gather data
   - The lead time until you can start estimating with confidence

8. Imagine that someone asks you to develop a security system such that people and computers can uniquely identify each other as being trustworthy. Some schemes work with specific knowledge about the other party, for example, identification codes and passwords. Other schemes require no knowledge about the other party. For each type of scheme,
   - Describe the problems you can expect.
   - Indicate how you would try to solve those problems. If you cannot resolve them completely, what would be your best-can-do solution?
   - Argue why it is, or is not, possible to develop one hundred percent secure systems.

9. Estimate and explain cost percentages for the development of a software project. Describe your assumptions and explain why you assign a certain percentage to each of the following categories:

. . . . %	For people in the development project, including the manager
. . . . %	For formal training of people
. . . . %	For share of software quality assurance for the project
. . . . %	For share of central development support
. . . . %	For share of supporting materials development
. . . . %	For share of costs for the development computer center
. . . . %	For share of costs for office and site facilities
. . . . %	For overhead costs and profit
100 %	Total development cost

Do you expect these percentages to change in the next five years? How? Why?

10. Make an initial business case for developing an information system to administer courses, classes, teachers, and students. Include the cost of development and maintenance, hardware, standard software, and otherware over periods of one year of development and five years of use. Make assumptions where necessary, and include the benefits of the system. Disregard interest and inflation rates, and assume that costs do not change.

- What items must this business case consider?
- Where is the crossover point at which the accumulated costs equals the accumulated benefits?
- If the crossover point is too far away, how can you bring it forward? What costs do you expect to change in the next five years? Why?

11. Some people believe that computers increase the flexibility of an organization to serve its customers while others believe that they make organizations bureaucratic because they require formal procedures. Explain your views on this, discussing options to

- Make the software simple or sophisticated, and the otherware belonging to it sophisticated or simple

- Introduce the software gradually or in a few major steps
- Postpone the point of no return in changing software specifications
- Develop software that is more flexible for the user

5

USING INFORMATION SYSTEMS

Because we are automating our administration,
you will get the invoice in three weeks.
—Neatly printed notice that I received in March 1988

This chapter discusses the use of computer systems. It describes the many plans and activities that are needed before an organization can use them and includes an example of the evaluation needed to computerize a particular application.*

Computers are different from most other tools in that they have such a strong impact on people, organizations, and procedures. If an electronic typewriter replaces a mechanical typewriter, for example, only the secretary who uses it must adapt and learn how to work with it; little changes otherwise. If a computer takes over a task, however, everything changes; and you must plan this changeover carefully to assure that both people and machine work together. Computers thus force everyone to work in a more formal manner. And because of their development lead time, information systems must be planned well in advance.

Nolan [150] discovered how computer use naturally evolves from dedicated computers to integrated systems. His description of the following six phases further explains the need for planning information systems:

I Initiation: A first group uses a computer.

II Contagion: Other groups start to use (other) computers.

III Control: Management establishes central control.

IV Integration: Computers get integrated into information systems.

V Data administration: Overall system's planning using models.

VI Maturity: The organization uses a well-balanced system.

In Stage I, the use of computers is explored by one group. In Stage II, other groups join, spreading the use of computers. In Stage III, management feels the need to control the many computers. In Stage IV, as a result, computers are connected to exchange their information. In Stage V, processes and data are modeled in advance so that computers can be in-

*As before, I will call developers those who plan and build an information software system, and users those who work with it. The user group owns and uses application software; this group may well consist of several departments of end users who serve customers of the organization. An application is the software and otherware of an information system. It includes all the actions that a user group needs to perform. A computer center owns the hardware and runs all the software.

tegrated in a proper fashion. In Stage VI, finally, integrated computer systems serve the purposes of the organization. Without planning, there is no chance that computers can be integrated. Remember, the rule in computerization is that nothing is ever right automatically and nothing ever happens of itself.

As more computers are used in an organization, they also become a more critical element of it. Proper planning must also consider this dependency on machines and include adequate security and backup measures.

5.1 Planning Computers in the User Organization

> If we could first know where we are and whither we are tending, we could better judge what to do and how to do it.
>
> —A. Lincoln, quoted in [4]

Any medium to large organization that plans to automate must have a master plan for all its computer systems. Such a plan contains a business model that details the organizational processes and information models, as shown in Figure 3-1. When you build an intersection of two highways, for example, you must have a master plan for extending it later or extensions will become costly. Your business model and plans for the information system {3.1} provide an overall framework so you can do the following:

- Decide which current applications to adapt.
- Decide which new applications to implement.
- Avoid and eliminate information islands, that is, applications that are incompatible and do not match with primary applications.

The first part of user planning involves creating the user business plan. It details the work area, the long-range objectives, and the strategy of the entire user organization for the next five years. It analyzes the strengths, weaknesses, opportunities, and threats (SWOT) of the organization during the strategic period. Some points in the business plan relate to how computers are needed to achieve the organization's business goals.

Figure 5-1 shows the hierarchy of plans that I will now describe (Blokdijk and Blokdijk [17]); many of the comments on similar plans for the development organization in {4.1} also apply here.

User business plan
↓
Information system strategic plan
↓
Information system tactical plan
↓
Information system operational plan
↓
Application plans

Figure 5-1. Hierarchy of user plans.

User business plan outlines the strategy of the user organization and indicates where computers are needed to

- Reduce operational costs
- Provide a wider variety of products or services
- Simplify ordering or access to services
- Improve products or service in a specific area
- Improve internal organization
- Integrate international subsidiaries

The success of any sizeable organization is becoming very dependent on computers. Having data available earlier, and being able to analyze it better, can give a strong competitive advantage. Increasing change and complexity are characteristics of today's environment; they, along with the use of computers, increase the need for strategic planning (Ansoff [4]). Therefore, general computer requirements must be stated in the business plan.

Information system strategic plan translates the user business plan into an information system strategy for the next five years. It gives the overall picture of how the user sees the evolution of information systems (functions needed), identifies key areas for the strategic period, and gives strategic direction to the user organization and the computer center. A decision to centralize or decentralize computers belongs to strategic planning.

Information system tactical plan translates the directions from the strategic plan into specific activities needed during the next one-to-two-year period. It considers the goals and factors critical to success and links the strategic and operational plans.

Information system operational plan is the overall summary of the current year's activities, consolidated from the specific application plans.

Application plans are the plans for installing and using each specific application project. They cover an application over its entire life cycle, which can be ten years, and contain detailed plans for the current year.

In addition, a similar set of plans can be made for large computer centers to determine the hardware requirements (computers and networks) that will implement users' new application plans. Networks represent a major investment and are an important consideration in computer center planning.

5.2 Planning an Application

Every application must support a user group within the organization. Before deciding to introduce a specific application, the user follows the procedure just described: First have an analysis done of the complete business or work done by the organization. The resulting business model is composed of two types of models: the process model, which identifies the organization's major processes in logical terms; and the information model, which identifies the information needed.

Having this overview, they can then decide which process to automate first in line with the strategic plan. Setting priorities is part of the tactical information system plan; actual decisions are part of the operational plan.

It is never possible to automate a group all at once; implementation has to be gradual. Therefore, before you begin, you must consider all computers (including personal computers) in the application plan so you understand how each fits into the information system.

The common denominator among organizational processes is data, that is, information. Every process uses information from a database. A goal of information system planning is to have common definitions of all data needed by users, their customers, and others. This provides the basis for integration of different applications at a later stage. A fairly new position is that of information manager, whose job is to coordinate the use of information among groups.

For actual planning, you can start with critical success factors (CSF) analysis, a method used to make an inventory of vital information needs of an application group. Through CSF analysis, you may realize that their business depends on telephone orders, use of computers, and availability of certain stock, for example. You can then reduce risks by paying more attention to those factors.

Critical success factors of an existing group are discovered by posing the following questions to its members:

1. What are your principal functions or goals?
2. What are the success factors necessary to achieve these goals?
3. What indicator or criterion do you use to assess the status of each of the critical success factors?
4. What performance do you desire for each of the indicators or criteria given for point 3?

The answers to questions 3 and 4 define the information needs of the group, derived from their mental models. If a group does not yet exist, as in the case of a new application, you must draw on your own knowledge and experience to make a CSF analysis.

In planning, you must then find a suitable balance between conflicting requirements, such as:

- How can people update a database during their daily work?
- Within how much time must actions be transmitted to the database?
- How much checking of human transcription errors is desirable?
- What are the information needs of users, their customers, and other people?
- Is one central computer system or several computer systems needed?
- If several computer systems are needed, what is their degree of integration?
  - At what level will logical coupling take place? For each level, will it be peer-to-peer or master-slave coupling?
  - What are the dependencies between systems?
  - How will you synchronize the various systems?
  - How will you connect systems?
  - How will communication between systems affect response time?
- What processing is done in interactive mode? What is done in batch mode (that is, processed at a later time)?
- What human interface approach ensures consistency to end users?

The answers to these questions will influence how people will work with computers. As I've said before, the first concern should be how people can work best, letting implementation support that. The application must enable users to understand the system architecture so they can see its implications and decide about its planning. Human experts need to be put in charge to control and check the operation of machines {3.5}.

Organizational procedures govern the workings of the otherware. As shown in Figure 3-1, they describe how the general tasks and detailed tasks are carried out and who actually performs them. Depending on their level, users are authorized to create, modify, use, view, or delete data. Realize however that setting up organizational procedures is only one of the many tasks to develop an application, discussed next.

5.3 Implementing and Using Applications

I distinguish seven activities to implement and use an application in Figure 5-2, in which the output, or result, is on the right.

Activity	Output
1. Evaluation	Selection of application software
2. Planning	Architecture of hardware, software, and otherware
3. Installation	Implementation of the application software
4. Customization	Adaptation of the application software
5. Conversion	Adaptation of the human organization
6. Migration	People moved to the new application
7. Operation	Exploitation of the application

Figure 5-2. Seven activities to implement and use an application.

As before, maintenance concerns major modifications to the system and requires the same seven activities, but on a smaller scale because the system's architecture is already established.

An implementation team usually carries out the first six activities as described here. Composition of the team depends on the people who are available, but it must include users and members of the computer center. User documentation, described in Chapter 8, supports implementation team activities.

Following is a general discussion of each of the seven activities.

1: EVALUATION

The first activity concerns the evaluation of alternative software products to determine which one best fits the organizational needs and user environment. The software must also fit within the general software architecture of the organization and be in line with computer center plans. Conversion and migration are key related activities because they often present roadblocks to computerization. An overall plan describes use of the software being considered. A business justification must support a decision of whether to develop the software in-house or to buy the software off the shelf.

2: PLANNING

The purpose of this activity is to plan Activities 3 through 7 and develop the otherware, making it complement the software for each task {3.1}. A detailed schedule is set up for each activity, and individuals are assigned responsibility for making it happen. The implementation team should make the overall implementation plan and coordinate the detailed plans.

3: INSTALLATION

The third activity is to install the software on the computer, often first as a test system, and to install any special hardware. This allows key users to try out the system so they can understand practical implications. This activity ends with a test, to check that the software works as specified.

4: CUSTOMIZATION

This is the process of tailoring software options and system data for the intended application. Special application programs are added for entering data, receiving data, sending data, and other software services. System parameters and variables are entered, for example, product codes and prices, tax rates, customer numbers, and so on. Help and message texts are adapted. Specific user documentation, consisting of manuals, reference cards, and so on, is developed.

5: CONVERSION

Conversion from the old way of operation to the new way involves preparing new otherware and converting information databases. At this time, a new organization, with new operational procedures, is set up; offices are adapted, new forms and other materials are designed, and so on. New end users are authorized to be on the system, and special password protections are set up. Another test may be conducted to check that the new system works as desired.

6: MIGRATION

This is the process of moving end users to the new way of operation, beginning with a few people. End users are educated and trained before they are put on the new system, preferably by the people who will support them in the future. Members of the computer center become familiar with new operational procedures.

7: OPERATION

This final activity begins with operating both the old and the new system in parallel. When correct operation of the new system is certain, you can change over to the new system. The implementation team will watch the initial operation and intervene when there are problems. When everyone is used to the new way of operation, the system will be in normal operation. Small modifications will keep it in line with changes in the real world.

There is often an informal phase process to review the seven activities to implement an application at the end of each phase. As before, you can combine activities in one phase. This phase process can be less informal because the user group understands the application and will make certain that it works properly.

5.4 Roles in the User Organization

Different people play different roles in carrying out the above seven activities. The following is a greatly simplified overview of the principal roles in an application group:

Application manager controls an application group. This includes reviewing the planning and installation activities, and deciding on alternatives proposed by the implementation team.

Key users/user support people are the experts on various aspects of the application. They decide on options and alternatives during implementation, perform the conversion test after installation, prepare documentation and education material, and train end users. After the system has been installed, they help end users with problems.

End users work with the application at terminals.

User staff are concerned about a variety of subjects ranging from process and data models to planning and tracking the system's operation.

An *information manager* coordinates application groups to make certain that their decisions are in line with strategic, tactical, and operational plans of the entire organization. In large organizations, a chief information manager may be responsible for an entire information system including all applications.

Some roles of people in the computer center {5.7} and staff groups are these:

Analysts and *programmers* handle the intended application from the software side. They provide the technical foundation for running the application along with other applications in the computer center. They coordinate the adaptation of the application software and establish operational procedures for running the software in the computer center.

Computer center support people help end users who have problems with the computer center service.

Network support people install end user facilities such as workstations, networking, and cable connections.

Computer operations people watch over the system, take care of disk and tape handling, run printers, handle system problems, start batch jobs for overnight processing, and perform many other operations in the computer center.

Facilities people prepare offices and install furniture needed to run the application.

Security people understand the special security and protection aspects of applications. They are concerned about security classifications of files, invasion by computer viruses, passwords, and so on.

Finance, administration, and *accounting people* handle financial matters for the organization, recording the costs of all people, costs of computer center services, and so on.

5.5 User Application Plans

The implementation team coordinates the creation of many new application plans, as well as the updating of those plans for maintenance. Here is an overview of the most important application plans.

Application plan specifies the purpose of the application. It states who is the owner of the application and describes how the project fits within the strategic and tactical plans of the user organization. It includes a plan for future functions of the application and new versions of the software to realize them.

Implementation plan describes how each software version will be installed, who will review the phases, and when reviews will be held. It describes the hardware, software, and otherware required.

Budget plan describes the financial side of operating the application, including an appropriate share of total computer center costs. It contains a consideration of alternatives, for example, external facilities management.

Brochures tell in nontechnical language what the application does and how it will fit into the human environment. End users need an extensive version to explain the new application in general terms (user training will explain the new procedures). Customers need another version of the brochure to explain details of the new operation.

Operability plan describes the application's performance (hardware configuration, throughput, and response time), possible performance degradations, reliability and availability of the system, and maintenance.

Fallback and recovery plan deals with disasters, ranging from accidental hitting of switches to power cuts, fires, and floods; their number and variety are unlimited. This plan includes options for fallback in case the system is not available, how often backup must take place, and to what point you can recover an application after a disaster and how. You must understand the cost of failure to plan proper emergency measures for each application. A critical failure factors analysis, similar to the critical success factors analysis in {5.2}, can uncover the most important causes of disaster.

User training and support plan spells out how to train users after initial implementation. (Training during migration is part of the implementation plan.) It tells how user support will help end users with problems.

Service agreement between the application manager and the computer center manager contains performance criteria for use of the application and costs for computer services. Performance has several aspects:

- End user response times, measured at the terminal under both typical and extreme conditions
- Reliability, including how often is the system expected to break down and for how long

- Availability, meaning during what periods must the system be up and running
- Security, describing the security measures taken
- Operability, including what factors are needed to keep the system in operation, how vulnerable it is to external factors, and how amenable it is to future changes

Liabilities plan contains an analysis of risks, including financial claims that others may put on the user organization.* This is an important area in view of the increased use of computers and the growing legislation on consumer protection. A risk manager can help users understand and reduce risks, for example, by checking whether they keep activity records.

Verification/certification plan identifies sensitive parts of an information system and specifies how to check an application and its data to see if they are correct. Hardware certification is generally done by the manufacturers. Software certification is done by an outside organization that gives a limited but formal warranty. Processed information is checked by the user group. Certification of a complete information system is an application manager's responsibility.

Auditability plan specifies how external auditors and accountants can audit an application so they can assess the effectiveness and efficiency of the investment. An audit considers, for example, reliability, security, organization, and management of the application.

Safety, security, and privacy plan gives any special safety and security considerations for users, their customers, and others. Safety is considered in relation to equipment used; security concerns the access of people to the system, the data in the system, and the application itself. It includes privacy considerations (Rule et al. [180]).

Security is rapidly getting more attention. Remember that computers cannot distinguish between good and bad; they can only determine what is authorized and what is not. Various security measures include password protection for system access, an authorization list that specifies which end users can use what transactions, information classified into categories with additional password control, and coding to transmit sensitive data over networks. You need self-assessments, peer reviews, and audits to make

*To understand liabilities, keep in mind that most paper documents have legal significance, whereas their electronic origin inside the computer has none. Business transactions with customers and important activities are therefore always recorded on paper. This paper information must often be kept for many years, which is not so obvious to users who regard computer information as being the original.

users aware of security. The suggestions in {4.3} for developers apply equally to users.

It turns out that most security offenders are people inside the organization itself who have the necessary knowledge and physical access. There is little you can do about them except to provide a reasonable level of security and create a climate that discourages illegal or harmful activity. Recommendations for accomplishing this are in Chapter 12.

It is certainly possible to "grow" many of these application plans {4.6}. You can start with outline plans and fill them in during planning (Activity 2). (An outline plan consists of headings and standard text describing what topics must be covered under each heading and during which activity they must be addressed.)

5.6 Practical Considerations in Using Computers

Like developers, users must also be right from the beginning, especially during the early activities. A wrong decision during the first evaluation activity may not be correctable when it is found out during conversion. Proper planning and a clear agenda are the keys to achieving a proper balance between hardware, software, and otherware.

Since the user group often lacks technical skills and may have difficulty assessing application details, computer center professionals must properly support users. But an application will be successful only if the user group has some computer expertise. An almost certain road to failure is when computer center people make decisions the users should make. It is the role of the user group to decide what system functions it needs; the computer center should only decide how to implement them technically.

A make-or-buy software decision concerns inhouse expertise. Developing your own software is often expensive but will give you the possibility to adapt it. Buying software is often less expensive but you may then have to live with its limitations and inflexibility. The choice depends upon the specific situation.

Proper introduction of a computer into an organization is important to convince people that it is their tool, not something that dictates how they must work. Support people (who do the implementation) are crucial for a smooth transition. It is a good idea to have the same people train end users and support them afterward. That way, they get to know each other and a human support network establishes itself naturally. The introduction of an information system must be an improvement for all people.

The information center is a group that makes information available to application groups, similar to a computer center that makes computers available. The center's staff use special software to provide large computer databases to many people and to help novice users get started.

When considering new software, talk to other organizations that are already using it. There is no substitute for practical user experience when deciding about software. And, if you don't have much expertise, don't be a first-time user.

I want to emphasize the need for proper cost recording and apportionment. Money is often the only common denominator to use in comparing alternatives. For example, when offering several services, use their real costs for pricing each one. Otherwise you risk going broke by offering services at too low a price or by being noncompetitive at too high a price.

The cost of people is usually by far the largest cost of an information system. But people often resist and even sabotage recording their time spent on different projects. Therefore, time recording must be simple and not be used in performance evaluations. People must understand that recorded time is used only to determine a proper price for their valuable work.

5.7 Running a Computer Center

A computer center actually runs the computers for application groups within an organization, and such centralization allows economies of scale, sharing of experience, and operational flexibility. Its purpose is to provide computer services efficiently.

The computer center consolidates the requirements of application groups for its own strategic, tactical, and operational planning. It must understand the implications of application group requirements, and install the necessary hardware and software in a timely fashion. The computer center manager reports to a financial director or is a director himself or herself.

A comparison of typical feedback times in reaction to problems shows how a computer center must operate to achieve its purpose:

- In a development group, problems take months before being detected.
- In a user group, problems take days before being detected.
- In a computer center, problems are detected within seconds, because a large number of users cannot work any longer.

Because of this immediacy and the importance of computers to people, computer center people must keep in close touch with the users, their customers. This is not so simple because computer center people must often work under time pressure on complex problems. To resolve this, computer center management must work on two sides. Internally, management should promote good social relations among computer center people who must often rely on each other. Externally, management should set up a centralized support group to let users talk to the technical people about their problems. In addition, management can appoint a manager for each major computer center service, who can represent users internally to various groups in the computer center on general matters.

Computer center services come in two basic modes: *interactive mode,* in which user requests are granted automatically and jobs are done in seconds or minutes; and *batch mode,* in which user requests are granted by a computer operator. Batch jobs are run only when interactive processing activity is low, for example, during a night shift. Batch jobs often necessitate special procedures, including loading magnetic tapes and printing voluminous output. Users generally need the results of batch jobs by the next morning.

A computer center can have more than a hundred thousand users, and several thousand users may be active at any one time. Many computer centers operate in two or three shifts, including weekends. The split between software and hardware people in a computer center is often about fifty-fifty. Many hardware and software alterations make change a way of life in the computer center.

There are many procedures in a computer center, including specific job procedures, fallback and recovery procedures, change procedures, and problem procedures. Actions are planned and spelled out in procedures that different people can use. Because people are in charge and can make ad hoc decisions, the detail need not be as exacting as in software. Procedures in the event of an emergency are rehearsed at least once a year.

5.8 A Taste of Practical Problems: Automating Expertise

After discussing many plans and procedures, I will get back to reality with an example of computerizing the expertise of a particular group. The experts in this example must judge a customer's situation and the risks involved in order to determine the details of an insurance policy. Currently, an expert records his or her decision about a particular applicant on a paper form, and when the decision is positive, all pertinent details are entered into the information system by another group.

There are four levels of experts: trainee, junior, standard, and senior. On average, it takes about five years for a trainee to reach the standard level, to master the very complex rules by which the experts judge applications.

Management of the insurance company wants to automate the experts' decision making process. The decision rules are complex and not always consistently applied, and management believes computers could help make the decision process more uniform. Automation would also help identify high-risk areas before they fully develop. Having all decision data in the computer, allows for "What if?" type of analyses.

These are all good reasons for automating the experts' group, but people's reactions are mixed. For the automation to be successful, senior experts realize that they will be needed more than ever before. Junior- and standard-level experts will become redundant and are not happy naturally, because trainees will replace them, with the knowledge contained inside the computer.

To begin the computerization project, an implementation team composed of people from many areas evaluates the situation and develops an initial master plan. They face the following questions during Evaluation (Activity 1):

- Can all decision rules be formalized sufficiently for implementing them on a computer or is human intuition required?
- If the rules can be formalized, how can they be established? And how can they be adapted later? What sort of explanation of the rules will people need to do their work?
- Will senior experts be able to explain all the rules they use? If so, can they assume responsibility for their use in the computer?
- How can all rules be verified to be correct, and correctly implemented?
- How will the new group work for other people?
    - What is the impact on other groups inside the organization?
    - How are customers and others outside the organization affected?
    - How is the group embedded and anchored in the organization?
- How will members of the new group work internally?

  - What are their jobs, and how are tasks divided between humans and machines?
  - What level(s) of experts are needed, and how many of them?
- What reassignments are needed? (Without a satisfactory people and work plan, any changes will meet with resistance, not cooperation.)
  - Where can redundant people be re-employed?
  - If necessary, how and where will new people be recruited?
  - What (re)training programs must be set up?
- What is the impact on the organization's information system?
  - Change in response time due to increased load?
  - Changes required to other software?
  - If new software must be developed, how will this affect current plans and priorities?
- What are user requirements of the new system, considering what is technically realistic?
- Is suitable software available or must it be developed?
- How can the transition be made from the old to the new system without affecting customers?

The report with answers from the implementation team must first be discussed with management, then with the expert group itself and the other groups potentially affected. This is necessary so that everyone understands the plan and can contribute to it; it must become their plan as well! There is likely to be an impact on every single group in the organization, and they all should start to think about how to cope with the change.

I repeat that when you introduce computers, everything changes and everything must be considered anew. To adapt computers to people is much more than designing a good human-machine dialogue. It takes much planning and, above all, much understanding and communication.

5.9 Summary

1. This chapter considered using information systems, and particularly how they must be planned at the strategic, tactical, and operational levels.

2. It also focused on how to plan and install a new application, as well as the operation of a computer center and the evaluation of a practical example.

3. Users must have a master plan to ensure consistency among applications and to allow for future integration.

4. Users must develop otherware, the human organization.

5. The major user's activities to plan and install an application are

1. Evaluation	Selection of application software
2. Planning	Architecture of hardware, software, and otherware
3. Installation	Implementation of the application software
4. Customization	Adaptation of the application software
5. Conversion	Adaptation of the human organization
6. Migration	People moved to the new application
7. Operation	Exploitation of the application

   An implementation team coordinates activities 1 to 6, and a support group assists end users during the final activity. Maintenance is the ongoing activity to modify an application as required.

6. There is often no need for a formal phase process to implement a user application, but the need remains to review implementation plans.

7. When deciding on an application, consider these items:
   - Strategic, tactical, and operational aspects of the application for the user group and the computer center
   - Business evaluation
   - Coverage of functional needs
   - Hardware and otherware required
   - Human factors
   - Implementation roadblocks
   - Available alternatives

8. Besides strategic and tactical plans, you must develop or adapt many other plans:
   - Application plan

- Implementation plan
- Operability plan
- Fallback and recovery plan
- End user training and support plan
- Liabilities plan
- Verification/certification plan
- Auditability plan
- Safety, security, and privacy plan

9. The computer center must maintain a close relationship with user groups because of their dependency on the computer service. A support group helps users handle problems. A service manager coordinates a computer service and represents the users.

10. Work in a computer center must be well planned. Many procedures describe planned and foreseen actions.

5.10 Review Questions and Exercises

1. Discuss why the seven user activities must be done in the given sequence. Give three examples of what could happen if you interchange two of the activities.

2. This book suggests that a formal phase process is often not necessary for installation and use of information systems, as opposed to development. Discuss under what conditions you would recommend the use of a formal phase process to a user organization and under which conditions you would not.

3. Find some newspaper and magazine articles that describe cases in which a new system did not meet expectations because of misunderstandings between developers and users.
   - List and summarize the problems.
   - How did the problems originate in the installation and use procedure (activities 1 to 7)?
   - What do you recommend to prevent such problems?
   - Explain why you do, or do not, agree with the statement in {4.9} that human planning errors are often the reason that things go wrong when introducing computers.

4. Find some newspaper and magazine articles that describe cases in which a new system did not meet expectations because of misunderstandings among users.
   - List and summarize the problems.
   - How did the problems originate in the installation and use procedure (activities 1 to 7)?
   - What do you recommend to prevent such problems?
   - Explain why you do, or do not, agree with the statement in {4.9} that human planning errors are often the reason why things go wrong when introducing computers.

5. An insurance company has two separate computer systems:
   - One system for insurance business operations to close insurance policies, to handle queries, to process claims, and to perform all financial transactions. A network connects five hundred branch offices and insurance agents.
   - One system for personnel registration and administration to process personnel data, producing a tape with employee salary information for final processing by the first system.

   Argue the pros and cons of integrating these two systems. Consider interconnection at the data level, the process level, the organizational level, the hardware level, and the software level. Discuss security and privacy aspects, and include relevant human considerations.

6. The value of information is difficult to define, but you can approximate it in at least two ways:
   - The cost to enter the information and to keep it current, made up of hardware, software, and otherware costs. Difficulties are how to apportion various costs and how to value future use.
   - The value the information has to you. What would it cost if you did not have it? What do you gain by having it? Difficulties are the many alternative work methods you can use and the time aspects (consider how quickly do you need the information and when it will lose its value).

   Discuss these and other ways to measure the value of information in your situation. Consider whether it does, or does not, make sense to appoint an information manager who coordinates, promotes, and supports the use of information in your organization.

7. Some Australian financiers have struck it rich in the mining business and are buying insurance companies all over the world. Their idea is that with satellite communications they can centralize all processing in Australia, leaving offices in the different countries to deal with customers. Country peak hours are divided over the entire day because of different time zones, causing a balanced load at the central computer center.
   - How would you distribute information processing tasks between a local office, a central location in each country, and the central processor in Australia? What processes must use interactive mode? What processes can use batch mode? To what extent does the human side (that is, customer and employee) influence your recommendation?
   - Name some differences in the human environment in various countries that could influence the need for alternative types of insurance policies. Do you expect a difference in communicating with people? Will this influence your answer to the first item?
   - The central computer system in Australia will be very large and must be in operation twenty-four hours a day, seven days a week. What are possible human bottlenecks in operating such a large computer center? Give recommendations to avoid them.

8. Imagine you are the security manager of the world-wide insurance company of Question 7. What measures would you take to prevent
   - Actions that would postpone the implementation of a country's system
   - Intruders from causing a disaster or malfunctioning in a country's computer center
   - People from causing a legal liability and suing the insurance company
   - People from publicizing alleged adverse affects of the computer system on the human environment
   - People from breaking through security and getting private information about employees or customers

   Give three recommended actions for each item and explain how you need the help of insurance company employees in each case.

9. Locate the people responsible for security of the information system on which you work. Ask if you can see the security plan, explaining that you would like to understand it and possibly contribute to it. If they object, explain that security is everyone's business and that you therefore must understand the plan. Read the plan, and discuss your conclusions and recommendations.

10. List what you consider to be the critical success factors {5.2} for your use of a computer. What are the essential processes and information without which you cannot do your work? For each factor, state

    - What alternatives you have in case of computer failure
    - How you would recover after a period of computer failure

    What emergency measures have been taken?

11. Section 5.6 states that failure is almost guaranteed when computer people make user decisions. Consider a user group and how familiar it is with details of the applications.

    - Will they recognize that the software must change when tax rates change and new legislation is introduced?
    - List ten external factors that affect functions of an application.
    - Propose actions that programmers can take to make certain that users understand all functional details of their applications.

Part III

COMMUNICATION, DOCUMENTATION, AND TRAINING

Chapter 6. On Language

Introduces language, the basis for human communication and thought.

Chapter 7. On-Line Communication

Compares on-line communication with oral and written communication
• Discusses specific ways of working with a computer.

Chapter 8. User Documentation

Elaborates on the written form of language to support people working with computers.

Chapter 9. Training

Gives an overview of teaching methods to give users the skills and confidence for working with computers successfully.

6

ON LANGUAGE

The individual's whole experience is built
upon the plan of his language.
—H. Delacroix, *Les Grandes Formes de la Vie Mentale,* quoted in [62]

Language is the basis for all human communication and thought. Both developers and users employ language to plan, develop, and use new software. Natural language is the key to understanding a problem, to saying how to solve it, and to doing what was said. This chapter introduces language as a framework for Chapters 7 to 9, which cover specific forms of communication.

Proper communication becomes increasingly important as we move from an agricultural society to an industrial society to an information society. The reason is food and industrial products are simpler to discuss than the use of computers.

Proper planning, developing, and using computers require extensive communication skills, because information systems are complex and have a strong impact on human activities. Good communication is needed to bridge the knowledge gap between developers and users. Users often know little about computers, and computer professionals know little about the work of users. Both groups require good communication skills to arrive at effective and efficient solutions.

With the advent of new software development tools, understanding a problem and discussing its solution is also gaining importance because programming is becoming automated. People who don't understand this trend may ask, "Why isn't Sam coding anything?" The answer is Sam must first read, talk, think, and write about what to program.

Two major forms of natural language are spoken language and written language. Spoken language has existed for many centuries but it is volatile. Written language is a permanent, coded representation of the spoken form. Sumerians started writing around 3100 B.C. The first alphabet was developed around 1000 B.C.; from that the Roman alphabet was developed (Paivio and Begg [156]). Roman letters are written from left to right and from top to bottom. Other written forms use pictographic, phonographic, or syllabic symbols. The blind use Braille, expressed with two by three elevated dot characters; the deaf use sign language, expressing concepts and letters with their hands.

Human culture transmits from generation to generation primarily via language. Language is a prerequisite to education. Both language and teaching are social inventions that make transmission of culture possible (Mowrer [142]). One reason that the French Huguenots fought religious wars in the 16th century was for the right to read the Bible in their native language. The power of words is clear when even today books are burned and writers are threatened.

Language serves as a binding element in countries and groups, reflecting social experience. Language can also keep people apart, even within an organization. Language reflects human creativity and changes constantly; it is an expression of the human mind, reflecting its complexity.

Thought and language are strongly interrelated. Language affects how we think, and how we think affects how we express ourselves (Halpern [81] Chapter 2). A text on the use of language is Rottenberg [179].

6.1 Imprecise Natural Language

> "Contrariwise," continued Tweedledee, "if it was so, it might be; and if it were so, it would be; but as it isn't, it ain't. That's logic."
>
> —L. Carroll, *Through the Looking-Glass* [32]

Whether written or spoken, the purpose of language is to convey meaning, and understanding occurs when the person gets that meaning. Of course, it is possible for a listener to hear the words but not get their meaning; it is also possible to not hear the words and yet get the meaning intuitively. How you express yourself and whether you get someone else's meaning depends on the interplay of the many levels that exist in language (Figure 6-1).

Words in natural language are notoriously imprecise. Words that we pronounce the same may be written differently, such as, "to," "too," and "two"; we must deduce their meaning from their context. Or the meaning of a word itself can be imprecise. Consider the word "beard." It means some hair on my chin, but how much? One hair does not make a beard, and a hundred fifty thousand hairs certainly make a beard—where is the crossover? And how long must they be? If the distinction really matters, different names emerge; Eskimos have as many words for snow as we in Holland have for rain.

Many words have several meanings, for example, the word "set" has at least thirty different meanings. You can use it as a noun, a verb, or an adjective. (During my final editing, I read that the 1989 *Oxford English Dictionary* uses sixty thousand words, about as many as this book contains, to define the word "set.")

Word ambiguity may result in a sentence's being ambiguous. For instance, "They are cooking apples" may mean that the apples are for cooking, or that some people are cooking apples (Paivio and Begg [156]). This ambiguity is more common when it is written rather than spoken because there are no visual or auditory cues to their sense. For example, the written sentence "What a nice program" can be spoken affectionately or sarcastically, taking on two entirely different meanings.

Figure 6-1. Illustration of the many different levels of language (adapted from unknown author).

Obviously, we resolve such ambiguities through the context or by asking for clarification. We draw on our personal knowledge, worldly knowledge, and common knowledge for meaning. We support correct understanding by adding redundancy. The sentence "*Both* programmer*s* *are* reading" contains three indications that more than one person is involved. We often imply redundancy across sentences, and use it to check our understanding through mind models.

Language ambiguity is a condition for human creativity. We could not be creative if there were a fixed relationship between a word and its meaning. For example, I can use a concept at an abstract level in ISVIC analysis and at a concrete level in ISVIC synthesis {1.6}. Four other levels in language are lexical (about spelling), syntactical (about grammar), semantic (about meaning), and pragmatic (about context). Ambiguity—using different levels—gives us the freedom to choose new meanings and be creative.

People employ cognition, feedback, and intuition as needed to make certain that they understand and are understood. The computer, unfortunately, falls short in all these respects because its communication is predetermined and uses a fixed syntax.

6.2 Precise Formal Languages

> . . .to convey my own wonderment at the intricacy of human language and at the kind of creature we are that we may master it.
>
> —T. Winograd, *Language as a Cognitive Process: Syntax* [212]

Unlike the ambiguous and imprecise natural languages of people, computers use *formal* languages that have a precise and unique syntax, spelling, and meaning, thus avoiding ambiguity and redundancy. These artificial languages serve specific purposes, for example, to write instructions for controlling a computer.

A formal, or programming, language must describe a process in exact terms, leaving no doubt whether something is this or that way. It has fixed syntax rules that determine how it is written. The spelling must be exact because their grammar has no redundancy. An early space probe missed the planet Venus because a comma was interchanged with a period. Winograd [212] discusses syntax and many other aspects of formal language.

Programming languages are not primarily concerned with meaning. Rather, they define a process that accepts input to generate output in some way. Only the input, starting from people, and the output, made available to people, have meaning. The process itself has meaning only insofar as it fits within the human environment. The written program is meaningful only to the programmer and to the computer.

Many programming languages serve as a metalanguage, as an intermediate, humanly understandable language that can be translated into a machine language for a computer to understand. Such translation makes software portable to different computers; it is fairly simple because all artificial language elements are unique.

6.3 Considering Natural Language Translation

As organizations and their products become more international, natural language translation becomes more important. To sell software in other countries, you must be able to translate messages and Help features as well as manuals. To integrate into a common market, West European countries have a need to translate much natural language text. Multilingual countries, such as Canada, Belgium, and Switzerland, have a similar need.

Computer translation from one natural language to another, sadly, is practically impossible to do completely without human intervention. (Nevertheless, research in computer translation is important and should continue because it sheds light on our use of language.) Incompatible grammatical rules, meanings that must be understood, and ambiguities stand in the way of practical natural language translation. This is unfortunate because computers already store much text, which could otherwise be readily translated.

If machine translation is not possible, what can you do to ease human translation of natural language text? The following are some recommendations:

- Separate text from programs so you can replace text without affecting program operation.
- Keep sentences as simple and clear as possible.
- Use simple English, without national idiom, technical jargon, or slang that could interfere with translation.
- Use correct and consistent terminology.
- Avoid abbreviations.
- Leave thirty percent empty space in screen areas and printed tables because some languages require more space than English.

- Avoid special character codes that other languages need for accented and national characters.
- Beware of writing conventions that differ among countries. For example, the English decimal point (as in 1.5) is a decimal comma (as in 1,5) in other countries. Also, some countries use a leading zero (0.5) and others do not (.5). There are also various country conventions on the writing of dates. The international standard is YY-MM-DD (year, month, day), but this standard will change before the year 2000. Finally, in English "I" is written with a capital and "you" is not, but that is not universal.
- Beware of special requirements for languages not written from left to right and from top to bottom and for languages using symbols.
- Always consult with future translators on specific requirements they may have, for example, on terminology, symbols, and artwork.

This chapter has considered the importance and richness of human language in general, considering meaning and ambiguity in language translation. Specific forms of communication are discussed in Chapters 7 to 9.

6.4 Summary

1. Natural language is an essential part of human culture. Use it correctly!
2. Natural language is a major ingredient in learning, thinking, reading, and writing. Its two major forms are spoken language and written language.
3. Human communication is often incomplete and imprecise. We employ cognition, feedback, and intuition in an ad hoc manner to make certain that we understand and are understood. The computer, unfortunately, falls short in all these respects because its communication is predetermined.
4. Important differences exist between natural and formal (or artificial) languages. People use natural languages; machines use formal languages.

6.5 Review Questions and Exercises

1. Language is an essential part of human culture. What is human culture? Look up the meaning of the noun "culture" in a dictionary, a thesaurus, and an encyclopedia.

    - Besides language, what else is part of human culture?
    - Do animals also have a culture? Do plants?
        - If so, how do their respective cultures differ from human culture?
    - How do human beings, animals, and plants transfer their cultures from generation to generation?

    (Read Russell's *A History of Western Philosophy* [183] for a general view of Western culture, and Bolter's *Turing's Man* [20] for a cultural perspective of computers.)

2. > The use of words is, of course, primarily social, for the purpose of suggesting to others ideas which we entertain or at least wish them to entertain. But the aspect of words that specially concerns us is their power of promoting our own thought. Almost all higher activity is a matter of words, to the nearly total exclusion of everything else. The advantage of words for purposes of thought are so great that I should never end if I were to enumerate them.
    >
    > —B. Russell, *The Analysis of Mind* Lecture X [181]

    Recall your activities of the past week, and consider the following:

    - What would you have been unable to do if you couldn't read?
    - What would you have been unable to do if you couldn't write?

    Argue whether you expect the importance of words to decrease, stay the same, or increase as graphics and images become more widely used.

3. Language is important for developing and using an information system, but it is only a means for communicating. What particular skills, understanding, insight, and disciplines do you feel are needed to develop and use an information system properly and effectively? How did you acquire those qualities?

4. Recall three important communications that you recently had with other people.

    - To what extent did feedback contribute to their result?

- What percentage of your communication do you devote to feedback? Explain your estimate.

5. Laws are examples of rules expressed in a more or less formal form of natural language. Discuss and give arguments for (a) using a more formal language in law, (b) using a less formal language in law, and (c) leaving language in law as it is. What is your considered advice on this issue?

7

ON-LINE COMMUNICATION

The only person who likes change is a wet baby.
—R. Blitzer, quoted in [153]

On-line communication is how users and computers "talk" to each other. Although on-line communication shares many of the characteristics of human communication via speaking and writing, it involves the use of different elements and is perceived as very foreign by many people. For one thing, unlike speaking and writing, on-line communication is predetermined by developers in computer hardware and software.

For on-line communication to be effective for all people, users and developers need to take into account such things as mind mechanisms that I discussed in Chapter 2. For example, an important aspect of on-line communication is computer response time because we lose our concentration if the computer takes longer to respond than our short-term memory can tolerate.

Other individual mind mechanisms also enter into considerations for on-line communication, including how users group related fields displayed on a screen (perception), what mental model users have of a system (conception), how users regard a computer (mind set), when a computer informs its users (feedback), what useful options a computer offers (selection), how adequate training is (confidence), and how users become experienced (learning).

Although humans and machines are quite different (Chapter 3), interpersonal mind mechanisms also enter into on-line communication: how pleasant the display presentation is (appearance), how intimidating or helpful the tone of the computer messages is (role), whether a user is warned of an irrevocable action (environment and time), whether the most common menu option is displayed first (suggestion), whether a user is prompted for a forgotten item (hidden agenda), the extent to which a user is in charge (assertiveness), and whether the computer can be trusted to perform in a predictable manner (integrity).

This chapter compares on-line communication with speaking and writing, explains the elements of a human-machine interface, and considers several forms of communicating on-line.

7.1 Writing, Speaking, and On-Line Dialogues

On-line communication is a new way of communicating for many people. A computer displays a panel on the screen of a video display terminal (VDT, sometimes called a CRT) and the user enters commands and responses. Panel* information is the message going back and forth in that panel. There are only certain responses that a computer will accept, and it will reply with an error message to other responses. To characterize communicating on-line with a computer, I will compare it with speaking and writing as follows:

- The computer displays panels on a screen, unlike speaking and writing, which can be done anywhere at any time. Also, using a VDT forces you to sit in front of it. Another difference is that with some displays, you can see only one panel at a time, which is often less than a page. A third difference is the way in which you search for a word or phrase. Searching for words or phrases on-line is easier than turning pages of a book and scanning text.

  Consequence: Because users want to get information quickly, words must be used sparingly on panels. Shorter sentences are better, but they must be understandable.
- The dialogue is predetermined in on-line communication. This is unlike speaking, which is an almost completely free form of communication, but similar to printed text, which is fixed but can be read in different ways. In an on-line dialogue, a user can choose options but all computer responses are predetermined.

  Consequence: Provide as much freedom as possible for the end user to control the dialogue. Dialogues must show whose turn it is and what actions are possible.
- On-line communication can be stopped and continued later unlike speaking, which you cannot just stop without greatly interfering with the communication. But it is like reading in that we can even quit reading entirely.

  Consequence: Provide controls for the end user to direct the dialogue, for example, by being able to quit at any time and to return from a started action, and to turn pages.
- Not all communication conditions are visible on the screen. This is unlike speaking, when we see most important condi-

---

*I use the word "screen" for the physical screen of a VDT and "panel" for the information displayed on the screen. Some VDTs display an entire panel at a time; others display the panel character by character. (Video is one of many techniques available to display a panel.)

tions affecting communication, but like reading, when we must assume conditions.

Consequence: Display important conditions on the screen; for example, display the meaning of function keys and the options available.

- Using a keyboard is a new and different skill. Unlike speaking and writing, which we learn at an early age, keying is a skill acquired later.

  Consequence: Be tolerant of keying errors in the dialogue. Ask for confirmation before destroying files or tying up the computer for a long period of time. Ideally, machines would be able to distinguish and accept keying errors that are of little importance, but such errors are difficult to determine for a machine.
- People deduce intentions from a computer. As in speaking and writing, we try to understand the purpose of a communication.

  Consequence: Be courteous in communicating on-line, be consistent, and create the impression that the user controls the dialogue.

People don't like to feel restricted or be forced to do things a certain way. They can easily feel that way, though, when working with a computer because responses are predetermined and the computer does not show any empathy. To avoid this feeling of being controlled by the computer, users must understand the information system so they can be in charge of on-line dialogues (as recommended in {3.5}).

7.2 Task Orientation

Task orientation is an important principle for designing the on-line dialogue, user documentation, and training to support human tasks. Tasks are units of work performed by people with the help of computers, and the purpose of task orientation is to structure the software and its supporting materials to make it simple for people to carry out defined tasks. To do so, the human-machine dialogue and the manual must focus on the tasks at hand and omit all other detail. A proper orientation eases the carrying of tasks and increases user satisfaction.

Tasks are determined during the Study and Analysis development activity when you decide upon the division of machine tasks and human tasks. This division determines the general and detailed tasks assigned to users

{3.1}. I will return to task orientation in {8.2} on documentation and {9.2} on training.

7.3 Elements of the Human-Machine Interface

There is a great variety of facilities available to realize a dialogue between the computer and the end user. Here are some elements of such a human-machine interface:

- A window is a panel displayed on part of the screen whereby a user can communicate with a program or use the Help facility. Program windows can overlap, using graphics and color to show their boundaries.
- Panel sequence may be a simple sequence or a complex hierarchy of panels to carry out a task with a computer.
- Panel layout may have a title, identification code, and date displayed in the top line and an explanation of function keys in the bottom line to help orient users.
- Panel fields are where information is shown by the computer or entered from the keyboard. The computer uses fields to display, for example, a header to prompt for data to be entered. Users enter data in input fields, for example, a "Y" or "N" for yes or no.
- Display attributes, such as color and intensity, determine how characters are shown on the screen. Different colors and intensities can distinguish characters entered by the user, those displayed by the computer, and errors that have been detected.
- Cursors exist for text and selection. A text cursor is a special (often blinking) symbol that shows where the next character from the keyboard will be inserted on the screen. A selection cursor highlights an option for immediate selection.
- Command line is where the user can enter commands to the computer.
- Message line is where the computer displays its messages to the user.
- A Help facility is displayed at the request of the user to clarify a situation. Help may be general for an entire panel, specific for a field, or contextual for specific data.

- Keyboard and mouse are used to enter characters, to select options, and to control the dialogue. Insert and Delete keys are used to change data in entry fields, and the Enter key can send data to the computer. Function keys call frequently used commands. Tab and cursor keys are used to move a cursor around the screen. A mouse moves the cursor to select items in a panel.

The VDT interface can be rather complex for end users who are accustomed to an electric typewriter, say. It is further complicated by manufacturers and developers who use different conventions for similar functions. Even keyboards for different computer models from one manufacturer may have different layouts.

A further complication is caused by the increasing use of PCs as mainframe terminals. Although this trend makes available all the capabilities of a powerful dedicated computer, integrating the PCs into the main computer system adds complexity.

Consistency in an on-line dialogue is very important because it causes users to reinforce their mental models. Inconsistency, by contrast, interferes with their model formation, and makes people feel insecure. An on-line dialogue must be consistent at different levels [201]:

- *Physical* consistency of the VDT hardware, including keyboard layout and the use of display attributes
- *Syntactical* consistency of the software, including the sequence of actions and responses
- *Semantic* consistency for the names and meaning of elements used in the dialogue
- *Pragmatic* consistency, which concerns the integration of human and computer tasks and how people regard the use of computers

7.4 On-Line Communication Standards

Standards provide consistency and increase the number of actions that users can perform intuitively (Norman [151]). There are standards for the terminal, the workstation configuration, and the human-machine interface. Different countries and organizations have different standards for on-line communication. An example of a manufacturer's standard is [201].

Workstation design can follow such common ergonomic considerations as placing screens at right angles to a window to reduce contrasts and reflections and to avoid direct sunlight [57]. People who suffer from decreased eye power, especially those wearing bifocals, should use glasses designed for a viewing distance of 16 to 28 inches (about 40 to 70 cm). Users can take an active role in ergonomic matters by getting up and stretching periodically to avoid getting stiff from sitting in a fixed position for too long. More recommendations for VDT users are given in Appendix A.*

The use of color and graphics is an important aspect of on-line communication standards, because they are somewhat akin to articulation in speech and punctuation in writing [79]: They can be used to emphasize different parts of the panel. Monochrome displays use a single color, often white, with text shown as either black-on-white or white-on-black. Although we are used to black-on-white in printing, there is no strong objective difference between them. With monochrome displays, high intensity, underlining, and a blinking cursor can be used to indicate different things.

Color displays use red, green, and blue with other colors resulting from mixing these primary colors. Color brightens things for most people, but use color judiciously or else it loses its ability to emphasize. Graphic panels can use many colors, but do not use more than four colors on alphanumeric panels. Also use it consistently; the same type of fields should always use the same color. Common choices are green and blue for low emphasis and white and red for high emphasis. Since red signifies danger, it can be used for error conditions.

7.5 Designing a Human-Machine Interface

To understand what is involved in designing a human-machine interface, consider the example of displaying a READ or RUNNING status on a VDT. What does the computer expect from the end user in each case? READ means that the terminal is being read or interrogated by the computer. When RUNNING is displayed, it means that the computer is working on something.

Most people will interpret READ to mean that they must look at the screen, not act. The result is a deadlock situation. It is not clear what users will make of RUNNING. What is clear, however, is that dialogue de-

*There have been efforts to make standards and laws to counteract presumed adverse health effects of using VDTs. A 1983 study, supported by the U.S. National Institute for Occupational Safety and Health (NIOSH), however, primarily found differences in judgment between VDT and non-VDT users, not differences in health (Sauter et al. [188]). It also found that a suitable chair and workstation layout were more important than the use of a VDT, as were proper eyewear and ambient lighting.

sign should take the human point of view, one that people easily understand, regardless of how the computer operates internally.

The point of view appears in considering many aspects of the human-machine dialogue. The keyboard, for example, has keys to turn pages on the screen. Should a key be labeled UP when it shifts up the viewing window or when it shifts up the displayed text? The results will be opposite in either case. The same question applies to DOWN, RIGHT, and LEFT. There is no single answer for all people.

One solution is to ask users to define the keys however they think about them, thereby making the keyboard conform to people's expectations. An alternative is to train people to expect keys to work as they are programmed. As I said before {3.5}, design dialogues so as to give people the feeling of being in command. Support this feeling by using proper wording, offering meaningful options, and taking the user's point of view.

Even more important than these semantic aspects are the pragmatic aspects of the human-machine interface as a user experiences it. Because people see tasks as a whole, many other items are included, for example:

- Workload peaks and pressure to finish jobs
- Forms, including their layout, size, and how people fill them in
- Task descriptions, both written and adapted orally
- Department procedures
- Training, including concepts and practice
- Conventions used for an application
- End user support facilities
- Restart facilities in the system for different types of errors
- Working relationships with other people and customers

Development groups typically decide on hardware and software aspects and user groups on otherware aspects. Unfortunately, users range from inexperienced to professional and from occasional to frequent, and there is little chance that you will meet the expectations of all people. To help them make these decisions, you need to find out who are the users of your product, listen to their requirements, and accommodate individual preferences.

Keeping things flexible will help users arrive at a suitable job design (as we'll see in {11.5}). But also remember that flexibility and alternatives increase complexity. The art of designing on-line communication is to keep it both flexible and simple for all end users.

Computers must help people do their jobs in a natural way, such as by offering meaningful defaults. A default function applies commonly used values to reduce the number of keystrokes for a user. There are two mutually exclusive ways to provide defaults. *Previous-action defaults* show what action was taken last; they are useful when someone switches between functions. *Fixed-value defaults* insert commonly used values in specific fields; they are useful when functions are used over and over again. Ideally, users should be able to select a default system that works best for their situation.

7.6 Specific Forms of Communicating On-Line

This section discusses eight specific forms of communicating on-line with a computer to illustrate the general discussion so far and to give more specific comments.

MAKING GOOD MENU PANELS

Menus are the signposts on computer displays; they contain words or icons (pictures) that express the available options. Menus make tailor-made system functions available via single keys. Pictorial menus let you connect, for example, a report icon with a printer icon to print a report.

Menu option descriptions should be simple and specific, such as "Enter new orders." Follow these guidelines in designing menus: Use common terms, capitalize only the first word of each option, group options logically for the user, don't display a restricted option that is not available to a user, and have the most frequently used option at the top.

Certain applications may have menu hierarchies, which are suitable for inexperienced or only occasional users. These menus guide them, step by step, to the desired function. But menu selection can be a nuisance for experienced users, who must wade through many levels of menus to get to the desired option. Therefore, allow experienced users to key options or commands directly. Of course, making available different command interfaces requires a decision early in the development process.

Menu hierarchies arise when available options do not fit on a single panel, requiring option selection in levels. There must be some trade-off between clarity and number of levels. Short-term memory demands no more than nine options per menu, but that may lead to long wait times.

If I must select a database from a list of sixty, I like to have all their names on one panel.

An article by Habinek and Savage in [190] describes the design and evaluation of a menu-driven interface. Norman [151] Section 3.1 discusses the design of task structures from a user's point of view.

DESIGNING EASY DATA ENTRY PANELS

In order for users to enter records into a database, developers must design data entry panels. Such design depends on the users and how they will use the panels. Careful design and extensive testing are necessary when a panel design is used in different ways.

A good general guideline is for the screen layout to follow the same sequence of fields as on the paper form because entering data in a different sequence is annoying, especially when data entry is a routine task. Another guideline is to put as many related input fields as is possible in one panel. This results in fewer panel changes and gives the user a broader view of data entered. To save time, frequent users like to be able to use nicknames or shortened versions (preferring to type the first four letters instead of the full customer name and address, for example) and have default values inserted.

SIMPLIFYING ON-LINE QUERIES

Users employ query panels to select database records. There are two basic types of queries:

1. Individual-information queries, which, for example, display the health insurance record for a specific customer during a telephone enquiry. For this type of query, let people enter ad hoc search arguments in fields of familiar data entry panels. Some systems allow use of a so-called wild character, such as an asterisk, in the argument. For example, the * in "m*gor*" stands for any characters or none, enabling a search for all MacGregory's. Some systems can even match on a phonetic basis, which is useful when names have been entered from a request by telephone and correct spelling hasn't been verified.

2. Grouped-information queries, which, for example, display a list of all health insurance customers who have not paid their bill by a certain due date. Three steps can create a simple list on-line:

- Specify the layout of the list. Select fields and their sequence and determine how the records must be sorted.
- Specify only those records you want listed by entering selection criteria in fields of the data entry panel.
- Specify the output device as to how the list is displayed, printed, or stored for future reference.

For reports that are complex and demanding on the computer, specialists can define them in a program instead of specifying them each time anew. Some database systems will estimate the processing time required for a long query and ask for a user's confirmation before starting it. Database structures in general are very complex and require much training and insight for specifying anything but simple queries.

ENTERING AND CHANGING TEXT INFORMATION ON-LINE

Editor programs are used to enter and change text. As of 1987, there were roughly ten thousand such programs, all different in varying degrees. They are one of the most useful and frequently used programs available for developers and users. Programmers can use them to enter programs and documentation, secretaries to type letters, and writers to write books.

Some word processing programs display the text as it is printed (called WYSIWYG or What You See Is What You Get). They insert invisible codes to format the text. Other programs use visible codes (called markup, like Standard Generalized Markup Language or SGML codes).

Editor programs are a major productivity tool and have the following features:

- They are faster than a typewriter.
- They separate typing and printing.
- They have many functions, including inserting, deleting, changing, searching, moving, and formatting text.
- They reveal the changes you make on the screen.
- They store and recall text and can send it to other people.
- They can call in standard paragraphs and other text.
- They can personalize a form letter with names entered from a database.
- Their key functions can often be redefined.

Editor programs range from the very simple to the very complex. Time to learn them is well spent if you use them frequently. Consult Carroll and Mack in [190] if you want to understand the complexities of learning to use the editor of a simple word processor.

DISPLAYING TEXT INFORMATION ON-LINE

Because much text information is already in computers for editing and printing, it is simple to display it on-line. Three basic uses for on-line text display are these:

- Reference use for looking up something specific. On-line searching is simple and easy, even in very large databases.
- Selective text use saves on paper, printing, and distribution costs.
- Full text use requires careful consideration because most people prefer to read from paper. Some recommendations are as follows:
  - Since people are used to scanning a table of contents or an index to select an item for reading, you'll need to provide quick access to a table of contents and an index in addition to the general search function. In a dialogue, this is a matter of using the cursor keys and a key to select a section.
  - Capitalize first words only; capitalized text is hard to read.
  - Condense the text; short words and simple sentences are keys to making text readable on-line. Rewrite printed text that will be put on-line.
  - Do not use right-justified text.
  - Display orientational information, such as chapter title, panel number, and the total number of text panels.

A new development at the time of writing is *hypertext,* which allows people to combine different text and image fragments by navigating through a variety of preprogrammed links. Hypertext avoids the linear structure of regular text, but it is often impractical to anticipate all links desired by users. Random searching in large databases may also be impractical.

In spite of many new developments, I find it hard to believe that on-line text will replace printed text to a significant extent. New printing technologies make it possible to print out on-line text in ever greater quantities (witness what we used to call "paperless offices"). Judging from that experience, the ability to print selected parts of on-line text holds more promise than full text display.

MAKING HELPFUL MESSAGES

For a change, I tried to write a small BASIC program, and got error message 67: "Too many files." As I was not consciously using any file, I had to look up number 67 in the (printed!) manual for the following explanation:

> You tried to create a new file when all directory entries on the disk are full, or when the file specification is invalid.

The second possibility turned out to be the case, and the correction was easy. I mention this incident only because it perfectly illustrates the following key points about error messages: First, an error message should tell what to do to resolve a problem. A user is seldom interested in what caused it. Second, error messages should be unique; never combine different problems in one message. My example consists of two problems served by one message. Users don't care that two conditions lead to the same error inside the program.

Programmers use messages to debug their code during development and they may forget to replace them by more user-oriented messages. In testing, therefore, check messages for the audience that they address.

Most information systems have several types of messages, often displayed in a specific location on the screen:

- Information messages, for the user's information only.
  Example: Computer busy processing report.
- Prompts, requesting a specific action from a user.
  Example: Please enter customer number.
- Warnings, informing the user of a critical situation, either an exception condition or an irrevocable user action.
  Example 1: Network not available now. Try again later.
  Example 2: Press ENTER to overwrite file or ESC to quit.
- System error messages, warning about system errors to which the user must react.
  Example: Memory parity check. Power off and try again.

- End user error messages, warning the user about erroneous actions.
  Example 1: Customer number must be 8 characters. Please reenter.
  Example 2: Valid options are 1, 2, 3, 4, 5. Please reenter.

A message is usually only one line long; it must be compact, helpful, precise, and user oriented. Some systems enable users to request a longer message for additional details.

PROVIDING USEFUL HELP INFORMATION

A Help facility is on-line support for end users facing a problem; it is usually available via a special key. Help is especially useful for explaining infrequently used details to users who understand system concepts. Developers, through software, can provide different types of Help:

- Panel Help, describing the purpose of an entire panel
- Field Help, describing the purpose of a field and its requirements
- Message Help, giving additional information on a particular message
- Key Help, giving information about the function of a key
- System Help, providing information about a system command

The facility should use the cursor position to determine what type is requested when the Help key is pressed. Pressing the Help key again should result in information on the Help function itself, for example, how to quit Help.

Help information often uses a separate window superimposed on the original panel, and different Help panels can be arranged in a hierarchy, parallel to the application panel hierarchy. Graphics and different colors can help to distinguish it. Instructions in the Help window must enable the user to navigate within the Help structure.

If you plan to include a tutorial {9.3}, you might well make appropriate parts of it available under Help. This may save work in development, and will reinforce the novice user.

COMMUNICATING WITH A KNOWLEDGE SYSTEM

Knowledge systems, a new class of system sometimes called *expert systems,* can solve information processing problems in another way. This section concentrates on their human interface; general human-machine considerations for knowledge systems are in {3.4}.

New possibilities of knowledge systems will lead to new ways of communicating with end users. There are no clear directions as to what is the best interface, but I can offer these observations on communicating on-line with a knowledge system. First, knowledge systems will integrate with conventional systems, requiring consistent interfacing and communication.

Because of their name and the publicity they attract, knowledge systems raise people's expectations. This requires them to have a smarter human interface than conventional systems. A knowledge system that does not understand the abbreviation "Y" for yes is not likely to be trusted to diagnose a complex situation.

You can use natural language to communicate with knowledge systems. Because of the ambiguity of language {6.1}, it is advisable to ask for user confirmation of a system's formal understanding before processing a natural language request.

Most knowledge systems have a facility to explain how it arrived at a conclusion. This explanation must be in a form that users can understand.

Knowledge systems demand much processing, requiring powerful computers to provide short response times.

Teaching many users to work with knowledge systems is a new field. Users must understand what a knowledge system can and cannot do. They must feel they are the human experts on the knowledge system.

People must decide to use a knowledge system's conclusions. Only simple and well-understood decisions can be left to a machine because only people can make a commitment and assume responsibility.

This chapter discusses points about on-line communication, a new area with many new developments. On-line communication is not yet as well understood as spoken and written communication, but I recommend that users participate in developing the human-machine interface. Developers and users should test different dialogues to find out which alternative is best. Proper training and support must give end users the necessary confidence to work with computers. (Chapter 8 discusses documentation and Chapter 9 discusses training. See Appendix B for on-line dialogue design principles.)

7.7 Summary

1. Compared to speaking and writing, on-line communication shares characteristics of both, especially in the areas of feedback and understanding of context. The computer displays panels, and the user responds by entering data in the panel and selecting dialogue options.

2. The basic division of tasks between people and machine is made during the Study and Analysis activity in development. Users, or their representatives, should develop the human-machine interface because they understand tasks in the user environment.

3. Task orientation is an important principle for designing the human-machine dialogue (and its supporting documentation and training).

4. VDTs have a complex human interface. This chapter discusses the elements of a dialogue available for creating an effective human-machine interface.

5. Display colors and graphics are akin to articulation in speech and punctuation in writing. Text panels should not use more than four colors.

6. Panels displayed by the computer must take the human, not the computer, point of view.

7. Workstation design and job content should be flexible and be adaptable to the individual.

8. There is hardly any general theory on how to design a suitable human-machine interface. You must test alternatives early in development and make adaptations during customization.

9. This chapter discusses several forms of on-line communication:
   - Making good menu panels
   - Designing easy data entry panels
   - Simplifying on-line queries
   - Entering and changing text information on-line
   - Displaying text information on-line
   - Making helpful messages
   - Providing useful Help information
   - Communicating with a knowledge system

10. End users must be properly trained and supported by a human network, especially when using knowledge systems. Confident users can be more important to the success of a system than a good ergonomic human-machine interface design.

7.8 Review Questions and Exercises

1. The introduction to this chapter compares communication aspects for speaking, writing, and on-line communication. List the elements that you consider important for all human communication, such as messages, medium, feedback, context, and understanding. Describe the importance you attach to each of those aspects for speaking, listening, writing, reading, and human-to-computer and computer-to-human communication.

2. Miller [136] and Shneiderman [193] Section 10.4 both deal with response time as a human-machine interface issue. Read that material and relate it to the way you experience response time when working with a computer. Extrapolate what would be acceptable response times for a knowledge system doing different jobs.

3. Select an unstructured instruction text, such as an explanation of how to fill out a form. Structure and condense the text into short verb-object sentences that would be suitable as on-line text. Discuss why the original text makes on-line reading difficult and whether structured text is also easier to read on paper.

4. As an exercise, consider an on-line dialogue with which you are familiar. Use points made in this chapter to assess it and make recommendations to improve it for novice users. What changes, if any, would you make? Which points, implemented to help novice users, would complicate use of the dialogue for expert users? What do you recommend to make a dialogue simple for both novice and experienced users?

5. Select a command from your editor program or some other familiar data entry panel. Write a Help panel for it, using no more than twenty lines of eighty characters each. Compare your Help panel with that supplied in the software. Describe your experiences and your findings.

6. Get a copy of the reference manual for the editor you are using. Tick off the commands that you are using daily. What other com-

mands are familiar to you? Browse through the remaining commands to find any others that you can use.

7. Find out what standards apply in your organization on workstations, user dialogues, and job content. Discuss whether they are up to date with regard to current technology. Consider what is obsolete because of new developments in hardware and software. Discuss your findings with people responsible for standards to make them reflect current technology when needed.

8. Some people argue that all parts of the human-machine interface should be developed by a single group to ensure consistency between its parts: panel sequence and content, messages, Help, user documentation, and tutorials. Others disagree, arguing that these parts require professionals who work and are managed in specialized groups. (Panels, anyway, are part of the program developed by programmers.) Discuss your position between these two extremes, considering the characteristics of your organization.

9. Carroll [31] describes an interesting strategy to approach unknown software. He explains what happens if software is regarded as a mystery game, in which the challenge is to discover the various functions *without having instructions.* Read the article and do the following:

   - Argue why you think such an approach is, or is not, a good suggestion for software that you know. What could happen?
   - Would a discovery tour be a useful approach for a printed primer or tutorial? Will it work, or not work, with a printed guide?
   - Imagine and describe another unconventional approach to get people to learn the use of application software.

   Read the article by Malone in [190] for more ideas on making an enjoyable human-machine interface.

8

USER DOCUMENTATION

I know that you believe you understand
what you think I said,
but I am not sure you realize that what you heard
is not what I meant.
—Anonymous

Writing and reading are important forms of communication in information processing. Writing gives permanence to our ideas and plans. We use it to document software functions and human procedures. Both developers and users spend much of their time reading different forms of software documentation.

This short chapter focuses on user documentation. It begins by explaining the various forms of user documentation, then discusses how to write so your readers will understand and how to read so you will understand.

Many of the points in this chapter are also pertinent to phase process documentation and development documentation {4.6}.

8.1 Importance of Documentation

Why are user manuals needed? Because they are often the only material evidence of a software product. Good user documentation will also enhance ease of use and reduce false error reports.

Although much software today seems to be self-explanatory, it really isn't. One of my manuals, for example, clearly explains how to change to a new version of an operating system but neglects to explain that it will destroy two files that personalize my use of it. A simple sentence could have saved me the hours spent to reconstruct these files. Programmers often underestimate the usefulness of manuals because they think their programs will speak for themselves. But they don't.

It is difficult to underestimate the importance and magnitude of software documentation. Compare for example, the documentation that describes an operating system for a PC: The one hundred fifty half-sized pages required for DOS version 2.1 have grown to more than three thousand full-sized pages for OS/2 version 1.1 and PM in only a few years (and that doesn't include the application documentation). Software documentation has made IBM one of the largest publishers in the world.

Users need information on various aspects of the software, such as:

- Uses for the software
- Capabilities and requirements of the software
- Installation of the software
- Customization of the software

- Conversion of and migration to the software
- Troubleshooting problems in using the software
- Operation of the software
- Maintenance of the software

Much of this information is used by the team that implements an application during the first six activities discussed in {5.3}; to be useful, documentation must be structured to support such team tasks. Other information is aimed at end users, for example, teaching how to use the software through examples (contained in tutorials), showing how to carry out tasks (task-oriented guides), and systematic descriptions (reference manuals).

Because so much effort is put into phase and development documentation and user documentation, it is a good idea to try to combine the material. But that sounds simpler than it is because they are developed for different audiences; also development documentation takes a system view. Much planning is required if parts of the documentation are to be shared.

8.2 Writing for Understanding

To write effectively, you must understand your readers and their needs. Writing is primarily for their benefit—not for yours—and you must think like they do.

To accomplish this, recall from the discussion in Chapter 2 that the conception and cognition mind mechanisms determine how readers interpret elements using their mental models. When you write, understand what your readers know and how they think. Other individual mind mechanisms also enter into writing and reading, for example: how a writer can shape elements for easy distinction (perception), limit their number to 7 ± 2 (short-term memory), shape reader expectations by a proper introduction (mind set), reinforce the reader by summarizing and asking questions (feedback), incorporate a task orientation (selecting what is meaningful), use a personal and helpful orientation (readers getting confidence), and provide useful material (learning).

Likewise, interpersonal mind mechanisms are at work when you write for people to read your writing: They judge how pleasing is the presentation of a manual (appearance), how intimidating or helpful is the tone of the writer (role), how timely is the manual (environment and time), how convincing is the writer (suggestion), how complete is the writer's description (hidden agenda), how much does the writer encourage reader's initiatives (assertiveness), and how well does the reader trust the writer (integrity)?

The specific content and style of guides, reference manuals, and user manuals will differ. But what they all have in common is the need to be clear—both in writing style and in format. To help achieve clarity, use the ISVIC procedure {1.6} to plan your structure and write for your audience. As an example, consider writing a user manual.

BEFORE BEGINNING TO WRITE: INVESTIGATING

Before you start to write, understand what you are going to write about and for whom. Clear writing builds on clear thinking (Flesch [62]). You will waste much time and effort if after you have begun writing, you discover you are on the wrong track. Make an outline first; it is much easier to change than a completed section.

Here are general guidelines for investigating before you start to write a computer user manual.

Purpose: Why? Be very clear in your own mind about the manual: What is its purpose and how will people use it?

Subject: What? What is the manual about? If you don't understand all the parts of the product or system, how will you get the necessary technical information? Who will check your writing? What terminology should you use? Is the product used in combination with other products? With what other manuals must you be consistent?

Audience: Who? For whom are you writing? Determine first if your audience is homogeneous. If not, for each group, develop a profile of typical users: age, education, skills, experience, and expectations. How will each group use your manual? Meet with prospective users to get a realistic idea of your audience. Then, you may have to consider writing different parts for different groups at different levels.

Style and tone: Whence? For your writing to be effective, choose a proper style and tone, depending on your goal and your audience. Avoid jargon.

Using situation: Where? How will the product you are writing about fit into the users' daily routine? How often will they use it? How much training will they get before they start using your manual? What support will be available to them?

Schedule: When? The time you have to write the manual will determine the work plan. Do you have time to prepare thoroughly and write a comprehensive manual? Or must it be a quick job? Be sure to allow time in the schedule for reviews and for production of the manual.

Writing tools and production: HoW? Select writing and editing tools that allow you to incorporate illustrations, do an index, and provide special formatting. Since tools also impose restrictions, you must understand them before starting to structure. Also consider production techniques because they influence what you write.

END USER TASK ANALYSIS: STRUCTURING

To structure your manual in a meaningful way, you must understand how end users will work with the product. They may prefer to have all information about each task in one place in the manual (called *task orientation* of the manual {7.2}). Or they may prefer *product orientation,* where the emphasis is on functions of the product, like in a reference manual.

Once you have determined the best orientation, you must determine the structure, which becomes the outline of your writing. Entries in the structure become your future headings; they are the table of contents and the architecture of your manual. Therefore, for headings to be meaningful to readers, entries must reflect what you will put in the section. Include introductions and summaries in your outline (following the 3T formula).

Structuring properly will save much time later. Remember, the further you progress with writing, the more difficult it becomes to make changes later.

PROVING THE STRUCTURE: VERIFYING

Make certain the manual has all the important elements to describe the product and that they are in a logical sequence. Before actually writing, verify your outline with a peer to get another view. Verification is easier if the entries in your outline (that is, the future headings) accurately describe what the sections will contain.

WRITING THE MANUAL: IMPLEMENTING

After preparing yourself and the subject and checking the outline's validity, you are ready to carry out your writing plan. As I said above, the better your outline, the easier your writing will be, the better the result, and the fewer surprises you will have.

REVIEWING AND TESTING: CHECKING

The manual can be reviewed and tested as part of the product review or as a separate task. Before the review, have enough copies of the draft manual available ahead of time, so that the reviewers will have adequate time to consider it and to make recommendations.

The reviewers should check for the following:

- Clarity: Is the writing simple?
- Conciseness: Is it brief?
- Completeness: Is it adequate?
- Courtesy: Is it fair?
- Correctness: Is it accurate?

Be sure to perform the five ISVIC steps in the proper sequence. Using this procedure, you will be able to plan in detail preparation of all computer manuals. As with software engineering, you can use measures based on experience, review progress regularly, and test the result. To avoid surprises, you can make a proposal with a description, a development plan, a specification, and a test plan for each manual.

ISVIC can help you get a sound base for your writing and give you a proper orientation. This is a good start, but it does not tell you how to write so that readers will understand. This requires experience and, for the best result, a person to edit your writing. Books on writing manuals are Marder [121] and Price [165].

8.3 Watching Your Style

There are two major aspects of style: *technical* style, which concerns appearance of the text, and *writing* style, which concerns expression. Both aspects of style must be appropriate for the audience and follow the meaning and content of your manual.

Technical style is the appearance of your text on paper, specifically its page layout and the type sizes and typefaces. What is a proper technical style depends to a great extent on the nature of the material, the type of communication, and the production means used. Good technical style brings peace to each page and promotes the understanding of your writing; a good general reference is *A Manual of Style* [120].

Writing style concerns the words and tone you use. The last chapter of Strunk and White's concise *The Elements of Style* [200] is devoted to writing style. Since I cannot improve on their phrasing, I'll borrow some of their suggestions:

- Place yourself in the background. Draw the reader's attention to the sense and substance of your writing.
- Work from a suitable design. Understand first what to write about.
- Write with nouns and verbs. They amplify your writing; adjectives and adverbs distract from it.
- Revise and rewrite. Shorten, improve, and rearrange whenever possible.
- Do not overstate. It will make all your other writing suspect.
- Be clear. Break sentences apart if they are too complex.
- Do not inject opinion. It may be in bad taste and not relevant.
- Prefer the standard to the offbeat. Use simple words and phrases.

Remember: Your purpose in writing is to inform readers. Therefore, write so that it will be read. And choose an appropriate technical and writing style that makes it easy to read.

8.4 Reading to Understand and to Remember

You read for a purpose and that purpose determines how you read. You may simply glance at pages to spot items of interest, or skim a chapter for sense, or read a section in its entirety. As you read, you remind yourself how well you must understand and remember what you read. Some parts you can skip without missing anything; other parts you must read carefully. Descriptive headings and illustrations help you to decide what to skip and what to read.

While scanning text, you are also scanning your mental models. If something seems all right, you go on to the next section. But if you see something unfamiliar, you read about it in some detail. If you detect a gross error, all the text becomes suspect and you read it critically. You also ask yourself what is *not* said but should have been, all the while checking the plausibility of what is written. If you anticipate the argument a writer develops, you need only check infrequently if you are right.

There are several ways to measure readability of a text. Readability depends on the subject and the readers. What is easily readable for a lawyer may be incomprehensible to a computer user, and vice versa. Here are some measures of readability (Flesch [63], and Paivio and Begg [156]):

- Average number of phrases or clauses per sentence
- Average number of words per phrase or clause
- Average number of syllables per word
- Ratio of abstract words to personal and concrete words
- Ratio of incidental or irrelevant facts to meaningful facts
- Frequency of using prefixes and suffixes
- Frequency of using predicate verbs
- Frequency of using passive sentence constructions

There are software tools that can determine readability using such measures and relate it to a grade level. These tools cannot understand meaning, of course, but they are useful to point out possible errors in grammar and weaknesses in phrasing. Some tools measure the use of adjectives and adverbs, indicate the use of passive voice, verify punctuation, find repeated words and jargon, and check spelling. The use of jargon is probably the strongest single factor influencing readability of information processing texts; avoid jargon but if you must use it, at least explain it.

8.5 Practical Points on Writing

Here are some final points about developing a manual for computer users.

1. Use professional layout and text preparation. Now that good layout and typesetting facilities are generally available, people expect properly printed text to support the software they use. For production of manuals for commercial products, however, the experience and assistance of professional people remains necessary.

2. Use descriptive headings. Headings in the text can be used to flag key points and to help guide readers through the manual. They

should describe the chapter and section content as accurately as possible. For example, "Choosing Parameters for REPORT Command to Make Monthly Sales Report" is much better than "REPORT—Option 5."

In an outline of a manual, descriptive headings indicate what will be in the section so that reviewers can easily understand and verify the outline. As headlines, they simplify a reader's decision about reading the details. A descriptive heading also serves as focal point for the section. They also can be listed in the table of contents, and they help to make an index since they describe all subjects, operations, and results.

Main part → Summary → Introduction

3. Write the summary and introduction last. Clearly, the summary can only be written after the main part is completed. But since the introduction must put the main part in a proper context, it cannot be written until everything else is done. The best implementation sequence of the 3T formula is to start with the main part, then write the summary, and do the introduction last of all.

This chapter touches on some aspects of preparing documentation, which is critical to the success of the developed product. Many books and courses are available to help you improve your writing so that you can prepare manuals and other documentation better, as well as to improve your reading skills, so you retain and understand everything that you read. (Appendix K lists the elements of a manual, and Appendix L making its index.)

8.6 Summary

1. Use the ISVIC procedure to investigate, structure, verify, implement, and check your writing.
2. Choose proper technical and writing styles to make your writing effective for the reader.
3. Reading can be speeded up by scanning the text, by selecting parts for reading, and by anticipating the argument.

4. Readability depends on your subject matter and your prospective readers. There is no good single readability index, and each group of readers requires special consideration.

5. Use descriptive headings as items in an outline for understanding future content and for helping others to verify the manual's content; as headlines for readers to describe the contents; as entries in the table of contents; and to simplify indexing.

6. Write the summary after completing the main part; write the introduction last. Introduce and summarize every part, using the 3T formula.

8.7 Review Questions and Exercises

1. Plan your next writing assignment as discussed in {8.2}. Structure descriptive headings in an outline, have them reviewed, and complete your writing assignment. Ask for a reaction from a reader, then answer the following questions:
   - In what respects did the ISVIC procedure make a difference?
   - How were descriptive headings useful?
   - How did descriptive headings delay your work?
   - What can you do to improve the planning of your writing?

2. Refering to the introduction to this chapter, give examples of how individual and interpersonal mind mechanisms enter into reading.

3. Plan how you will read your next book. Look at the introductory text and table of contents first:
   - What is the book about? What is its purpose?
   - Why was it written? For whom?
   - Read the recommendations given on how to use the book.
   - Browse through the index and the glossary to check concepts and terms used.
   - Determine what you want to get out of reading the book.
   - Finally, determine your reading strategy:
     - — Will you glance through the book first?
     - — Will you read from the beginning to the end?
     - — Will you just read selected chapters?

Was the book organized to help you determine the above points? After reading, do you feel that planning helped you read the book more efficiently? Why?

4. Try to increase your reading speed by using different reading strategies. You can take in chunks of words at a time, scan for key words, sample lines, look at illustrations, or use any other method that works with the chapter. Breeze through the chapter and carefully read the summary at the end of it. After breezing through the chapter, read it again thoroughly and note what points you missed.
   - In each case, why did you miss the point?
   - How can you adapt your reading strategy to pick up those points?

5. Offer to check and edit a piece written by a colleague. When you are done, answer the following questions:
   - Was your effort worth the result? How?
   - What was the reaction of your colleague?
   - What did you learn from this exercise?

6. Select some one-page samples of writing. First, rank the samples intuitively on readability. Then check the readability of the samples using the following criteria:
   - Average number of words per sentence
   - Average number of words per phrase or clause
   - Average number of syllables per word
   - Ratio of abstract words to personal and concrete words
   - Ratio of incidental or irrelevant facts to meaningful facts
   - Frequency of use of prefixes and suffixes

   What conclusions can you draw by comparing your intuitive estimate with the measures? In what way has this exercise changed your views on readability?

7. Check a user manual of a program that you use daily:
   - How well does the preface introduce the manual?
   - Compare its organization with the elements listed in Appendix K.
   - How useful is the table of contents?
   - Do chapter divisions make sense to you?

- Do the title headings properly explain section contents?
- How complete is the index?
- Is reference information located in the text or in the appendices?
- What do you think of the technical and writing styles?
- Are graphics used? Are they helpful?
- How well is the manual oriented either on tasks or on product functions?
- How clear is it?
- How concise is it?
- How complete is it?
- Does it use a proper tone? Why?
- To what extent is it correct?

How effective is the manual overall for your use of the program?

8. The people who write user manuals can be positioned differently in a software development organization:

   a. Manual writers are in a group that is separate from software developers, reporting directly to the director of the development organization. The manager of the writers is responsible for manual quality.

   b. Manual writers are in a group that is separate from software developers, as in (a), but they are assigned to and located in the development groups. As in (a), the manager of the writers is responsible for manual quality.

   c. Same as in (b), but manual quality becomes the responsibility of software development.

   d. There is no separate writing group. Manual quality is the responsibility of each development group, where the manual writers are also located.

   e. Manual writing is the responsibility of a user (representative). How would you position the user in the development organization?

   What are the advantages and disadvantages of these five approaches. What positioning do you prefer? Why?

9

TRAINING

But it is not enough to be told.
You must see for yourself.
—O. Sacks,
The Man Who Mistook His Wife for a Hat [186]

As the use of computers grows, more and more people must learn new topics in information processing. Developers need continuous training to keep up with new software techniques and hardware technology, and users need training to work with applications. Managers need training in management skills and everyone in communication. Training is a special, intense form of communication.

After a general discussion of learning, this chapter explains how learners' needs* and teaching objectives lead to choosing the appropriate instructional strategy, and how different forms of training can be justified financially. (Learning is also discussed in {2.9}.)

9.1 Characteristics of Learning

To be told what something means, to understand it, and to check that we understand it is the important process of learning. Reinforcement through feedback increases the effectiveness of learning. Gazda et al. [71] say that no topic is more basic to human existence and behavior than learning. Learning is essential in human life to adapt to changes. We have learned to act the way we do, and we can learn to act differently. We learn attitudes and values, and indeed we can learn how to learn.

We learn all the time, but how we do it is a secret of the mind. To learn something, we must first become conscious of it and aware of its use. Thorndike developed the notion that all mental processes depend on connections between situations (which provide stimuli) and responses. He formulated three laws in 1906 that are basic to learning (Gazda et al. [71]).

1. *Law of Readiness:* If we are prepared for something, its completion is satisfying and its noncompletion or meaningless repetition is annoying. Completion gets it off our mind; noncompletion doesn't.
2. *Law of Effect:* The strength of a connection increases when we enjoy it and decreases when it annoys us.
3. *Law of Exercise:* Doing something the first time is the most difficult; it becomes easier each successive time.

*I will use the word "learner" to indicate an adult student.

Learning by adults has special characteristics with important consequences, as I'll discuss in the next sections. First, let me briefly list them: Adults are generally motivated to learn, so there is less need to check their progress. They often have a specific need and can usually decide what they need to learn.

Adults are oriented toward what they can use tomorrow and they require practical training. They want to understand things, not memorize facts; they want to understand the why and how rather than the what. Since they are often afraid of failing, they must know beforehand in detail what they will be learning.

Adults often need more time to learn, so they should determine their own learning pace, not the teacher. Adults learn effectively in groups from examples set by others.

Teachers must adapt their methods and materials to learners' needs. Flexibility, practicality, and encouragement are the key to teaching learners successfully. It would be nice if learners could select their own learning strategy, but practical considerations often dictate a single strategy for the whole group. Developing a course for such a group is discussed next.

9.2 Beginning With Learners' Needs and Teaching Objectives

There are three basic components of learning:

- Knowledge: We learn by being told.
- Skills: We learn by doing, from experience.
- Attitudes: We learn by example.

To truly learn something, we need all three elements: Basic knowledge of a topic is obviously critical in a technical field; skills are equally important for all people in information processing in which productivity is key; and attitudes are becoming increasingly important as people must make more decisions in today's information processing world.

For example, take learning how to program. You must acquire knowledge of how to write instructions and how to enter them. You must gain the skills to do so from performing exercises. Last, you must gain the proper attitude for using your knowledge and skills, including being motivated to program in a team.

The first step in developing a course is to establish realistic learners' needs. Learners' needs can be best described in the form of teaching objectives, or what learners should be able to do after training. General objectives describe the goals in precise, concrete terms, and should at least specify the desired behavior and the content of tasks. Specific teaching objectives may also be necessary. They specify performance (how learners must demonstrate competence), conditions (under what circumstances), and criteria (to what level of performance).

Bloom devised a classification of cognitive skills to describe increasing competence levels that training can achieve. Davies extends this list as follows [41]:

- Knowledge: Reproduce/select/describe facts and details.
- Comprehension: Recognize/explain relationships.
- Application: Find/construct/predict/use relationships.
- Analysis: Identify new relationships and structures.
- Synthesis: Combine/discuss new relationships and structures.
- Evaluation: Judge from evidence, using given criteria.
- Skills: Operate/handle/perform an action.
- Attitudes: Accept/prefer/value/select a way of behaving.

Learning objectives should contain verbs that describe the competence level desired. The above list gives some of those verbs; Davies gives many more in [41]. He presents a rationale for thinking about and working with teaching objectives in [40].

9.3 Choosing an Instructional Strategy and Medium

From learners' needs and teaching objectives, trainers must develop an instructional strategy to meet them. Davies gives five aspects of instructional strategy that trainers need to consider to arrive at a successful framework for course development [41]:

1. Efficiency and effectiveness: How can trainers teach the right things in the right way? To plan a course properly, they must set priorities in selecting subjects and depth of coverage.
2. Choice of instructional method: What method can trainers best use to teach a subject? The method depends upon the nature of the task and the learners' needs (see Bloom/Davies classification).
3. Structuring lessons: What is an appropriate structure for a lesson? A lesson has an introduction, a body, and a reinforcing summary.

4. Preparing lessons: Where can trainers start? How can they proceed to the goal? Trainers must plan their approach to teaching and prepare teaching material.

5. Settings for instruction: What environment is best for teaching? Consider group size and facilities.

Finally, the trainer must choose an appropriate instructional medium for the course; refer to Heinich et al. [89] and {9.3} for examples of different media. You need keyboard practice to learn typing skills, watching others and exercises to master communication, and discussion to learn new procedures, all requiring different media.

Because of the intensity involved, training must be well planned. You can use the ISVIC procedure {1.6} to prepare a course.

INVESTIGATING THE FOCUS AND DIRECTION

Use the seven W's to carry out this step.

- *Why* do you want to teach? Clarify learners' needs and your own motivation.
- *What* do you want to teach? Define the subject matter you want to teach, putting aside irrelevant topics.
- *Whom* are you planning to teach? Adapt your teaching to the learners by carefully knowing them. Create a mental picture of them so that it will be easier for you to prepare your teaching and the result will be more effective.
- *Whence* are you making the teaching? What is your position and authority for teaching? Are you the right person? Were you asked to teach or is it your idea? Your role depends on your position and authority relative to that of your learners.
- *Where* do you start from? What are the starting conditions for yourself, the learners, and the teaching environment? What do your learners know? How well can they learn?
- *When* will the teaching take place? Analyze when is the best time to ask for the attention of learners, and for how long. How much time will you have to prepare your teaching?
- *HoW* can you best move from learners' needs to learning results? Teaching implies structuring teaching matter, putting it in its sim-

plest form for teaching. Select a suitable combination of instructional media [88], depending on available facilities, to make the course effective for the learner. This question involves decisions on

- Teaching control whether by an instructor, a computer, or the learner
- Active or passive learning
  - Ratio of telling to letting learners find it out themselves
  - Ratio of telling to showing
  - Ratio of telling to doing
- Level of understanding to be achieved
- Amount of feedback required; the interaction and reinforcement depends upon how important proper understanding is

STRUCTURING THE COURSE

The course structure must incorporate all essential tasks, including the teaching context and an introduction to you as the teacher. Describe all tasks in the form of an action, such as "Understand options of the COPY command." These descriptions become the titles of your sections. The verb in such a teaching objective is chosen depending on the desired competence level (Bloom/Davies).

VERIFYING THE STRUCTURE

As before, ask one or more of your peers to check that the course outline is complete and does not contain irrelevant matter.

IMPLEMENTING THE COURSE

The nature of your implementation depends on the teaching medium, the scope of your teaching, and your "hoW" decisions. Learners' needs and the subject will determine the best implementation form and approach.

A proper course structure isolates the major parts so you can work on one part at a time. Each module should use the 3T formula; the first T to introduce the part and its overall plan and the third T to reinforce major points, in line with the Law of Readiness. After preparing the course, verify that the parts fit together and are consistent. Prepare questions that allow learners to verify their mental models and to let you understand whether they are still with you.

CHECKING THE COURSE IMPLEMENTATION

Checking the implementation of the course is the last step in course preparation. Since checking your own work, especially teaching a course, is very difficult, ask colleagues or the manager of your learners to be your critical audience for a test run, and ask them to consider the following in respect to your course:

- Clarity: Will learners grasp it easily?
- Conciseness: Will learners understand it rapidly?
- Completeness: Is everything included?
- Courtesy: Is it fair to all?
- Correctness: Is it accurate?

Also ask them to review the course against a course description. The course description is the "contract" between teacher and learner. It specifies the following:

- Course objectives: what goals and what level you want to achieve
- Prerequisites: what starting level you assume
- Teaching process: how you will teach
- Course schedule: what subjects are taught when
- Course preparation: what learners must do beforehand
- Work during the course: what work you expect from learners
- Materials that learners must take to the class
- Any other matter learners should know about beforehand

Learners must accept beforehand what they are getting into and understand what they will get out of it. The whole purpose of this description is to avoid surprises for the learner by shaping expectations to the course. A learner in the wrong course spells disaster for the teacher as well as the learner.

9.4 Some Specific Forms of Training

A course often combines several instruction forms and media. Implement each form so that it conforms to the required Bloom/Davies competence level, the number of learners, and a financial justification {9.4}. This section briefly discusses eight basic forms.

PREPARING AND DELIVERING CLASS INSTRUCTION

Ragan [169] gives an overview of a teacher who prepares and delivers instruction. According to him, a class teacher

- Provides an attractive full-color, three-dimensional visual display
- Is self-programmed, using instructional strategies as needed
- Gives immediate or delayed feedback as required
- Is learner controlled and can branch to any requested subject
- Shows understanding and empathy
- Explains and shows context where necessary
- Is self-storing and portable, not requiring electricity

Moreover, a human teacher is flexible and senses the need for adaptation; this is important when teaching adults with varying needs. Last but not least, a teacher can best motivate learners and inspire their confidence. For example, during the first session in a computer initiation class for older people, the instructor asked the learners to pound with their fist on the keyboard, conveying the idea that they can trust the keyboard. After turning on the computer, the instructor made people press some keys, conveying the idea that pressed keys show on the screen. The instructor then made them type and enter a print command, conveying the idea that they control the computer from the keyboard. In fifteen minutes, the instructor overcame their fears, got across the idea that they control the computer, and made them enjoy what they were learning.

SETTING UP PRACTICE ROUNDS

Practicing skills during a course is important, according to the Law of Exercise. Practice rounds are the beginning for future achievement as well as providing the necessary variation in a course. It is a good idea to alternate one-hour class sessions with one-hour practice rounds. People can get refreshments and move around during the breaks.

ON-THE-JOB TRAINING

On-the-job training, or sitting-with-Nellie, is an informal way to train someone when there is no course available. It serves two purposes: training and getting to know the people in a department.

Trainees first watch others and then do the work under supervision. This approach works well if one person joins a new department during a quiet period. It is simple and inexpensive if done occasionally and in groups in which relationships are good. But it becomes disruptive if many people train this way.

PREPARING AND GIVING GROUP INSTRUCTION

Group instruction is different from class instruction in the following ways: A group can discuss and do, instead of being told. It also can be split into smaller groups to do exercises, to provide for variation, and to learn by doing. The seating arrangement, in a circle or circles, emphasizes that leader and participants are more equal than in the usual classroom arrangement.

Group instruction can be an effective way to teach conceptual subjects that have many aspects, such as creative thinking, mind sets, or counseling. The leader starts and guides the discussion, illustrates a concept, and suggests exercises to demonstrate a concept. The various views of the subject will come out naturally.

AUDIO COURSES

Instead of having a teacher/classroom situation, a teacher's voice can be recorded on magnetic tape. The cassettes can be played repeatedly, at any time, even in the car or while jogging. In addition, they can be copied easily.

Use the paper insert in the cassette box to describe the course and summarize key points. An optional workbook can contain illustrations, exercises, quizzes, and reference material.

There are obvious limitations to the use of audio teaching, such as in the case of teaching programming skills. But it is suitable for teaching conceptual aspects of communication and management because it can include real examples.

VIDEO COURSES

Video is powerful in its ability to show things. It may be the only good substitute for practice when it comes to teaching how to service a machine, for example. Printed drawings with pointers can show locations but a video can show exactly how to replace a defective unit.

Making a video need not be expensive; you can record a class course using only one TV camera. But professional results require much planning and effort.

The advantage of video over audio is the addition of moving images and color. Although video is basically passive, a teacher can pose a question and wait for an answer, forcing the learners to think about the answer. A workbook can give exercises and a summary for future reference.

PROGRAMMED INSTRUCTION AND SELF-STUDY

Programmed Instruction (PI) is one of the oldest forms of self-study. It began in the early 1950s when a machine was used to present printed questions sequentially (Hughes [93]). It was then used in textbooks, where learners filled in the blanks; see, for example, *Teaching: A Course in Applied Psychology* (Becker et al. [13]).

A PI book contains text, questions, answers, and branching instructions. The learner covers the answers while reading the text and the question, then checks the answer, and finally follows the branching instructions. PI has most of the advantages and disadvantages of self-study courses. Some general advantages of self-study are these:

- No teacher is needed.
- It is self-contained, including a course description and instructions.
- Learners can take a course whenever and wherever they desire.
- Courses can be modular, letting learners select parts.
- The learner controls the pace and can repeat parts.
- Correction and reinforcement are possible by adding text.
- Quizzes can use the same format as questions.
- Course materials are inexpensive to reproduce.

The disadvantages of self-study, including PI and other forms, are the following:

- The learner may not use a good way to learn.
- The learner must have enough self-control to hide the answer.
- It is difficult to bring variety to keep the learner's attention.
- The course is rigid, independent of learner understanding.
- Self-study courses must be very good to make learners enjoy them, which is important in view of the Law of Effect.
- There is often no record of how well a learner learns.
- Not all subjects can be explained in frames and panels.
- Only one answer is right, limiting answers to elementary facts.
- Some learners will need human help, which may not be available.

You can circumvent some of these disadvantages by using computers for self-study, as discussed below.

AUTHORING COMPUTER-ASSISTED INSTRUCTION

Consider the following scenario. You are given a course program with instructions. You find a computer (either PC or mainframe), load the program, and take a self-study computer-assisted instructional (CAI) course. You can stop whenever you like and you will resume automatically from where you stopped. You do not have to cover the answers. The computer displays questions, answers, and reinforcing messages. Depending upon the quality of your response, it either automatically takes you to the next topic or rehearses the current topic. It measures how well you are doing and automatically puts you on the right instruction level. At the end, you are told how well you did.

And that is only the beginning. The computer can use color, graphics, and animation to illustrate the material. It can use other forms of learning material, including the following:

- Demonstration program, or demo, which shows panels with text and graphics to demonstrate, for example, how to use a spreadsheet program; a window, superimposed on application panels, gives explanations.
- Tutorial to explain a program's details using words and examples. A tutorial can be combined with a Help function {7.6}.
- Video sections to illustrate an action in a CAI course through a video player controlled by a PC.

- Practice system for exercises, letting the learner work with an actual application.

The basic elements of a CAI course are a panel and a learner's response. The panel can contain text information, a question, or a simulated application panel. The CAI program evaluates the response and branches to a next panel, a mechanism that opens the door to the world of possibilities just sketched.

Whether CAI is practical and economical may be another issue. Some of its limitations are

- All functions of a CAI course are programmed, meaning a comparable program complexity and expense as for the application itself.
- The software maintenance problem applies equally to CAI programs.
- Good teachers that can also develop and program a CAI course are scarce.

In the 1970s, computer-assisted instruction was one of the major promises in the computer field; witness the *Proceedings* of the IFIP first World Conference on Computer Education [99]. But the promise has not been fulfilled.

9.5 Justifying Training Financially

The commitment to develop a course requires planning and a financial justification; training must never be an afterthought. This consideration is last in the chapter only to emphasize its importance.

Developing and giving training cost a lot. Therefore, financial justification must always accompany training plans. The justification forces you to think about teaching a subject in different ways. Only then can you select a best approach. The following factors can play a role in the financial analysis of proposed training:

- Number of learners for a course: Self-study has advantages if there are many learners.
- Learning time, which is determined by time away from productive work multiplied by the number of learners.

- Learners' travel time and expenses are a major factor to justify self-study when learners are scattered geographically.
- Elapsed time between availability of the software and the end of the training. Consider how quickly learners must use the new skill or knowledge. An advantage of self-study courses is that many learners can take them simultaneously.
- Ability of holding the course outside normal working hours, which is important to people who work night shifts.
- Need for course availability on demand after the first wave.
- Quality of teaching. How important is it that all learners reach a specific level? What are the benefits in productivity, error reduction, and support? How long does it take to reach proficiency? Are quizzes needed to check correct understanding?
- Development and maintenance costs, which include teacher's time, support, validation, and equipment.
- Production costs, which depend on media used.
- Operational costs, that is, costs and availability of special rooms, equipment, and support for course teaching and practice. Be sure to include sufficient human support to give learners the confidence they need to learn effectively and efficiently.

You must assign a value to each item, no matter how difficult that is. However, there are often intangibles you cannot express in money. I remember when I was interviewing end users from all over Germany who were trained yearly on a new program version. They made it perfectly clear that self-study should never replace their once-a-year training. Central training made them feel they were doing a job together and gave them a chance to meet with people at the head office. Besides, they enjoyed the central training—it was an outing for them. Replacing it by a CAI course would have been seen as a setback and would have had a tremendous toll on morale.

Computer companies especially spend much money on training their people. User organizations with computers follow their example. Much training is necessary for all computer users to avoid costs due to their ignorance, incompetence, incertitude, and indifference.

This chapter presented some aspects of training in connection with computers. Many books and courses are available on specific aspects of training. Read Dow [48] for a personal account of teaching, and Nickerson et al. [149] on the teaching of thinking skills.

9.6 Summary

1. Learning is basic to human existence. When you learn, you modify your behavior and possibly your attitudes. Teaching and learning are important because of the many changes arising from the use of computers.

2. Thorndike has formulated three laws that are basic to learning:
   - Law of Readiness: Completion of an expectation is satisfying.
   - Law of Effect: A connection is stronger when it is pleasant.
   - Law of Exercise: Things become easier to do each time.

3. Teaching adults requires a practical orientation.

4. The first five steps in developing instruction are
   - Establish learner needs.
   - Establish teaching objectives. Describe the desired competence level (Bloom/Davies):
     - Knowledge: Reproduce/select/describe facts and details.
     - Comprehension: Recognize/explain relations between them.
     - Application: Find/construct/predict/use relations.
     - Analysis: Identify new relations and structures.
     - Synthesis: Combine/discuss new relations and structures.
     - Evaluation: Judge from evidence, using given criteria.
     - Skills: Operate/handle/perform an action.
     - Attitudes: Accept/prefer/value/select a way of behaving.
   - Decide upon an instructional strategy.
   - Make instruction plans and a financial justification.
   - Get management commitment.

   Choose an appropriate instructional medium based upon your findings.

5. Use the ISVIC procedure to prepare for teaching.

6. A computer-assisted instruction course is at least as complex as its subject, the application program.

7. Financial justification is needed to get management commitment and to select the best teaching approach (see {9.4} for some cost and benefit items).

9.7 Review Questions and Exercises

1. One of the primary objectives of teaching is to create learner confidence. Confidence removes anxiety and uncertainty, which gets in the way of effective functioning.
   - Give ten ways in which you, as a teacher, can inspire confidence in learners.
   - List ways for you to inspire confidence in yourself.
2. Consider the statement, "Most books on a technical subject have some instructional purpose."
   - Discuss the statement, referring to examples and counterexamples of books you have read.
   - Characterize the instructional approach of this book.
   - Make a rough justification of your use of this book, using some of the factors listed in {9.4}.

   Consider alternatives to reading this book. Argue why reading this book is, or is not, an efficient way to gain an understanding of the many human sides of computerization.
   - Compare course notes to a book. How are they different? Why do most people keep books and throw away course notes?
3. Mastery learning assumes that most learners can learn well. For example, ninety percent of the learners will achieve ninety percent of the objectives ninety percent of the time. *Mastery Learning* (Bloom in [16] Chapter 4) suggests procedures to achieve this. Read it and write a one-page abstract.
4. Mastery learning acknowledges that some learners may take longer and require more perseverance than others to reach the same degree of learning. Consider the learning abilities of some people in your environment. Make a list of factors that could cause differences in their learning ability as a result of their personality and the environment. You may begin with the following personality factors from Shneiderman [193] and Snyder and Fromkin [197]:
   - Attitude: assertive ⟷ passive

- Competitiveness
- Social style: introverted ⟷ extroverted
- Cooperativeness
- Locus of control in one's life: internal ⟷ external
- Self-confidence
- Anxiety: high ⟷ low
- Happiness
- Motivation in work: high ⟷ low
- Tolerance for ambiguity: high ⟷ low
- Intelligence
- Compulsive precision (attention to detail)
- Variety of interests
- Humility (feeling insignificant)
- Tolerance of stress

5. Using the description of the last course you took, do the following:
   - Check whether it contains all the course description items listed in {9.2}. What is missing and what is extra? If there are missing items, would you like to have known them beforehand?
   - What parts of the course were effective for you?
   - What parts of the course were less effective for you? If possible, discuss your conclusions with your teacher.

6. Suggest to the education department of your organization that you participate in the review of courses on subjects with which you are familiar.
   - Study the financial justification and planning of the course before you assist with the review.
   - What did you learn from assisting with the review?

7. Watch a few installments of an educational television series for an adult audience on a subject you understand reasonably well. Characterize the instructional strategy.
   - How does the program introduce the course (teaching objectives)?
   - How is the learning matter structured?
   - How is learners' motivation stimulated?

- What methods are used to activate the learning process?
- How is the learning matter reinforced?
- Is the course theoretically or practically oriented?
- How are visuals used to illustrate key items?
- Is the 3T formula used? How?
- For what competence level (Bloom/Davies) does the course aim?
- How does the course check correct understanding?

8. A didactic approach says that in teaching you should proceed
   - From the simple to the complicated
   - From the near to the distant
   - From the easy to the difficult
   - From the concrete to the abstract

   In this chapter, I have used the opposite direction, starting with the theory and ending with examples.
   - What are the pros and cons of both approaches?
   - What is your preference in a course? Why?
   - What is your preference in a book? Why?

9. Make a list of the factors you would use to evaluate external courses. Explain how you would measure each factor.

10. Section 9.1 states that we learn knowledge by being told, skills by doing, and attitudes by example. Describe for each of the eight categories in the Bloom/Davies classification {9.2},
    - How people can best learn them
    - What self-study method is best suitable to learn them and how much additional human assistance is required

11. The training department of your organization faces the problem that some teachers are falling behind in new developments. It has the choice of either
    - Recirculating present teachers in development projects to refresh their technical knowledge
    - Letting the teachers teach other courses and training some good technical people to become teachers on new subjects

    What is your advice? What are your considerations?

12. Imagine you are a teacher in the training department of a large organization. Your department trains adults in a wide variety of subjects using different methods. Learners fill in an evaluation form at the end of each course, which your manager uses to evaluate courses and teachers. At the next department meeting, present your views on the following:

- How to evaluate the quality of courses more objectively
- How to evaluate the quality of teachers more objectively
- What other measurable factors to use for the yearly appraisal and rating of teachers

4 Teaching

Part IV

ORGANIZING AND MANAGING FOR QUALITY

10

DEFINING QUALITY

What concerns me is not the way things are,
but rather the way people think things are.
—Epictetus, quoted in [153]

Because computers in organizations have such a strong impact on so many people, they must be carefully planned and introduced. Remember that in automation nothing is ever right automatically and nothing ever happens of itself; everything must be planned.

Up to this point, I have only implicitly considered quality throughout planning, developing, and using information systems. In this chapter, I give quality the attention it deserves. Here, I distinguish between objective and subjective quality and emphasize that service to customers must be the main goal for organization and management.

Quality control in industry began as a focus of attention during World War II, when the Allies needed to produce equipment for the war effort in unprecedented quantities. The quality of each part had to be inspected after each step in the work process to make sure that the assembly would satisfy a statistical criterion. This led to many quality control departments and massive quality control organizations. Their success was not one hundred percent, however, because of the complications and time lag that quality control introduced into the work flow.

Following the war, Japan was left in a desolate state. In the early 1950s, Japanese industrialists met to discuss their unsuccessful strategy of making poor quality products and selling them at low prices. They consulted D.E. Deming, who had been unsuccessful in convincing American management of his views on achieving quality in a better way. The Japanese listened carefully and devoted much effort to assuring quality (Mann [119]). They instituted the notion of quality circles (a small group of competent people who produce a whole product) with the understanding that only motivated individuals can produce quality (Ouchi [155]).

Obviously, inspection alone doesn't assure quality. Quality must be designed into the product by considering how customers will use a product or service. The following sections discuss both the measurable and unmeasurable aspects of quality.

10.1 Objective and Subjective Quality

We all have distinct notions about the quality of things. Some of these notions are easy to describe while others cannot be put into words. Let me illustrate with two examples:

1. *Developing software:* A programmer spends four months redesigning the structure of a program and documenting it to make the program compatible with a new software architecture. He corrects some errors but possibly introduces new ones. He improves operation in parts of the program but impairs it in others, increasing the number of instructions from 267 to 271. How can we express the quality of this program so that we can measure how much the quality has increased or decreased? Software experts could intuitively understand the difference in quality before and after the redesign, but they could not express it in words or numbers.

2. *Using computers:* An instructor spends two months preparing a course to train end users in a new application. She designs the course to concentrate on motivation and attitudes of end users, so that they will be confident in using the application. She also concentrates on teaching them to understand how the system works and how important their role is to the organization, spending little time on the needed skills to enter data into the system. How does the quality of her course compare with that of another course that concentrates on improving users' skills to enter data without discussing the system itself? We may expect better work quality from the first course and higher initial productivity from the second, but how can we measure or describe course quality?

Both examples show how difficult it is to define quality. If this definition is so difficult, we can at least try to understand something about the mechanism by which people judge quality. Figure 10-1 illustrates two aspects of quality: objective quality and subjective quality.

As the left side of the figure indicates, a person measures a thing and compares it to specific objectives and criteria. For example, an objective would be that every part must be 10 cm long within $\pm$ 0.05 cm and a criterion would be that 98 percent of all parts must satisfy this objective. Another example is that under certain loading conditions, the system's response time must be less than 1.0 second (objective) 97 percent of the time (criterion).

We express objective quality in terms of something's fitness for use and its conformity to requirements. Note that as in the examples, we use statistical criteria when it would be too expensive and impractical to have every part meet the objective all of the time. We add "on time" to express that we want things on a certain schedule, not a month later.

On the right side of the figure, we see how a person perceives and judges a thing, based on his or her personal values and opinions. To stress the individual aspect of subjective quality, the figure shows two people. Since the evaluation goes on inside the mind, we cannot measure it. The evaluation is unique because no two people feel exactly the same about something. People have an intuitive feeling for quality that cannot be put in words because they consider many different aspects of a thing. Subjective quality, contrary to objective quality, is a moving target because people's views and needs can change their appreciation of something.

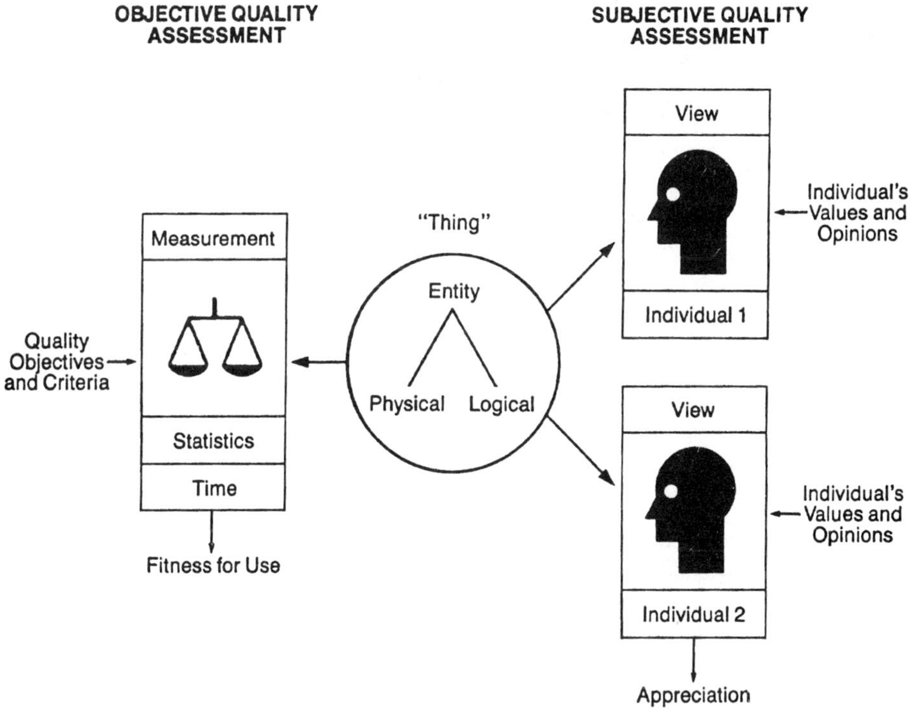

Figure 10-1. Two views of objective and subjective quality.

The proportion of objective and subjective quality changes over time. In the beginning when a new product or service is introduced, the customers' needs are unclear and suppliers must try to anticipate what people want. At this point, the quality of the particular product or service is more subjective. As the technology matures and becomes more well known, there is a consensus on the product's use and quality becomes more objective. Realize that computers are still in the early stages and will remain so until the continuing flood of new developments lessens.

10.2 Objective Quality: Conformity to Requirements

The original approach to quality control used a three-step engineering methodology: First, define the level of quality that will make customers of a product or service happy (called the *acceptable quality level* or AQL). The underlying assumption is there exists an optimum in the relationship between quality and cost. Higher quality will make a product unnecessarily expensive and lower quality is not acceptable. Second, with the understanding of the complete production process and the use of statistical methods, determine the necessary quality of parts to arrive at the final AQL. Third, establish an inspection and control organization to make certain that all production stages achieve the intermediate levels of quality needed for the final quality level.

Juran's books on quality [104, 105] describe the application of this approach, using statistics and other procedures to control quality in production. Juran shows how a statistical approach enables you to determine the cost of quality, but it turns out that quality control adds high costs. Some reasons why this approach is becoming less acceptable today are the following:

- The increasing number of stages in production processes are making inspections and quality control very expensive.
- Mass-marketing requires one hundred percent product quality because the cost of repairing or replacing an inexpensive product often is prohibitive.
- The world is depending more on manufactured products, which increases reliability demands because we use them in such large quantities and in critical areas.
- Trade barriers between countries are disappearing and multinational companies are evolving, thus increasing competition. If you don't make high-quality products, consumers will buy from someone else who does.
- Japan succeeded in producing nearly perfect products at a reasonable cost. As a result, customers no longer accept products that are only 97 percent good.

These reasons may serve to explain today's move toward zero defects by all companies that want to succeed. If you know you'll do it right at the start, you hardly need quality control. As often is the case, the solution is intrinsically simple: To avoid defects, don't make them in the first place. Savings on inspection, quality control, and correction pay for the time and effort spent to prevent errors initially.

There remains the question of how to prevent defects. The answer is twofold: First, organize a work process to prevent defects; and second, create an environment in which people make no errors. International standards ISO 9000 to 9004 [168] offer a possible quality system and its management to implement the first part of the solution.

To implement the second part, you must set quality goals, establishing a mind set of quality. But most of all, you need the cooperation of the person doing the work, as he or she is the only one who can really affect the product's quality. Zero-defect quality can only result when everyone involved understands the process and has a commitment to quality.

As often happens in history, events coincided. Similar quality problems also appeared in the area of software development. As information systems became increasingly complex, the software crisis emerged. Software engineering {4.8} provides only a partial answer to the problem of quality because it uses techniques and statistics only to improve estimating, not to control quality of the product as such.

Proper development procedures and methodologies can prevent a certain percentage or type of software errors, but two important problems remain: One, the most important properties of software are immaterial; that is, they concern meaning, not matter. Software can be viewed as text, but its essence is its logical meaning. How can you measure the quality of immaterial meaning? Second, even if you produce defect-free software, how do you know whether it meets users' needs? In the end, users determine whether an information system meets their quality expectations and requirements.

User requirements are considered during the first two activities of software development {4.2}. The difficulty facing both developers and users to do so is that they must define an immaterial moving target. This brings me to the topic of subjective quality—how people view quality.

10.3 Subjective Quality: How Each Person Sees It

People are the ultimate judge of things. In Figure 10-1, two individuals perceive the thing in the center. But each judges quality according to his or her frame of reference, or value system. Because different people have different values, we all judge quality differently.

We consider many different aspects when we judge the quality of a thing. For example, when choosing a stereo system, everyone wants reliability, but each person judges cost differently. We each judge whether something is too expensive or is a bargain for what it offers. Size is of concern to some and appearance to others. A turntable is important to a buyer with many records, while others want a compact disc player; still others consider the quality of the radio important. Some people want undistorted sound; others want big sound. These are just a few of the many aspects involved in judging the quality of a stereo system, which is a well-established technology. Computers have many more aspects because they use an evolving technology and have a stronger impact on us.

Quality Is Free by Crosby [36] presents the thesis that quality is not a gift, but is ultimately free because of the savings realized by doing it right the first time. Unfortunately, because of its complexity, doing it right in information systems is different from doing it right in a product that you can feel and see. Software is just too complex for it to be planned in every detail. But even if the hardware and software were designed perfectly, the otherware would also have to be defect free.

Where does this leave us? We can do our best to define certain aspects of quality, but most aspects are subjective and cannot be defined. They must be left to people—developers and users alike—who understand their customers. Quality is not a matter of working harder, but of understanding what you are doing and for whom you are doing it. Everyone must have the insight and the motivation to do things right, rather than having to do them over. Read Pirsig's book on quality [163] to understand how quality exists in the minds of people and how only quality-aware people can realize quality.

10.4 Providing Quality Service to Customers

> If you treat your customer as a nuisance or a "necessary evil," you're in for trouble. Think of the people you dealt with in life when you were a customer.
>
> —P. Metzger, *Managing Programming People* [133]

For whom do you work? Your answer may be the name of your manager or your organization. Or it may be the people who continue building on the results of your work. Or it may be the ultimate customer of the product or service. As discussed in the previous section, you will provide a better product or service if you want to please your customers, instead of pleasing yourself, your manager, or others in your organization.

Objective quality is not enough; what counts in the end is subjective quality. This means that you have to understand your customers and their needs and requirements. It may please your manager when you produce zero-defect software ahead of schedule, but what is its use if no customer wants it? It pays to provide a superior service to customers; see Peters [161] C-3 for examples.

Thus, quality starts and ends with the customer. The road to quality is found from the answers to these four important questions:

1. *Who are your customers? What do they want and why?* Understanding why customers want something helps you decide upon alternatives for details that were not planned.

2. *What work process can provide your customers with what they want?* Consider how you can efficiently make what customers want.

3. *How can you organize to make what your customers want?* The work process must be embedded within the organization to achieve quality.

4. *How can people produce what your customers want?* Motivating people properly is necessary to perform the work process for high-quality results.

I discuss the first two questions below, and I deal with questions 3 and 4 in Chapters 11 and 12, respectively.

WHO ARE YOUR CUSTOMERS? WHAT DO THEY WANT AND WHY?

To consider how to answer these questions, compare these two cases: a nurse in a hospital, who works directly for the customer (the patient in this case), and a programmer in a software development organization, who is far removed from the customer. The programmer interacts with the customer only through many layers: a proposal leads to an analysis that leads to user requirements that lead to design specifications that lead to programming specifications from which the programmer works. Because of these many layers, programmers have much more difficulty than the nurse in understanding who their customers are.

What is a possible solution to this problem? How can programmers get closer to the customers, to understand them and even think like them? Theoretically, you could subdivide a large process into subprocesses with intermediate customers. For example, an analyst writes requirements for the designer (the analyst's customer) and the designer makes a design for the programmer (the designer's customer). But such a quality chain is only a theoretical consideration; only end customers count when you want to achieve subjective quality.

How can you introduce direct feedback when customers may not even know what they want? The answer is you must try to involve customers as much as possible in personal contacts so developers know for whom they work, forming a partnership. Show developers how the software will be used and let them talk to end users. When it is difficult to involve customers directly, assign a user representative to play the customer role in the development process, as discussed in {4.4}.

To be effective, feedback must be direct and must cover the entire process. Use the Deming circle, which consists of four steps for achieving quality: plan, do, check, and improve. In the last step—improve—the circle repeats itself. For the nurse, this may take a couple of minutes. In software development, it may take a year or more, which is why you need intermediate checkpoints in a phase process to make it a self-regulating process.

WHAT PROCESS CAN PROVIDE CUSTOMERS WITH WHAT THEY WANT?

The second step is to define the best work process for producing what the customer wants. Because all work processes are different, I can only make some general recommendations to emphasize the customer aspect:

- Look at the entire process: from trying to discover what customers want at the start to fulfilling actual customer needs.
- Shorten communication lines on customer needs, making feedback as immediate as possible.
- Consider how you can listen throughout the process to customers to anticipate changes during your work.
- Discuss the division and content of tasks with workers because they know the process best and know how to adapt it to changing customer needs best of all.

Providing service to customers also improves workers' motivation. People in an organization prefer to work for customers whom they know than to achieve a zero-defect program one month ahead of schedule. Also, instead of a manager controlling people to realize zero-defect programs on schedule, a manager can work together with people to satisfy customer needs; this gives a better working relationship.

Service to customers requires that workers understand customer needs and have the means and controls to determine quality. Such a mode of operation is especially important in information processing where quality primarily depends on how people use their mind. The resulting quality is almost free if people are properly organized and managed, the topics of Chapters 11 and 12, respectively.

This chapter discusses two aspects of quality: objective quality, which is measurable, and subjective quality, which is defined by customers. Quality is achieved only through service to customers. To reach that goal, you need good organization, management, communication, and planning.

10.5 Summary

1. Quality is becoming a vital part of our world of manufactured things, especially with software. To achieve software quality, make people responsible for it.

2. There are important movements toward total quality control and zero defects. To avoid defects, don't make them. This is difficult to practice in developing immaterial things such as software and information systems in general.

3. Objective quality can be expressed in terms of objectives and statistical criteria.

4. Subjective quality is an individual judgment and therefore difficult to describe. The proportion of objective to subjective quality changes over time as people acquire more experience with a particular technology and as the technology matures.

5. To realize subjective quality, emphasize service to customers in the work process. Stress the notion of providing service to customers instead of achieving some objective quality.

6. You can travel along the road to quality by answering these four critical questions:

    - Who are your end customers? What do they want and why?

- What process can provide customers with what they want?
- How can you organize to make what customers want?
- How can people produce what customers want?

7. The concept of providing service to customers allows managers to work with people rather than controlling them to achieve an objective goal.

10.6 Review Questions and Exercises

1. In the twentieth century, people depend much on the quality of many manufactured things. Make a list of twenty manufactured items whose quality can be a matter of life and death to you today (adapted from Juran [105]).
   - How have people determined the quality of each item?
   - How do people continue to assure their quality?
2. The Pareto Principle, also called the 80/20 rule, is a rule to approximate statistical distributions (Juran [105]). For example, twenty percent of customers account for eighty percent of revenue; twenty percent of people account for eighty percent of the mistakes; and eighty percent of the cars cause twenty percent of the traffic. The 80/20 rule is useful to determine where you can make major improvements most easily.
   - Check this rule on some statistics you have available.
   - Read some of the examples in [105].
   - Give your conclusions and list areas where you can use the rule.
3. Compare and give examples of the measures for quality inspection and control needed in the following two cases of getting milk from a cow to a customer:
   - A cattle owner milks his cow, treats the milk, and delivers it to his customers.
   - The milk from cattle owners is picked up by truck, transported to a consolidating storage plant for initial processing, moved again to a plant for further processing, storage, and packaging in cartons, and transported via a distribution center to a supermarket where customers can buy it.

What characteristic makes the two situations different from the point of view of quality control? What are the consequences of this difference?

4. Does your organization have a quality assurance program?
   - If yes, how effective is it? If it isn't effective, check with members of the quality program to see whether your impression is correct. Find out how you can help them do a better job.
   - If no, and if you feel there are quality problems, propose to set up a quality program. After all, the future of your organization is at stake.

5. Is an acceptable quality level approach sufficient for your organization to survive?
   - If yes, consider the advantage for your customers if you provide products or service that completely cover their needs.
   - If no, what is being done in your organization to understand and satisfy real customer needs? Are these actions sufficient? What can you do in addition?

6. Consider your present work:
   - Who are your end customers?
   - What are their requirements?
   - How do you learn of changing customers' requirements?
   - How long does it take before you are informed of their change?
   - What are your objectives/directives from the organization? Are they oriented to your performance or to your customers?
   - What situations may cause defects in the product you make?
   - How can you prevent or detect those situations?

7. Section 2.7 states that reinforcement is essential to achieve quality in everything you do. Consider your organization: Explain how feedback is designed into its work processes. Illustrate what could go wrong if there were no feedback. What additional feedback would improve quality? How can you make feedback more direct?

8. In a software development organization, it is difficult to include changes in customer requirements (Metzger [132, 133]). Basic decisions made early in the development life cycle can be very diffi-

cult or impossible to change later. Propose procedures that make the development process more flexible to achieve more customer satisfaction.

9. List three quality goals for each of the following groups or people connected with an automobile garage:
   - Mechanics
   - Stockroom manager
   - Sales representative
   - Office administrator
   - Manager
   - Director of the chain that owns the garage

11

STRUCTURING AN ORGANIZATION

Sound structure is a prerequisite to organizational
health; but it is not health itself. The test of a
healthy business is not the beauty, clarity, or perfection
of its organization structure.
It is the performance of people.
—P. Drucker, *Management* [51]

To many people, "organization" is a nebulous concept, just something discussed by top managers or illustrated on charts.* However, organization is an important subject requiring careful consideration. It affects everyone and determines how people work together. Organization concerns the division of labor into tasks and the coordination of tasks to accomplish the work. A good organization provides the means for people to work effectively and efficiently for customers.

The purpose of organization is to position people so they can best serve customers. In a fairly stable world, a centralized organization serves that purpose. In today's world of change, a decentralized organization may be more effective.

After an introduction to the various theories of organization and their evolution, this chapter explains the mechanism of delegation, describes aspects of job design, and discusses the health of an organization.

11.1 Theories of Organization

Organization is a figment of the mind. People, managers and subordinates, act as agents to make up an organization, to give it its purpose, and to fulfill that purpose. The base of an organization is the role behavior of its members, the norms that lead to these behaviors, and the resulting values (Katz and Kahn [106]).

There are many ways in which people can be organized. Theories X, Y, and Z serve to illustrate three extremes in organization. McGregor [127] proposed Theory X and Theory Y as follows:

Theory X (autocratic organization)

1. People dislike work and will avoid it if they can.
2. Therefore, people must be controlled in order to make them achieve.
3. People prefer to be directed; they want security above all.

*I use the word "organization" to mean the human structure of what may be an enterprise, an institution, or a true organization. From the context, it will be clear whether I mean the whole organization or its human structure.

Theory Y (participative organization)

1. Physical and mental work are as natural as play and rest.
2. People can exercise self-control toward committed objectives.
3. Commitment to objectives depends on the rewards.
4. People can learn to accept and seek responsibility.
5. People can be creative in finding organizational solutions.
6. Capabilities of people are only partly used under Theory X.

McGregor suggests that under the assumptions of Theory Y, integration and self-control of the individual can make an organization more effective. Ouchi [155] has added Theory Z as follows:

Theory Z (egalitarian organization)

1. People must create trust because distrust lowers productivity.
2. People need subtle human relationships to maintain productivity.
3. People need intimacy and caring to encourage human relationships.
4. People need to have a management style and organization that has roots in society.

Ouchi suggests that the structure of an organization results in different social mechanisms, and he characterizes the three extremes as follows: In a hierarchy (that is, a bureaucracy), workers do not have a clear sense of the value of their work. In a market, workers are competitive and pursue selfish interests. In a clan, workers have a common goal, work on the basis of trust, and reject outsiders.

Characteristic of Theory Z is the clan, which has a more holistic concern for people and shared values than does a hierarchy or a market. Ouchi gives several examples of companies in the United States that exhibit the characteristics of this theory, including major computer companies.

After explaining these three extremes in organization, I present some general thoughts on organizational structure. Galbraith [67] discusses organization and its design. Besides structure, he includes reward systems, jobs, information technology, physical location, and many communication and decision processes. My approach is to emphasize structural aspects in this chapter and discuss management in Chapter 12.

Basically, organizational structure determines what is produced. If an organization is structured in two parts to make products A and B, for example, that is exactly what you will get. Such an organization cannot make product C unless it is reorganized so that an individual becomes responsible for product C and gets the resources. That's why organizational structure must reflect the goals of an organization.

When computers are introduced into an organization, it must often change to reflect the new division of labor. People and computers perform work processes carried out previously by people alone; these must be properly integrated with the remaining noncomputerized processes in the organization (see Figure 3-1). To achieve this integration, you must organize before you automate, and make information system design match the organization.

Above all, the main purpose of organization is to provide high-quality service to customers. Providing quality of working life, job enrichment, and participatory work structures may be necessary, but they are not the primary goal of organizing (Goodman et al. [76]).

11.2 Moving From Centralized to Decentralized Organizations

The structures of large centralized organizations have their origin in history. In ancient Egypt, the Pharaohs organized people to exploit the Nile River. During the medieval period in Europe, the Catholic Church, as one of the most powerful organizations, became the largest landholder there. Then, at the turn of this century, the subject of organization elicited many theories, and during the Industrial Revolution, the concept of division of labor was implemented to manufacture products efficiently.

Fayol and Weber are important early representatives of this period. Fayol's fourteen principles of management, notably unity of command and unity of direction, lead to a hierarchical organization, as I'll discuss in more detail in {12.1}. Weber propounded the bureaucratic organization theory to make administration faster and more accurate. (It was only later, after World War II, that bureaucracy became associated with inefficiency.) Weber defined bureaucracy as having a well-defined hierarchy of authority, a clear division of work, a system of rules and duties, a system of work procedures, impersonality of interpersonal relationships, and selection of people based on their technical competence.

After 1930, organizational theories were affected by new work tasks, which demanded more creativity on the part of employees, and by the human relations movement. The following people contributed to the evolution of the theory: Simon distinguished between routine and creative decision making, making the case for decentralized decision making. Barnard emphasized that the organization is a network of decision makers, and placed particular importance on the role of the informal human network. Finally, Katz and Kahn [106] stressed that organizations are open systems, continually influenced by and having to respond to their environment.

With the addition of management science, organizational theories further developed to become situational theories. Emphasis changed from concerns for efficiency to needs for diversification and adaptability. Dessler [47] and Galbraith [67], among others, concluded that organizational uncertainty should determine the structure of an organization, ranging from central and formal to creative and adaptive {11.3}.

Peters and Waterman [162], investigating excellent companies in the early 1980s, found that a fairly stable and simple organization provides the clarity needed to cope with day-to-day complexities. The influence of leadership on organizational culture provides a framework of values {12.5}.

Peters, in *Thriving on Chaos* [161], explains that increasing changes and uncertainty now require a management revolution. This situation requires managers to motivate people and invest in them; first priority for all managers is to manage the human resource. Peters anticipates greater decentralization of the organization in order to get its decision makers closer to customers for responding better to customer needs.

11.3 Organizing to Deal With Uncertainty

Organizational theories remind me of a sketch I once saw in which a hospital sergeant explained how different countries transport wounded soldiers. In France they do it this way, he explained, in Great Britain that way, and so on. He ended after ten minutes of explanation, stammering, "But folks, if there is a real war, it's done all different again." There is more to organization than just theory.

The problem in real life, as this story illustrates, is that practical considerations often determine what is a best organization at a given time in a given situation. That is, you not only have to determine what is best in situation B, but you must also consider how to get from A to B while continuing to work.

Organizational structure must be designed to handle the future in the best way. The direction must come from the organization's strategic plan, which sets the goals and the overall framework. A flexible organizational structure must then simplify the primary work processes most exposed to environmental uncertainty; their planning must also consider how to exploit the power of computers.

Dessler [47] and Galbraith [67] conclude that if there is a central theme for structuring and managing organizations, it is the uncertainty with which the organization must cope. There is little uncertainty in organizations performing routine tasks and much uncertainty in fast-changing organizations. Examples of organizational uncertainty are good and bad publicity causing large fluctuations in the work load, unusual requests for bidding, and a competitor's challenge in offering a new kind of service.

Galbraith notes that an organization has five ways in which to cope with such uncertainty: controlling and modifying the environment, creating slack resources to handle unexpected demands, creating self-contained tasks, improving information processing, and lowering the level of decision making. If properly incorporated in organizational processes, computers can help an organization in all five areas. First, computer networks and terminals can change the environment, like telephones did earlier. Computers can allow human effort to be redirected to get closer to the customer, and support people in performing whole tasks. Computers obviously improve the availability of information. Lastly, knowledge systems and computer networks can push decision making to lower levels in the organization.

The question remains as to what processes and tasks can be decentralized and what must be centralized. Recall from Chapter 1 the need to make and keep things simple for people, and Figure 3-1 showing task-oriented design of organizational processes. Good organization simplifies communication and decision making where uncertainty is greatest. Delegation of decision making to the lowest possible level in the organization may be desirable anyway.

Not all functions can be decentralized, however. Personnel and administrative functions, quality assurance, and the computer center work most efficiently when they are centralized. But staff functions should be under constant scrutiny to keep them lean and efficient. Since money is a universal unit to express material values and service costs, you can achieve visibility of centralized functions by charging for their services to decentralized operational groups. This way, operational and staff groups can challenge each other on effectiveness and usefulness: a check and balance both ways to achieve the mechanism of a free market.

11.4 Rules, Procedures, and Delegation

Society has many written rules in the form of laws and regulation. Organizations also have rules and procedures for dealing with routine operations such as hiring people and promoting them. Rules and procedures are decisions made in advance to deal with expected forms of uncertainty; they imply a kind of delegation, for if a rule sanctions something, no one will argue if you comply with it.

To see the effects of a rule in a large organization, consider this example. Imagine a project manager whose programming project is six weeks from system test and who discovers the user documentation is not yet written. All in-house writers are busy, but the manager locates a person outside who can write the documentation quickly and cheaply. But the manager bumps up against this rule: "We only subcontract people from certain large agencies to work for us."

The rule is enforced by a higher-level manager (who refuses to sign the request), contracting people (who refuse to write a contract), and administration (who would refuse to pay for the services). The project manager must now either accept a more expensive subcontractor from a large agency or try to justify an exception to the rule.

An example of a procedure is the sequence of steps needed to get someone promoted to a new position. First, the manager fills out a form, which is signed by his or her supervisor. This form is discussed by the divisional director and others who are concerned with hiring and personnel. If the proposal is accepted, the Personnel Department must update its records, Administration must change salary information, Communications must prepare a notice for the bulletin board, and so on. In this way, the form reflects the details of a procedure so that people will not forget them.

Every person in an organization faces rules and procedures, which limit the room for initiative. If there is little room, the situation is authoritarian; this structure is effective when there is little uncertainty. If there is much room for initiative, the situation is self-directive, which is effective when there is much uncertainty. Unexpected forms of uncertainty require making ad hoc decisions.

The need for procedures depends upon the size of an organization. In a one-person business, there is no need for special procedures; the owner makes ad hoc decisions. The same is true when there is one manager and only a few subordinates. The problem starts when there are many people in different departments. In an organization of a hundred thousand people working in a thousand locations, there must be rules and procedures or chaos would result.

There are four simple criteria on rules and procedures:

1. They must be reasonable, consistent, and meaningful, or else no one will use them.
2. They must be simple, or else no one can remember them.
3. They must be verifiable or else people will not feel responsible to obey them.
4. They must be enforced, or else no one will use them.

A first principle of organization is that everyone must know what needs to be done and who is responsible. People will settle by power the matters that are not formalized in rules and procedures (Farnsworth [59] and Robbins [174]), possibly using contention and conflict. Contention and conflict are essential in organizations because they provide the feedback necessary to avoid a hidden agenda and to give people a proper direction. Organizational culture and management style determine how contention and conflict are handled, as I'll discuss in {12.5}.

An organization is structured by delegation, which is an essential aspect of a hierarchical organization. As shown in Figure 11-1, the basic mechanism of delegation implies authority and commitment. A manager can delegate a task and sufficient authority to a subordinate; that subordinate is authorized to perform a task. The person may refuse if the task is too big, the schedule is too tight, or the means are unavailable. But once committed, the person is held accountable for achieving the tasks.

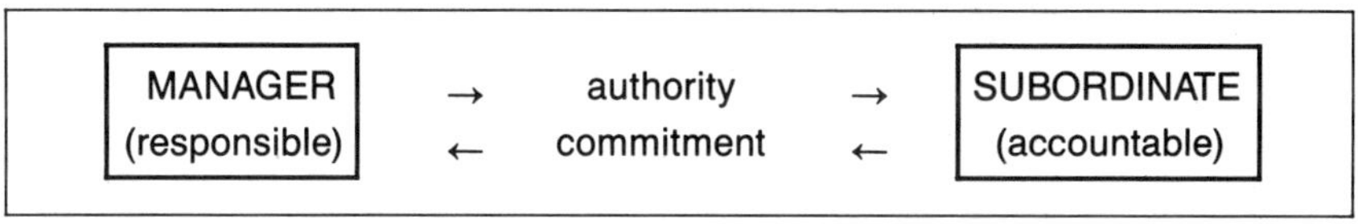

Figure 11-1. Basic mechanism of delegation.

Managers are responsible for achieving goals with people and other resources, and are held responsible for the results of their subordinates; they cannot delegate responsibility to subordinates or to computers. A responsible manager can be guilty or innocent of an act committed by subordinates.

Everyone responsible for making a decision must understand the decision, why it must be taken, and when it must be taken. Delegation may give freedom to make a decision, to select a work approach, and to resolve problems. People get rewards for carrying out tasks; rewards can range from salary increases to a simple thank you.

11.5 Individual Job Design

This section looks at an organization's structure from the bottom up. It considers what developers and users like to see in their job definition and what consequences this has for organizing. First, here are some criteria for structuring jobs from a human viewpoint in a development environment:

- Job autonomy, so people have a say in their work situation, can determine a work approach, and can identify with the job. Delegation can promote a feeling of importance and self-respect.
- Variety and job rotation, so people do not feel they are locked into a certain type of work but can broaden their experience.
- Natural work units, so the work has only a minimum of dependencies on other people. Work units should match the skills of the individual to make the job a motivating challenge.
- Proper division of work, so people can stimulate each other to do their job. Everyone must feel that the workload is properly balanced among members and that skills are used in the best way.
- Clarity, so people understand what they need to do and why and what other people and groups in the organization are doing. There should be no question about personal responsibilities and who makes decisions.
- Feedback at natural checkpoints, so progress becomes visible for the individual and for the manager.
- Human network, so people can set up informal contacts for getting work done. Contacts with others give them a sense of belonging, widen their horizons, and encourage efficiency.
- Optimal group size, so group cohesiveness is strengthened. The group should not be too small (because that limits the potential to succeed as a group), but not too large (because that limits getting an overview of the work and the growth of relationships within the group).
- Encouragement of initiative because there is no substitute for individual initiative. "Thinking out a plan and ensuring its suc-

cess is one of the keenest satisfactions for an intelligent man to experience" (Fayol's thirteenth principle of management, from Dessler [47]).

- Flexibility of operation because people will move from project to project during the development cycle. People must be able to break through organizational barriers to get help from key people when needed; formalities must not stand in their way.
- Stability of key personnel, so experts in key areas remain available in the organization to provide continuity. Whenever necessary, special expert functions or groups can create stability.

In a user environment, by contrast, there is often more stability than in a development environment. People stay longer in the same job, and the work is more predictable and can be better planned. As a result, the structuring of a user organization is simpler. Here are the corresponding criteria for structuring a job from a human viewpoint in a user environment:

- Job autonomy remains important in the user's environment for the worker to get a sense of achievement.
- Variety and job rotation remains desirable but is not so easy to implement in a user environment.
- Natural work units are more stable and more easily adjusted than in a development environment.
- Proper division of work is more easily adjusted.
- Clarity of the job is needed, as in a development environment.
- Feedback at natural checkpoints is clear from the results as the work proceeds.
- Human network, in which relationships are set up informally.
- Optimal group size poses similar problems as in a development environment.
- Encouragement of initiative is needed as in a development environment.
- Flexibility of operation demands that users control the use of computers.
- Stability of experts is assured, as they are part of the formal network.

We are social creatures, even at work. Job design must motivate us to take responsibility and to delegate it, especially when working with computers because they force people to work more formally. The criteria expressed above point toward decentralized organizations and flatter organizational structures. Thus, they reinforce the need for more delegation, resulting from the increased organizational uncertainty noted in {11.2}.

11.6 Diagnosing an Organization's Health

If an organization is in trouble, it is often because its members are having problems. As I mentioned in {2.10}, fatigue and stress result if the working environment is not properly adjusted to the human being. Argyris's basic hypothesis [5, 6] is that organizations develop unintended results when individual needs are not congruent with organizational demands. He gives five signs as possible indicators of problems:

- Absenteeism and turnover: When people are frustrated on the job, they stay at home or try to find another job.
- Aggression: People take out their frustrations on the manager or others. People also cheat, create waste, and make errors.
- Requests for increased pay: People ask for raises to compensate for the degree of dissatisfaction, tension, and stress they experience.
- Alienation: A sense of powerlessness and helplessness may lead to alienation of the individual from himself or herself and others.
- Lack of involvement: Poor involvement leads to apathy and disinterest in work.

Conducting opinion surveys is one way to measure the health of an organization, so long as they are designed by professionals (this assures that the proper questions to organization members are asked and that results can be compared over time). Another simple test of an organization's health is by having customers call different people about a problem. The amount of time required and the number of referrals needed to get the problem resolved are an indication of the organization's ability to serve customers.

The best way to keep an organization healthy is to prevent problems in the first place. To do this, assign the individual with the right skills and the appropriate responsibilities to each task. Another key to improving the health of an organization is encouraging workers' satisfaction by serving a customer. Remember, organizing is not an end in itself—serving customers is. People often must cut across organizational lines to get a job done in time; this requires a healthy organization.

This chapter discusses the meaning and theory behind organization and sketches some of its implications for the human sides of information processing. Organization is an abstract subject, closely linked with management (Chapter 12). Dessler [47] gives an extensive overview of organizational theories. Galbraith [67], Handy [83], Mintzberg [138–140], and Robbins [174] provide further reading.

11.7 Summary

1. Organization is a concept that concerns the division of labor into tasks and the coordination of tasks to accomplish goals.
2. Practical considerations and continuity often determine what is a best (re)organization at a given time in a given situation.
3. The shape and structure of an organization should be in line with its strategic plans because reorganizations often require much time to take effect, and because organizational structure determines what products and services you can provide.
4. How to deal with uncertainty—an important part of the strategic plan—sets the tone for structuring an organization. Delegate decision making to the lowest possible level in areas in which the uncertainty is highest so people can best respond to changing customer needs.
5. In the ideal world, decentralization enhances the autonomy of groups and individuals but keeps certain functions central.
6. An organization's rules and procedures limit the room for individual decisions; their number and rigidity depend on the size and nature of the organization.
7. Delegating authority and making commitments are essential aspects of a hierarchical organization.
8. Criteria for individual job design are job autonomy, variety and job rotation, natural work units, proper division of work, clarity, feedback and natural checkpoints, informal network, right group size, encouraging initiative, flexibility, and expert stability.

9. Use opinion surveys to help diagnose the health of an organization and its people.

10. Prevention of organizational problems is easier than their correction.

11.8 Review Questions and Exercises

1. Name some typical uncertainties of organizations, and what could have caused them, in the following areas:

   - Home insurance
   - Medical liability insurance
   - Private banking
   - Investment banking
   - Commercial banking
   - Airline seat reservation
   - Computer service bureau
   - Software development
   - A chain of shoe stores
   - A chain of supermarkets

   What, if any, are the connections between uncertainty and the possible use of computers? What connections exist between critical success factors {5.2} and organizational uncertainty? Give arguments for and against such connections. Illustrate with examples.

2. Section 11.1 states that the organizational structure must reflect the goals of an organization. Describe the strategy and the structure of your organization and some other organizations. For each organization, give arguments why structure should follow strategy, and counterarguments why strategy should follow structure.

3. Consider a working group of people whom you know. In what respects is the group independent? For what matters does this group have to ask for authorization? What other rules or procedures limit the freedom of the group to act?

4. Here is an adaptation of Metzger's [132] two alternative managerial structures for a group of forty people in software development.

(a) Two-level managerial structure
  Group manager
  — Staff manager
  — Analysis and design manager
  — Programming manager (3)
  — Integration manager
  — Test manager

(b) Three-level managerial structure
  Group manager
  — Staff manager
  — Analysis and design manager
  — Programming manager
    - Programming manager (3)
    - Integration manager
  — Test manager

- What are the advantages and disadvantages of each structure from the point of view of human relationships, efficiency, effectiveness, uncertainty, and product/service quality?
- When would you choose solution a? Solution b?
- A single project usually starts with a few people, grows to a peak during design and program development, and tapers off to a few people after installation and cutover. How would you handle the changing size of projects in both structures?
- How would you structure the organization for a development group of four hundred people? What would you change?
- How would you structure the organization for a development group of four thousand people? What would change?

5. Section 11.5 gives eleven criteria for job design. Describe how each criterion applies in your own work situation. Next, consider whether its current design is optimal for doing your work. If it isn't, describe what you want changed and discuss that with your manager.

6. Imagine you are on the staff of a large organization that develops or uses information systems. List twelve areas for an outside agency to explore to assess the organization's health. Include the most important aspects of the organization from the employee point of view. Explain why you include each area. (The agency will phrase the questions for the opinion survey.)

7. Section 11.1 discusses Theories X, Y, and Z as three models for thinking about organization.
   - Read McGregor's [127] and Ouchi's [155] books to fully understand the differences between Theories X, Y, and Z.
   - How does your organization fit into Theories X, Y, and Z?
   - Explain why many computer companies conform to Theory Z.
   - What type would you like your organization to be? Why?
   - If you had freedom to change your organization, how would you realize the change? Are social mechanisms rooted in knowledge, skills, or attitudes? How difficult is it to change them? Give examples.
   - What would be your objective in the reorganization? Explain what you would want to achieve and why.

8. Imagine that you get a brainstorm and suddenly realize that you can place responsibility for achieving work only on the people who do the work. A manager is put in an awkward position of being responsible for others doing the work. No wonder so many managers have ulcers. To put responsibility directly on the workers and to use lower managers as coordinators who assist the workers become the central ideas of your Theory W:

   Theory W (worker-oriented organization)

   - Workers must have sole responsibility for getting work done.
   - Lower and middle managers become coordinators (linking pins).
   - Top management sets the goals for each group.
   - A top management team directs all the groups; its role is coordination of goals and formal management.
   - Coordinators and staff help establish individual objectives.
   - Workers are rewarded on how well they achieve objectives.
   - Individual objectives are combined for each group.
   - Group objectives are combined for the entire organization.

   Compare Theory W to Theories X, Y, and Z.

   - What are the pros and cons of having objectives and rewards by group? By the individual?
   - Which theory do you prefer—Theory X, Y, Z, or W? Why?

12

ON MANAGING AND BEING MANAGED

We can improve our ability to control
only if we recognize that control consists
in selective adaptation to human nature
rather than in attempting to make human nature
conform to our wishes.
—D. McGregor, *The Human Side of Enterprise* [127]

Bring together some people at random and the chance that they will act as a coordinated group is rather slim. As Nietzsche observed, madness is the rule in groups. It follows, then, that there must be a leader for a group to do useful work. That leader is the manager.

Managing is making people want to achieve the goals of the organization, by influencing their minds, will, and imagination. This chapter deals with managing human, not material, resources. After an overview of management theories, I will discuss managerial tasks, management by objectives, being a manager, and leadership. The second part of this chapter is devoted to being managed, discussing self-actualization.

12.1 Management Theories

Since the shift from family-oriented farming communities to industrial societies, much attention has focused on management as a means to influence productivity. Interestingly, management theories as described by Dessler [47] and Stoner and Wankel [199] have evolved from a technocratic to a human orientation.

In the beginning of the twentieth century, Taylor's scientific management theory proposed a science of work to make it most efficient. This process often led to a specialization of work that now is regarded as reducing people to the level of machines (a standardized man), resulting in work monotony.

In 1916 in France, Fayol's classical organization theory provided the first systematic description of managerial behavior, contrived in fourteen principles of management:

1. Division of work or specialization, which increases efficiency
2. Authority and responsibility, required to get things done
3. Discipline, resulting from leadership and fair agreements
4. Unity of command, by which a subordinate* reports to one manager only

*The word "subordinate" indicates the relationship of a person to a manager. A manager directs subordinates and is subordinate to a higher manager. Different aspects of managing may actually be divided among several people; nurses in a hospital, for example, get functional guidance from different people.

5. Unity of direction, by which those performing similar functions report to one manager
6. Subordination of individual interests to general interests
7. Remuneration, which must be fair to both employees and employers
8. Centralization, so as to decrease the employee's role in decision making
9. Hierarchy, running from top to bottom
10. Order, so that materials and people are available when needed
11. Equity, meaning managers must be friendly and fair to subordinates
12. Stability of staff, which is desirable for continuity
13. Initiative, so that subordinates can choose their own work method
14. Team spirit, giving people a sense of unity in purpose

Mayo's human relations movement aimed to improve human relationships within the work environment. From the Hawthorne experiment conducted in the early 1930s, Mayo accidentally discovered that physical conditions had little effect on workers. Rather, the act of changing environmental conditions caused a feeling of importance by the workers that resulted in cooperation and high output.

In the late 1950s, Argyris's immaturity-maturity theory predicted that autocratic and bureaucratic value systems lead to poor human relationships. Rules and restrictions lead to immaturity, which results in decreased interpersonal competence and subsequently decreased success. People behave passively because managers encourage them to behave passively (the Pygmalion effect {2.14}).

In the 1960s, Likert proposed four management systems, from which you make a selection depending on the maturity of the group being managed:

1. Exploitive authoritative management, using fears, threats, and downward communication.
2. Benevolent authoritative management, using rewards, delegation, and primarily downward communication.
3. Consultative management, using rewards, involvement, and some upward communication.
4. Participative management, making full use of group participation and involvement; decision making is integrated into the formal or-

ganization, and people called "linking-pins" coordinate the work between groups.

In the late 1960s, Blake and Mouton developed a managerial grid that integrated economic and human aspects. Their theory balanced concern for production with concern for people on a grid of 1 to 9 in either direction. They suggested that a 9,9 style of team management, with high concern for people and high concern for production, is always best.

To Blake and Mouton's grid, Reddin [171, 172] added a third dimension, indicating that a manager's effectiveness depends upon adapting leadership style to the situation at hand. In Reddin's method of management by objectives (MBO), the three dimensions are

1. Managerial task behavior: How are member roles defined and how much emphasis is placed on tasks?
2. Managerial relationship behavior: How much emphasis is placed on personal relationships within the group?
3. Managerial effectiveness: What management approach is chosen to be most effective for the needs of the situation (technology, subordinates, co-workers, superior, and organization)?

Around 1980, Hersey and Blanchard's [90] situational leadership suggested that the most effective leadership style (task and relationship behavior) depends primarily on the maturity level of workers. Maturity consists of job maturity (the ability to do something) and psychological maturity (the willingness to do something). The manager must select and use a management style appropriate for an individual. There are four styles from which to choose:

- A telling style for low maturity
- A selling style for below average maturity
- A participating style for above average maturity
- A delegating style for high maturity

The trend in management theories has been toward an increasing focus on the human resource, as people are becoming more vital to the success of organizations than ever before. This is especially true in the use of information systems.

See Dessler [47] and Stoner and Wankel [199] for a more extensive overview of management theories. See [85] for a discussion of the human relations aspects of management.

12.2 Basic Managerial Tasks

Mintzberg [138] gives six basic reasons why organizations need managers: to assure the organization serves its basic purpose (that is, the efficient production of goods and services); to design and maintain the stability of the organization's operations; to take charge of the organization's strategy-making system and to adapt the organization to its changing environment; to ensure that the organization serves the ends of those in control; to serve as the key informational link between the organization and its environment; and to be responsible for operating the organization's status system.

Mintzberg concludes that the manager must be the contact person, the political manager, the entrepreneur, the insider, the real-time manager, the team manager, the expert manager, and the new manager when entering a new job. He explains the use of rituals to strengthen the role of the group and the cohesion of its members.

A group (that is, manager and subordinates) must handle the uncertainties of the environment to achieve work. To reduce the uncertainty of subordinates, a manager makes decisions that allow them to work effectively. A manager, on behalf of the organization, must also invest in subordinates through training and learning from doing, to increase their future usefulness. Fayol defines five elements of managing:

- Planning, including unity, continuity, flexibility, and precision
- Organizing, depending on how many people there are
- Commanding, making the organization perform planned tasks
- Coordinating, streamlining the work of the various groups
- Controlling, checking work results, and intervening whenever necessary

Management must be achieved over time, keeping in mind both the short and long terms. Stoner and Wankel [199] use an illustration by Steiner to show how the planning time horizon varies from one week for a supervisor to several years for a corporation president. They regard planning as a straightforward process: Determine a goal, define the present situation, identify aids and barriers, and develop a plan.

Planning is an important part of a manager's work. Use the ISVIC procedure to Investigate, Structure, Verify, Implement, and Check a plan, as follows.

INVESTIGATING

Why do you want to plan? What is your real goal? What do you want to plan? Are all subjective impressions removed? Who is involved in the planning? Who is affected? Whence are you making the planning? What is your role? Where will the work take place? Where are the roadblocks? When will the work take place? What schedules must be met? How will you do the planning? How can you make people part of the plan?

STRUCTURING

After completing the investigation, you will understand the plan's structure, specifically the sequence of items in the plan. Consider how to get from situation A to situation B, not just consider new situation B.

VERIFYING

Others must verify that the structure of your plan is complete. They can easily check that a plan's structure is complete.

IMPLEMENTING

Your analysis will show the best way to implement the plan; its items are in a logical sequence from structuring.

CHECKING

- Clarity: making sure your plan conveys the elements properly
- Conciseness: omitting all unessential matter in the plan
- Completeness: including all essential items in a logical manner
- Courtesy: showing respect for the dignity and character of people
- Correctness: being correct both in logic and implementation

Planning is closely linked with budgeting, to express the use of human and material resources in a single unit. This allows the manager to plan the work in the most effective manner. Obviously, the manager must have planning and budget responsibility so the budget can reinforce the planning.

12.3 Management by Objectives

A formalized procedure to plan and control human activities is known as management by objectives (MBO), popularized by Drucker in the early 1950s [51]. Reddin integrated MBO [172] into his method described in {12.1}. Characteristic of MBO are the following requirements:

- A list of objectives, in order of priority, is agreed upon by the manager and the subordinate.
- Individual objectives are part of the group's objectives, which are in turn part of the objectives for the entire organization.
- Objectives are measurable so they can be controlled and checked.
- Objectives are specific, result centered, and time bounded.
- Objectives are balanced and realistic for everyone and do not result in underload or overload for anyone.
- Objectives are limited in number and are ranked.
- Objectives are reviewed and updated when necessary.
- Objectives are used to evaluate people's performance and to determine awards and reprimands to motivate and reward people.

MBO is a popular system for performance planning and appraisal that should stimulate communication between manager and subordinate on working toward goals for a specific period. To be useful, the objectives must be centered on quality and customer satisfaction, instead of milestones and results. To be effective, MBO must be practiced rather rigorously and must have top management commitment. MBO can be an important aspect of management but it is exercised only at appraisal time. McGregor takes a look at performance appraisals in [128]. Appendix I discusses talking person to person, whether to plan objectives or to appraise subordinates.

12.4 On Being a Manager

Management theories typically concentrate on the manager's behavior to realize objectives through subordinates. Other schools of thought that are not as well documented stress the importance of internal processes, rather than external behavior, to accomplish objectives. These theories propose that since behavior is a result of attitudes, emphasis in management training should be on managers' attitudes, rather than external behavior. No matter what school you subscribe to, it takes many skills to be a good manager, for example:

- Leadership: the ability to influence people
- Trust and confidence: the ability to inspire these qualities in people
- Open mind: the ability to listen to people
- Communication skills: the ability to communicate with people
- Understanding: the ability to know people and how they work
- Knowledge: the ability to direct technical people
- Vision: the ability to see things in perspective
- Clear mind: the ability to organize and rank items
- Memory: the ability to remember special events and to forget incidental slips
- Resilience: the ability to recover from surprises
- Stress resistance: the ability to dismiss thoughts from the mind
- Versatility: the ability to handle all of the above at the same time

Add to this list the ability to manage conflicts, both inside and outside the organization. A manager can often prevent role conflicts by making certain that people understand their role and that of others. Contention for the resources of an organization makes people aware of their value, and keeps a group self-critical, creative, and efficient (Robbins [173]).

Another difficult job for a manager is to get people to accept changed rules, procedures, and plans. People often resist such changes because they affect their relationships and interfere with their views on work. Hersey and Blanchard [90] explain that it is increasingly difficult to make changes in knowledge, in attitudes, in individual behavior, and in group behavior. Read Goodman et al. [76] on the many aspects of change in organizations.

Extreme change may start a so-called change process similar to that experienced by someone who loses a dear friend or partner. We overcome an imposed change by adapting our frame of references {2.6} in two phases. The first is a *downhill reactive phase* to become conscious of the change. The first reaction is often a denial: This cannot be true. When it finally sinks in, anger develops: Why me? Anger then converts into questioning ourselves: What have I done or neglected to do? The second phase is an *uphill active phase* to adapt to the change. During this phase, we find new vision and other values and gradually accept the change. We try to find our way into the new situation, then adopt it, and finally participate in it.

The period of adaptation depends on how severely we experience the change; it can be minutes, days, or years. Managers must allow time for the reactive phase and provide timely new vision and values for the active phase.

12.5 Top Management Style and Organizational Culture

Top management can be the bottle opening and the bottle neck at the same time: They can stimulate or suppress needed initiatives. Drucker [51] says that top management is essentially different from other management. They are often a team that must

1. Think through the mission and strategy of the organization
2. Set standards for achieving that vision and for the values in key areas
3. Build and maintain the human organization
4. Establish and maintain relationships outside the organization
5. Perform ceremonial functions inside and outside the organization
6. Be a standby function in case of crisis
7. Do the things that need to be done and that no one else can do

Items 2 and 3 are key, and their importance cannot be overestimated. Let me illustrate them with three examples of organizational culture.

1. At a meeting in which all top General Motors executives agreed to a proposal, President Alfred P. Sloan, Jr., said, "I propose that we postpone further discussion of this matter until our next meeting to give ourselves time to develop disagreement and perhaps gain some understanding of what the decision is all about" [51]. Such a top manager's attitude toward critical thinking has effects that ripple down through the entire management line and will be noticeable throughout the organization.
2. Drucker [51] discusses how in Western countries, the emphasis is on getting an answer to the question, whereas in Japan the focus is on defining the question, from which the answer usually follows directly. The advantage of the Japanese approach is that it achieves consensus among the people who must carry out the actions that

result from the decisions. They may take longer to reach an answer, but they can then act faster. In the West, by contrast, people spend much time "selling" the idea to the people who must carry out the actions. There are pros and cons to both approaches, and people are made part of the plan in either case. My only point is that the approach to decision making is an important part of organizational culture.

3. President Thomas J. Watson, Jr., describes IBM's first principle, "Respect for the individual," in *A Business and Its Beliefs* [204]. Such a principle is not exactly lubricating oil in the heat of daily work, but in my experience, IBM's management take IBM's principles very seriously; they are a touchstone to which you can appeal. There are not many companies, however, that have respect for the individual as their basic belief, let alone as first principle. Thomas Watson, Sr., was the charismatic leader who set this example (and many others) during the depression years of the 1930s.

As Drucker points out so well, "It is character through which leadership is exercised; it is character that sets the example and is imitated" [51]. Managers get authority from their superior manager and leaders get power from the people they lead. A big book on leadership is Burns [26], a medium book is Ellis [55], and a small book is Heider [88]. Ouchi [155] and Pascale and Athos [157] compare Japanese and North American organizational culture.

12.6 Managing in an Information Processing Environment

Managing people in an information processing environment has several unique considerations. Among the most important are these: First, people in information processing are highly paid people doing creative work. Many have a college degree and an above-average intelligence. They are a scarce resource.

Second, the product they produce is immaterial and very difficult to check for being correct. Developers and implementors must often make decisions on complex matters that have far-reaching, often irreversible, consequences a year later. Responsibilities are often shared. As a result, information system management must trust subordinates to a higher degree than in other areas.

Third, because information processing is a rapidly developing field, the means and tools often change and there are many dependencies. Changing and learning are a way of life when working with computers.

Finally, because computers can be used for almost everything, only people's imagination limits their application. A motivating environment is needed for people to realize their creativity.

A manager in information systems must manage events and set directions, coaching workers to achieve instead of controlling them. A congenial atmosphere in working relations is essential because people have to work creatively as a team.

Good social relationships are therefore the key to providing the conditions necessary to develop and use information systems effectively, especially since the computer does not promote social relationships: Apart from sending messages to other people, working with a computer is a solitary effort.

To foster social relationships, an information processing manager should encourage people to talk with each other and to participate in extracurricular activities. Because managers often begin their careers as programmers, they tend to concentrate on technology instead of the people. They must understand the human world because that is where the results of their efforts are used. Communication skills (discussed in Appendices C to N) and knowledge about the human world are of prime importance to people who develop and use computer systems.

For additional information on managing in information processing, see DeMarco and Lister's book on managing people in software projects [46] and Weinberg on understanding the professional programmer [209]. Metzger [133], who gives a lively account of daily life in a U.S. development group throughout the development life cycle, defines a manager's role as one of preventing stagnation in the work flow. The manager must make people understand what is needed when, and assure that people work together as a team.

12.7 On Being Managed

> The fault, dear Brutus, is not in our stars,
> But in ourselves, that we are underlings.
>
> —W. Shakespeare, *Julius Caesar* [192]

Almost everyone is a subordinate, yet I have not found much written on how to be a good subordinate. Does this mean that it is not important to know how to be managed? Or that knowing how to be managed comes naturally? Or that managing is only a matter of good management, regardless of how the subordinate reacts? Is your manager the person who must teach you how to be managed? I don't think so, and that's why I want to devote the second part of this chapter to being a good subordinate.

Managers and subordinates both must take care that their relationship does not end up in a downgrading self-fulfilling prophecy. If a manager thinks that a subordinate is acting like a child and treats the person accordingly, the subordinate may indeed react like a child. (See, for example, Livingston's article [85] that describes Pygmalion management.)

To avoid such self-fulfilling prophecies, consider the other end of the stick. Herzberg et al., who have investigated the motivation to work in the United States in the mid-1950s [91], found the following motivation factors ranked in the order of their importance:

1. Achievement and recognition
2. Work itself, responsibility, advancement, and growth
3. Salary
4. Other factors, including the potential for growth, interpersonal relationships, status, technical supervision, company policy and administration, working conditions, personal life, and job security

The first and second factors, which Herzberg called the *motivators,* were most important and relate to the working group. The third and fourth factors, called the *dissatisfiers* or *hygiene factors,* can only bring peace, not motivation; they relate to the organization as a whole. This shows the importance of human relationships in the direct work environment.

I believe that the introduction of computers since the mid-1950s has only increased the importance of human relationships at work: Because working with a computer is a solitary effort, people may need such relations to make their work meaningful. Another reason may be that computers increase the span of work, forcing more people to work together in more different ways and at a greater distance than before, which strengthens the need for good human relationships.

Alvesson [3] extends Herzberg's factors to make the case for self-actualization. He describes the use of quality circles in the Volvo factory at Kalmar, Sweden, in which a small group of workers determines their work situation and job content, combining productivity and work satisfaction. Volvo president Gyllenhamar [80] gives a top management rationale for creating this work environment.

If you as a subordinate agree with the way things are done at work, everything is fine. The problem starts when you feel that things should be done differently and other people do not immediately agree. You then have a choice of reactions:

- You can ignore the matter and brush aside your disagreement; this is not easy if you must face the situation every day.
- You can put up with the matter and tell yourself that other things in life are more important; that is, you find a compensation.
- You can accept the matter and convince yourself that apparently this is the way things are.
- You can quit the group and find a job elsewhere.
- You can fight the matter head on and try to enlist support from others.
- You can propose a reasonable alternative that achieves a similar result in a more acceptable way.

The last reaction is what is needed most in an information processing environment, where important decisions are made by subordinates without management's being aware. It requires self-driven and competent people. Choosing the last reaction gives a sense of achievement (meaningfulness) and helps combat a hidden agenda {2.15}.

I believe the most important goal for a subordinate in an information processing environment is the inner desire to realize full human potential.* For want of a better word, I use "self-actualization" to describe this feeling. It starts from inward motivation, not by a manager enriching your job or telling you to be competent. Self-actualization requires self-awareness, self-control, and self-competency. My postulate is as follows: The information processing environment strongly needs self-actualized subordinates. All human beings require some degree of self-actualization to deal proficiently with their work environment. It is a true joy to achieve something that you feel is important. To be competent in a team, you need to communicate properly with others, which requires self-awareness. Another requirement is a desire to improve your own functioning.

Achieving gives self-respect, which is basic to self-acceptance and to feeling like a human person. The feeling of achievement strengthens your effectiveness in a team. The environment must confirm achievements because confirmation is a basic human need to determine meaningfulness.

---

*Arguments for this are in Argyris [5, 6], Maslow [124, 125], Morse and Lorsch [141], and Rogers [175–177].

To understand how self-actualization works, picture a department in which things have settled down to routine operations. You reflect on your working situation and see that work should be done differently (awareness). For the sake of this illustration, I will consider only two possible reactions:

1. Why bother? No one is asking you to act. The manager will not accept your proposal anyway. This reaction decreases your feeling of self-actualization and your efficiency in the department.

2. You try to assess the situation objectively and propose a change (control). You convince people that indeed things should be changed (competency). After a while your manager and colleagues confirm your contribution as being useful (confirmation). This reaction increases your feeling of self-actualization and your efficiency in the department.

You may say that you can never convince your manager that a situation can be improved. I can only respond that you need to use the right arguments. The premise must be that things can change (your self-confidence) and that they will. To put it another way, you get the manager that you deserve: The Pygmalion effect also works the other way around.

We can find within ourselves most things important to self-actualization. What you need is vision so you can put a proper goal in your mind, something useful that you can realize.

12.8 Becoming a Self-Actualized Subordinate

> No man is free who is not master of himself.
>
> —Epictetus

Choosing self-actualization as an individual goal serves both personal needs and organizational needs. Achievement increases your effectiveness through self-confidence. To become self-actualized, however, you must make conscious limitations that you were not conscious of, so you can change them (Heider [88]). You must also break out of self-deceptions (Goleman [75]).

Here are some first thoughts on how to become a self-actualized subordinate: Develop your communication skills, for they are essential to achieve work together with others. To communicate well, you need to be aware of yourself and of how others see you. The more you enlarge your self-concept, the greater is your potential to understand and control your behavior (Argyris [5]).

Develop your competence and understanding of your work environment. There is a ninety-nine percent chance that your solution will not work if you don't understand your work environment.

Understand how your manager tries to manage you. If you feel your manager is not effective, ask yourself how you can adapt. Take the initiative to discuss with the manager how you can make your relationship more effective.

Use your assertive human rights {2.16}. Choose a role that you feel is appropriate, effective, and efficient. Be reactive or active as the situation demands. Reflect on why you should do something, when you should do it, and how.

Assume ownership of your tasks and feel responsible for their successful completion. Put into practice what is likely to be successful: "Deeds are the pulse of time" (G. Eliot). Thinking is a deed only when you express the thought to the right people. Only through practice and success are you able to develop your feeling of competence. Take on responsibility, but try to avoid failures that may break down your feeling of competence. Ask for help when you need help; the goal is to get something done, not to do it all by yourself.

Use your energy to achieve things for others instead of trying to live up to your self-image. "...man should be able to achieve happiness, provided that his passions and interests are directed outward, not inward" (B. Russell [182]).

Accept the easy way only after thorough consideration. Because of subjective impressions, the real solution often is not what you thought it was. "We must continually learn to unlearn much that we have learned, and learn to learn that we have not been taught" (R. Laing, quoted in [1]).

Be honest with yourself and others. Refuse to seek scapegoats. If you are not honest with yourself, someone else will be. Being found out will break down your feeling of self-actualization. To get recognition, give it away (R. Pascale in [85]). The give-and-get formula works for many things, including confidence, trust, power, caring, and uncertainty. It works best in unexpected situations; it is not give *to* get.

Assurance is two-thirds of success. Feel confident, and you will be confident; make confidence a self-fulfilling prophecy. See Hambly [82] for how to improve your confidence. "All Greeks know what is right, but only the Spartans do it" [110]. Be a Spartan, starting today.

If you have lost genuine interest in your work, break the daily routine and renew yourself. Take the time to reflect on how you function in your group and in your organization, and determine what interesting new activities you can undertake. Especially in automation, there are always many opportunities available that are valuable to the organization and that do not require a financial investment. An alternative is to seek responsibilities outside your work. In either case, finding a new balance will make you feel better and increase your usefulness.

Managing yourself effectively is what becoming self-actualized is all about. You may not realize the opportunity to do this in most situations, nor the need. But self-driven people are becoming essential in a world full of computers; become a technical leader (Weinberg [207]). For one thing, the environment is becoming too complex for people to manage other people. For another, if people manage themselves, they can protect themselves against unfair treatment and being burdened with too much work. A bird's-eye view makes it possible to assess your situation objectively and to avoid rising to Peter and Hull's level of incompetence [160]. The better you are master of yourself, the more freely you can communicate with others. You need these achievements to plan, develop, and use information systems properly.

Managing and being managed is an involving subject. This chapter can give only an overview, with some first thoughts on being a good subordinate. Recommended further reading are Dyer [53, 54], Hambly [82], Handy [83], Robbins [173], and Rogers [175–177]. Read Stoner and Wankel's *Management* [199] Chapter 11, on authority and delegation; Chapter 13, the section on how organizational culture affects the organization's ability to change; and Chapter 22, the case study on electronic advisers, "The Management Edge," a software package to help managers change their behavior.

Take the following exercises in Robbins [173] to develop your self-awareness: (IIA) value assessment, (IIB) locus of control, (IID) supervisory attitude, (IIE) needs, (IIIA) status ranking, (IIIB) management communication skills, (IIIC) leadership, (IIID) power orientation, (IVA) bureaucratic orientation, (IVB) your job's motivation potential, (IVC) your classroom culture, and (IVD) rate of life-change.

12.9 Summary

1. The goal of managing is to make people want to achieve the goals of the organization. Management's primary tasks are to decide what things are worth doing and how to get them done.

2. Management theories have shifted their emphasis from work to human relationships and the integration of people into the organization. An organization will not survive if its people don't care.

3. Top management sets the tone for the organization's culture.
4. Managers get authority from their superior manager, and leaders get their power from the people they lead.
5. Communication is a major part of a manager's work, working as a coach to make people achieve.
6. Use the ISVIC procedure to analyze management problems and planning.
7. Budgeting is a way to plan and control human and material resources. Management by objectives can be used to plan and control human activities.
8. Being managed has received little attention so far, yet almost every person is a subordinate.
9. Feeling self-actualized is a central goal for a subordinate in an information processing environment. Self-actualization implies self-awareness, self-control, and self-competence. It makes both the organization and the subordinate more efficient.
10. You need knowledge of yourself, your environment, and the world to become self-actualized and to manage yourself effectively.

12.10 Review Questions and Exercises

1. Section 12.1 states Fayol's fourteen principles of management, which lead to a hierarchical organization. Section 11.2 gives the basis for Weber's bureaucratic organization theory.
   - Do you think that any Fayol principle needs changing today? Why?
   - Consider why bureaucracies have become synonymous with inefficiency. What makes them inefficient? What must you add or change to make them more efficient? (Toffler [202] argues that bureaucracies cannot handle change, but you can also consider other reasons.)
2. Consider how your manager typically selects solutions in the light of the following dimensions described by Harrison [84]:
   - Power, selecting a solution that will reinforce the power of the group or its manager
   - Role, selecting a solution that is strictly in line with the role of the group

- Task, selecting a solution that reaches the desired goal
- Person, selecting a solution that will glorify a person, either a manager or a subordinate

Refer to Harrison's list of questions to help you plot these four aspects on a four-dimensional graph. Explain, with examples, why the manager's orientation is due to organizational culture, to personal character, or to both.

3. Discuss the following section from Farnsworth [59] Chapter 12:

> In management, as in life, you can be anything you want to be, provided that you want it badly enough and have the courage to persevere. And since as a manager you are expected to be successful, you have a clear vested interest in getting the best out of your people for it is *their* performance and results which determine *your* success. After all, if you could do everything single-handed then you wouldn't need subordinates, you could play every role yourself.

4. List what motivates you to do things on your own initiative. Then list what demotivates you to take initiative. Who or what primarily motivates you? Who or what primarily demotivates you?

5. In "Beyond Theory Y" [141], Morse and Lorsch report on a study of four organization units. They explain differences in performance as a result of differences in competence motivation. The following paraphrases their argument:

    a. A central need of human beings is to achieve a sense of competence.

    b. Human beings can fulfill a sense of competence in different ways, depending on their other needs.

    c. Competence motivation is most likely to occur when the organization is designed to fit human beings.

    d. When people achieve a competence goal, they set a higher one.

    e. Competence motivation can occur in any (X, Y, Z, or other) type of organization.

    Give arguments for and against each of those statements. Discuss the consequences of the argumentation on (1) hiring and firing policies, (2) moving people in an organization, and (3) dividing tasks among people and computers. Besides the sense of success, what else will motivate you? Compare competence motivation with feeling self-actualized. Give examples.

6. In management by objectives, a feedback system to reinforce work objectives, much depends on defining the proper objectives.
   - What can go wrong if the requirements given in {12.3} are not met?
   - What are some other requirements for objectives?
   - Besides wrong objectives, what else can go wrong with MBO?
   - How would you determine what is a suitable MBO review period?
   - What are the objectives for your current work?

7. Blanchard and Johnson's *The One Minute Manager* [14] teaches you how to use one minute goal setting, one minute praisings, and one minute reprimands. The basic system appears similar to management by objectives.
   - What are the differences between the two methods?
   - When can you best use each method?
   - Will a one minute manager encourage self-actualization? Why?

8. Oncken and Wass [154] devised a useful "monkey-on-the-back" analogy to identify who has a problem, which is important in manager-subordinate communication. You can use this analogy to shift responsibility onto others and to refuse responsibility.

   The analogy makes responsibilities clear in the mind. The monkey appears when someone identifies a problem and disappears when you resolve the problem to mutual satisfaction. The person who owns a problem has the monkey and may try to make it jump on you. You should only take over the monkey (the problem) knowingly and willingly, but you can also refuse it by using arguments. You get the monkey if you don't say anything. The rule is to keep the monkey where it belongs. Everyone must solve his or her own problems or ask for help and get rid of their monkeys as soon as possible.
   - Watch a TV play or comedy where people work together. Identify when monkeys appear, how people try to give monkeys to others, how they accept or refuse them, and when monkeys disappear.

- Does a one minute manager [14] make clear where the monkey sits?
  - If yes, in what ways?
  - If no, how is responsibility made clear?

9. Machiavelli wrote *The Prince* [117], a book often referred to for its insight into politics and power. Read it and translate M's situation into your situation, making a list of recommendations for your manager. Then construct an opposing set of recommendations for a subordinate to survive a Machiavellian manager. Compare your recommendations for a subordinate to my recommendations on how to become a self-actualized subordinate, and discuss any differences.

10. Assess your state of self-actualization in terms of Argyris's general immaturity-maturity continuum [5, 6]:

Immaturity		Maturity
Passive	→	. . . . Active
Dependence	→	. . . . Independence
Behave in a few ways.	→	. . . . Capable of behaving in many ways
Erratic shallow interest	→	. . . . . . Deeper and stronger interest
Short time interest	→	. . . . . Long time perspective
Subordinate position	→	. . . . . . Equal or subordinate position
Lack of self-awareness	→	. . . . . Awareness and control over self

Consider your technical job maturity, communication maturity, and psychological maturity separately:

- In what ways can you be more active, if you wished?
- How often can you take more initiative, if you wished?
- How often do you adapt behavior to suit the situation?
- What other interests can you develop, if you wished?
- How far ahead do you plan?
- How do you think people at work see you? How often do people seek your advice or help?
- How often do you regret having done things a certain way?

11. Section 11.2 explained that reducing uncertainty is a primary factor in determining an organization's structure. There could be a

relationship between people working effectively and efficiently when confident and not when uncertain. Describe the relations between environmental and individual uncertainty. What are your critical success factors—your uncertainties?

12. A director of a large company, who is seeking your advice, explains that he has many good ideas to shape the organization in such a way that people would be more happy and the organization more effective. An opinion survey shows, however, that he is not successful in making it happen. He compares his organization to a sand hill that he tries to shape with a spade and with his feet. No matter what he does, he explains, the hill is back in the same shape the next morning.
    - What questions would you ask him in order to understand the situation?
    - Assuming some answers to these questions, what are your conclusions?
    - What would you advise the director to do?

13. Peters says in *Thriving on Chaos* [161] Section I-6, "Everybody can (must) be a champion" and we must find ways to unleash the power in people to cope in a world turned upside down. Make a list of items that you can (must) improve on, and add what is holding you back. Consider your inhibitions, to see what you can do about them.

13

COMMITMENT AND SELF-ACTUALIZATION

The human mind has to ask
"Who, what, whence, whither, why am I?"
And it is very doubtful if the human mind can answer
any of these questions.
—R.D. Laing, *Wisdom, Madness & Folly* [113]

In this final chapter, I will draw conclusions based on the thoughts I developed in the previous chapters. The theme of the chapter—as well as the book—is that people must make computerization happen, people who have a vision of quality and are self-actualized.

13.1 Commitment to What?

> Everything's got a moral, if only you can find it.
>
> —L. Carroll, *Alice's Adventures in Wonderland* [32]

As I write this section, there is much commotion in Holland over a remark made by a soccer player. (I use this incident solely as an illustration, not to judge. I have no idea what really happened, and I don't know a thing about soccer except that unlike in rugby and American football, knocking down other players is forbidden.)

In the incident, player C was quoted in an interview to this effect, "Player A knocked down player B, which was first class at that point in the game." Player C was penalized by the European soccer association (UEFA) for making this remark.

The knocking down represented quality in a sense: The team of player A won the match. But the UEFA apparently wanted to set an example to denounce the moral decay in soccer. They punished player C for his attitude and for expressing his admiration for player A's commitment to winning.

I include this example only to show that, in the close alliance between quality and success, quality also has a moral aspect. If you become number one because of your commitment and dedication, you may be penalized when you hurt other people on the way. (For a discussion of management and ethics, see Blanchard and Peale [15].)

Unfortunately, you cannot always avoid hurting others. Take a company that decides to aim for one hundred percent quality. It may succeed very well in the market, but at the same time put another company that disregards quality out of business. Most people regard such a commitment to quality as correct, presumably because it moves society forward.

The definition of what is accepted ethical behavior is often the subject of discussion in professional organizations so they can establish a code of ethics. In the medical and engineering professions, for example, it is not uncommon to refuse to do certain work. Some computer professionals refuse to work for military organizations. There is not much publicity about professionals who refuse to develop and use poor information systems. One reason may be that they can easily find another job.

My point in this section is that quality has a moral aspect too, relating among others to personal integrity {2.17}. We all make (conscious and unconscious) choices and are responsible for the consequences they have. Self-actualized people achieve results for others and must take responsibility for their quality.

13.2 Self-Actualization: The High Road to Quality

> It seems that we are very good at finding reasons for what we do, but not so good at doing what we find reasons for.
>
> —S.P. Robbins, *Organizational Behavior* [173]

Pirsig [163] quotes Kitto [110] to say that what moved the Greek warrior was not duty toward others, but duty toward himself. This reflects an idea of efficiency that encompasses everything and that exists in life itself. Self-actualization can be thought of as the road to fulfilling such a total concept of quality.

Seneca remarked that "things" are not good or bad. It is our attitude and the way we use things that make them good or bad. An automobile, for example, can be a murder weapon and a valuable means of transportation at the same time. It is not the car itself that is good or bad; what counts is how it is used, or the driver's attitude.

Self-actualization is such an attitude, whereby we strive to be as competent as possible in our job and elsewhere. Not everyone will reach as far but there is no need for that either; each person is unique.

The road to self-actualization is not easy. Teilhard de Chardin remarked that animals and humans both think and know. Their distinction is that only humans know that they think and know. This self-consciousness is our Achilles heel that can either help us to reach new heights in achievement or make us feel miserable about our failures and conflicts. Because we will suffer from feeling miserable, it must be our personal decision on how far we want to go. Others must respect this decision, which is part of our individuality.

Others can help us to achieve goals—I learned to do pushups in a group session. They are also effective in serious matters, such as getting rid of an addiction or attaining a higher degree of self-actualization. However, the decision to participate in such group sessions must be an individual one, not made under pressure from others.

We are prisoners of our own assumptions, our hidden agenda. I repeat: If we want to change something, we must first make it conscious. If we want to become more conscious of people and their situation, we must learn to live with uncertainty and unanswered questions. Living with uncertainty requires intelligence; the more uncertainty, the more intelligence. In any case, the decision to become more conscious of ourself and our environment is and must be our conscious decision.

The road to self-actualization is also not simple because attitudes are difficult to change. It requires much conceptual blockbusting (see Ackoff [1], Adams [2], Goleman [75], Halpern [81], von Oech [153], and Perkins [159]). The first and most difficult step is to notice our situation and to see how we can improve it. To help begin, let me suggest some examples of attitudes that could change for the better.

- The jargon used by technical professionals makes it difficult for nontechnical people to understand what computers can and cannot do. Yet nontechnical people are the customers for computers. Wouldn't it be great if professionals would talk in an understandable language so customers could see what they are buying?
- Technical professionals make many decisions that will affect nontechnical people without even consulting them. They often view consulting users as asking for trouble. Wouldn't it be great if professionals would take the time to consult with and understand the needs of customers—to show that they work for them, not to please themselves.
- Telling a client that the computer has made a mistake may be the simplest way to handle a problem, but such an attitude will not lead to improvements. Computers make very few mistakes; people make most mistakes. Wouldn't it be great if people wouldn't use the computer as a scapegoat? Wouldn't it be great if clients wouldn't accept such an answer and demand a true explanation of the problem?
- Users often have neither the interest nor the time to think about a new computer application. They leave decisions to technical people. Wouldn't it be great if the real users (that is, the customers of the developers) would actually take a strong interest

and express their opinions beforehand? And not complain afterward about shortcomings that could have been avoided?

- Managers spend much time on administrative detail and arguing with people outside their group. They often leave technical decisions to their professionals. Wouldn't it be great if managers would take more interest in the implications of technical decisions?
- Professionals must make many technical decisions. Wouldn't it be great if they tried to understand and discuss their implications?
- Different software systems use different keys for the Help function. They also use different keys for other standard functions. Wouldn't it be great if developers refused to do this and users refused to accept it?

A change in attitude requires awareness first. After becoming aware, you need self-discipline, knowledge, and skill to remove roadblocks to quality. "Man is limited not so much by his tools as by his vision" (Pascale and Athos [157]).

This book has tried to increase your awareness of the many human sides of automation, and to provide a framework of attitudes necessary for achieving quality in computerization.

13.3 Summary

1. There is an important moral aspect to quality and excellence.
2. As Seneca remarked, "things" are not good or bad. It is our attitude and the way we use things that determine their quality. Computers are examples of such "things."
3. Self-actualization is the attitude required to realize the goals for computerization stated at the beginning of this book.
4. How far you go on the road to self-actualization is a personal decision that must be respected and not influenced by others.
5. Use the vision gained from reading this book, to adapt computers to people in a better way.

13.4 Review Questions and Exercises

1. Think of a person in your environment who "knocks" people down on his or her way to the top. Describe how you could introduce the consequences of such behavior to that person, that is, give the right feedback. (For ideas, read the article "The Abrasive Personality" and its appendix by Levinson in [85] and *Power Plays* [59] by Farnsworth.)

2. Suppose the director of your organization asks you to manage a prestigious project that will change the organization's future. While the director is explaining the project and its ramifications, you become uneasy. Not only is the project too big and complex for you, but its undertaking is also risky. How do you communicate your uneasiness to the enthusiastic director so that he or she has a true opportunity to remove it?

3. Think of some people who you feel are not behaving in a self-actualized way. Make a list of the items that you feel they could improve upon.
   - Why do you think those items are not up to par?
   - Can the people improve by changing their attitudes? Why?
   - How can you motivate them to change their attitudes?

4. List items that you should improve upon.
   - Why have you not done better on those items?
   - Can you improve by changing your attitude? Why?
   - How can you motivate yourself to change your attitude?

5. List five activities that you find difficult. For each activity, ask yourself whether the difficulty is due to a lack of proper knowledge, a lack of skill, or a poor attitude. How can you learn to do them better?

6. Consider an information system that you know fairly well.
   - List ten ways in which an incompetent person can impair the system.
   - List ten other ways in which an unmotivated but competent person can impair the system.

- Is it possible to make a completely foolproof system that end users cannot impair?
  - If yes, discuss why it has not been done.
  - If no, discuss why not.

Discuss whether you think an atmosphere of trust can or cannot help to prevent systems from being impaired.

7. Describe how an increase or decrease of trust would affect the atmosphere and working relations in your working environment. What is the origin of trust? Why is trust important? (For ideas, read the article "Managing the Paradox of Organizational Trust" by Barnes [12].)

8. Give arguments for and against each of the following statements:

   a. Because the essential matters in information processing are immaterial, you cannot tell people what they must do to achieve quality.

   b. To achieve quality in information processing, you must rely on people's initiative and their intuitive idea of quality.

   c. If people like to do things, they do them on their own initiative.

   d. Understanding what is important and to be self-actualized is traveling the high road to achieving quality.

   e. Trust and respect for others are conditions for creating an environment in which self-actualization can flourish.

9. In the article "Intelligence Is Mental Self-Government" [198], Sternberg explains that the main functions of government are to set rules (that is, to plan), to perform, and to judge (that is, to evaluate). These functions must check and balance each other to achieve good results. Consider his view: "The essence of intelligence is that it provides a means to govern ourselves so that our thoughts and actions are organized, coherent, and responsive to both our internally driven needs and to the needs of the environment."

   - Discuss Sternberg's choice of internal and external needs as goals. What other goals do you prefer? How do you attain such goals?
   - What are the facets of intelligence? Can someone be intelligent in one or more specific areas? How?

- Why is intelligence such an elusive subject?
- What is your opinion about Sternberg's definition?
- Discuss implications of your opinion on the concept of "artificial intelligence."

10. Develop your self-competence to speak, listen, write, and read by considering how you can use individual and interpersonal mind mechanisms {2.2 to 2.17}. Read the recommendations in Appendices C to N to improve your communication qualities.

Epilogue

Things and living organisms both exist, but only living organisms have a culture. A culture can be described as how organisms survive, satisfy their own needs and those of others, and improve their condition. Like quality, human culture has an outward objective aspect, concerning the results that can be seen and measured, and an inward subjective aspect, concerning matters of the mind.

I set out to write a psychology of automation, but according to this definition, I have described an automation culture, that is, how we can use computers, adapt them to our needs and those of others, and improve our use of them. In this book I have endeavored to strike a proper balance between outward and inward aspects of automation, which I hope will be useful to you in the difficult task of making computer technology improve human conditions.

A characteristic of human culture is that people expand on and use the work and experience of predecessors. Today's software, for example, could never have been developed without the work of yesterday's programmers. But what is common practice in software, also needs to take place on a more personal level, incorporating computer technology in human society.

Realize, however, that such a change of general society may take decades, as it requires that most people adapt. Because technology is moving so fast, it is vital that all people involved join forces to realize the automation goals stated in the introduction. Or else, computerization will score a Pyrrhic victory, winning the battle but losing the war.

Appendices

A: Recommendations for VDT Users

B: On-Line Dialogue Design Principles

C: Preparing and Making a Presentation

D: Attending a Presentation

E: Having a Productive Meeting

F: Daydreaming and Brainstorming to Generate Ideas

G: Writing a Meeting or Activity Report

H: Conducting an Interview

I: Talking Person to Person

J: Negotiating for Agreement

K: Elements of a Manual

L: Designing and Making an Index

M: Keeping a Diary as an Aid to Memory

N: Nonverbal Communication

APPENDIX A
Recommendations for VDT Users

As I mentioned in {3.5}, *ergonomics* is the discipline that involves adapting the work environment to people. It derives from the Greek words "ergon" (work) and "nomos" (laws of) and is another word for human factors. The following ergonomic aspects of working with a video display terminal (VDT, also known as a CRT) are important for everyone who interacts with a computer.

Arrange for proper lighting. Avoid light reflections and strong contrasts that require your eyes to adjust every time you look at a display. Indirect daylight may be better than artificial illumination because it contains the full range of the visible spectrum and is more restful as a result. Some people feel that a window gives them an important mental orientation on the outside world, but others may find it a distraction.

Use special eyeglasses for viewing a VDT screen, especially if you wear bifocals. The typical reading distance with VDTs is 1.5 to 2.5 feet (.50 to .75 meters), which lies between the distance for reading and for normal viewing (1 to 16 feet or .3 to 5 meters). Opticians typically add about 1.5 diopters to your normal lens specification for such a special use. Have an eye checkup if in doubt.

Sit properly. When you work with a computer, you often sit in the same position for a long period of time. An estimated eighty percent of the population will have back pain at some time in their lives. To avoid lasting back injuries, pay attention to your posture and follow these good practices—your body will appreciate it!

- Look down at the screen to avoid a pain in the neck.
- Keep your back vertical to reduce tension and torsion in the spinal column.

- Support your lower back to help you keep a proper posture for some time.
- Position the keyboard at a proper height to let your upper arm hang down straight, reducing torsion in the shoulder joint. Many people prefer arm rests.
- Don't bend your wrists when typing.
- Make sure the front end of your seat does not cut off the flow of blood in the arteries of the upper leg. Use a foot rest if necessary so that your entire sole is on a surface.
- Use an adjustable chair with a sturdy base.

If you still feel uncomfortable after following these guidelines while seated at your workstation, consult your company's health or facilities group for advice. Your workstation probably uses standard ranges for table top height, arm reach, leg space, and so on [57, 126, 213], and you probably require an adaptation if your dimensions are outside the standard ranges* (see Figure A-1).

Be active. Stretching periodically is important to restore a blood flow restricted by sitting too long in one position. Shift both your physical position and mental focus once in a while. All people need changes in sensory stimulation and react adversely to their absence.

Get proper training and support. Train properly for productive work, and have people support you when you cannot continue. Training must explain the overall concept of the system and give hands-on experience. Human support is necessary when working with computers because, as we've seen, it is impossible to foresee every situation you may get into. Make certain you are confident about working with the computer before you must become productive. Do not accept inadequate training—you must fully understand what you are doing.

Get regular exercise. Certain parts of the body degenerate when you don't use them, some muscles starting to deteriorate within only a few days of non-use. Also, sports and exercises can improve your physical well-being. Some people feel that mental exercise is as important as physical exercise: Take courses, read books, and participate in activities outside the sphere of your work.

---

*In 1988, the American National Standards Institute and the Human Factors Society developed a ninety-page document on the engineering of workstations, giving details about the ranges.

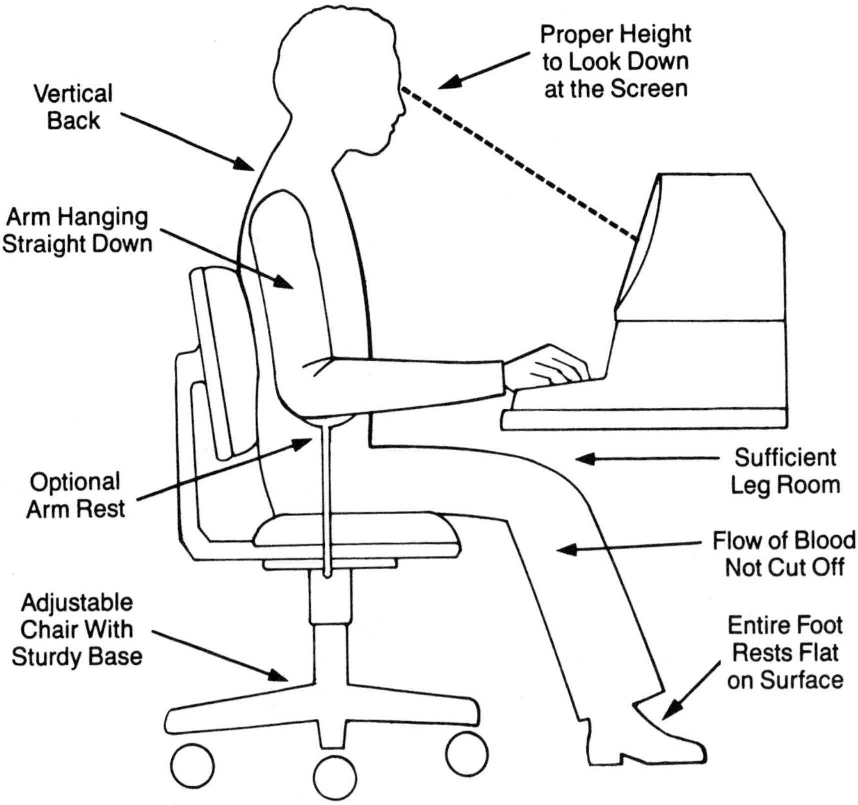

Figure A-1. Proper posture while working with a VDT.

Avoid strain caused by repetitive actions. Beware of repetitive activities that can easily strain your muscles. For example, alternate working at the VDT and writing by hand. If you cannot avoid doing a certain activity, look for ways to vary the activity.

APPENDIX B
On-Line Dialogue Design Principles

Here are the eleven most important principles for considering the human user in designing on-line dialogue.

Make computers do what people want them to do. Understand future users and how they work. How will they want to use computers in their setting? How will they judge the efficiency and effectiveness of working with a computer? What problems can the computer help them with? How can you avoid introducing new problems? How will users work with customers? To answer these important questions and to offer insights into a particular user situation, include someone in the development group who is familiar with the user environment—a user or user representative.

Design the dialogue early in development. In design, start with dialogue design so that system design will support it, and not the other way around. To create human-friendly systems, begin with how people will view the system and let internal system design support that view.

Provide a clear task orientation. Start with a task analysis of the entire information system. Then decide which tasks will be done by people and which will be done by the machine. Task design must be part of total system design, and task definition clear and consistent at different user levels. Information processing tasks must blend well with other human tasks. Above all, consider how users can serve customers.

Make and keep the dialogue simple for all people. If you make procedural details too complex, people will find an alternative way to do it. Keeping it simple makes it more likely that it will fit in with other human tasks. Overview panels should show all available options, with the most frequently used one on top. Suppress options not available for a specific end user. Use no more than four colors. Accept abbreviations whenever possible, displaying the full version for checking. Try to handle an entire logical operation on one panel. Don't force end users to remember (or write down) information from one panel to the next. Let the system insert data that are already available; don't demand another entry.

Make the dialogue meaningful and efficient for people. End users, their customers, and all other people affected must experience the task as meaningful and the implementation as efficient. For example,

- The task should be complete, not partial.
- End users must understand the task in detail.
- The task must fulfill a clear role in the organization.
- Task automation must improve efficiency, compared with the old way of doing the job, for all people.

It may be efficient to use people as robots, but not meaningful in terms of any but simple, well-defined tasks. If possible, people should enter information whenever and wherever they create it. Avoiding duplication of effort and of information is the key to making dialogues meaningful and efficient for people.

Provide adequate support for the task. After some basic training, people should be able to work with the system in a satisfactory manner with only occasional help from a specialist. Make all needed information available within the critical response time {2.5}. The system should determine where to store input data, and not need to ask the end user.

Conform to end user expectations. Be consistent with the way an end user works in other areas and consistent within the application. For example, use the same meaning of keys for common keyboard operations like Help and End. Also conform to the expectation of people in the Western world to read from left to right and to work from top to bottom (but understand that this is not universal). Be consistent in the use of color, terminology, and position of messages. Input fields must have the same name and appear in the same sequence as on the printed form. Documentation must conform to the system.

Make the on-line dialogue self-descriptive. Make basic information available from the application. Include a panel title, help information for every field and every command, messages explaining options, and indicators of system and user status. Show only options that are available, and give information about special keys on the keyboard.

Put the human experts in charge. The application must give the end users the feeling of being in control—it must empower them. The end users should be able to choose between command interfaces. Provide tolerance to erroneous actions from the human experts. They must be able to continue after making an error, and they must also be able to change plans, to undo the previous operation, and to cancel the current one. People must be able to determine their own pace of work.

Give adequate feedback to people. The system must show where the end user is in a procedure and what the system is doing when it is busy for some time. Acknowledge an accepted transaction, and show that a new one can be entered so the end user can mentally close the first one. Give "sorting records" or "preparing report" messages when the computer is going to be busy for some time. Give a "report ready" message when the computer is done. Messages and other displayed text should take the end user's view. Display READ when the end user must read the screen, not when the computer "reads" the terminal. Computer feedback must be intuitively clear, and not cause delays. Similarly customers must be informed when information about them in the computer changes.

Properly introduce computers and support users. Proper training must explain the overall concept of an information system and should give hands-on experience (Chapter 9). Users must understand the organization, job descriptions, and their tasks with the computer. Users must also understand the part performed by a machine before they can assume responsibility for a task using that machine. Technical support must help users who get stuck on items not covered during the training; provide a human network for this purpose.

Section 3.5 discusses how to put the human experts in charge, Chapter 7 is devoted to communicating on-line with a computer, and Chapter 9 covers training.

APPENDIX C
Preparing and Making a Presentation

Speaking is an act of self-expression, to put forward information, a point of view, and plans. Both formal and informal presentations are a frequent activity in information processing, and they require advance preparation that is proportional to the importance of the presentation.

To speak properly and effectively, you need a desire, an affection, a purpose, and a plan:

- Desire because it is easier when you feel the need to speak
- Affection because speaking is easier to people you know and like
- Purpose because you and your audience need a reason for the presentation
- Plan because the presentation must be effective

There is a wide range of preparation required, depending upon the situation: Thinking a moment will suffice for answering a short question from a colleague. An informal presentation may require fifteen minutes to prepare, and a formal presentation may require several days. As Mark Twain said, "A good improvised speech takes three weeks to prepare."

PREPARING A PRESENTATION

You can use the full ISVIC procedure {1.6}, or parts of it, to prepare a presentation. Prepare more thoroughly if you anticipate little feedback, consider the subject important, and have little experience. The following is a recapitulation of the ISVIC procedure, tuned to designing a formal presentation:

Investigating to answer seven questions (seven W's):

- Why do you want to present?
- What do you want to present?
- Whom are you going to present to?
- Whence are you making the presentation?
- Where will the presentation take place?
- When will the presentation take place?
- HoW will the presentation take place?

Structuring the communication to make the subject matter clear in your own mind so that it will be for your audience: Organize the presentation of the subject matter as you want to convey it to your audience, building from the simple to the complex and from the concrete to the abstract.

Verifying that you have all the important elements of meaning, no more and no less, and that they are in the proper sequence. Before starting to implement, have a colleague review your plan to get a second opinion.

Implementing the elements in a form that helps to convey their meaning. The investigation revealed what form is most suitable for your audience. Implementation is the preparation of overhead slides, handouts, and other props.

Checking the implementation to ensure the following (five C's):

- Clarity: Is it simple?
- Conciseness: Is it brief?
- Completeness: Is it adequate?
- Courtesy: Is it fair?
- Correctness: Is it accurate?

A rehearsal can complete your preparation.

Designing overhead slides: Use an overhead projector to support, not distract from, your talk. There is no point in duplicating what you say on slides; otherwise, visual communication will dominate verbal communication. Rather, use slides to show the structure of your speech and to illustrate it. Use a maximum of twenty overhead slides per hour of speaking; of those twenty, no more than ten should show the structure of your speech. Some recommendations for using slides are as follows:

- Use key words only; discard even short sentences to avoid duplication of what you will say.
- Include headings on every slide to show the particular part and topic you are discussing.
- Use no more than 7 ± 2 text entries on each slide in view of the limitations of short-term memory {2.5}.
- Capitalize only the first word of each line and use a legible letter size that is readable for even those at the back of the room.
- Use emphasis, such as color and underlining, judiciously and consistently.
- Use graphics to show relationships, and illustrations to give details.
- Be consistent in terminology.
- Be aware that even the smallest error on slides gets noticed.

MAKING A PRESENTATION

Before the actual presentation, begin by readying your props, such as handouts, reference material, a pointer, and samples. Handouts will give permanence to your words, if you so desire. I like to have a handout of overhead slides during a talk for members of the audience to make notes. Handouts will also come in handy if the projector fails. Use overhead slides to present key words and graphics to support your speech. The slides, however, must never be a distraction. After gathering your props, prepare yourself and your audience as follows:

Personal appearance is important, so you must dress appropriately for the occasion. To avoid surprises, check out the equipment in advance and become familiar with its operation. If necessary, have someone help you to start a video recorder or slide projector and dim the lights. Have a backup plan if the equipment fails.

To help your concentration, clear your mind of all unrelated thoughts. Have your props and everything else directly at hand. Nobody really minds the time you take to organize before speaking. But it's a nuisance for you and your audience if you have to search for something during your speech.

Prepare your audience. First, you need an opening to establish rapport. Some speakers use an anecdote, but if you do, make it personal and pertinent to the topic. It may be useful to mention your background and how you relate to the subject. If possible, interweave that information with your anecdote. Being personal (and being honest) establishes trust, which is vital to being an effective communicator.

You will have to advise your audience of procedures. Are handouts available? If so, when? Will you take questions during your speech or after? What is your schedule? Will there be breaks?

Start speaking. Now that you have prepared your subject, yourself, and your audience, the real speaking can begin. Use the trusted 3T formula {2.3} for every part of your structure:

- Tell them what you are going to tell them, and why!
- Tell them.
- Tell them what you told them.

You must then start to tell your audience what you expect as a result of your talk. Remind them of this result as you continue. The summary at the end recapitulates what you have said.

To speak effectively, pay attention to these key oral communication elements:

- Articulation
- Emphasis
- Eye contact
- Body language
- Audience feedback
- Handling questions
- Performing and directing yourself at the same time
- Summarizing

Speaking and listening properly require much effort. Provide variation in your presentation if you have to speak longer than one hour and schedule breaks.

APPENDIX D
Attending a Presentation

Proper listening is important to avoid subjective impressions while planning and developing information systems. If listening is so important, why is it so difficult? One reason may be that we are flooded with all sorts of communications, ranging from television to telephone calls and meetings. This abundance may well result in our not paying enough attention to communications for which listening is important.

Most of the time we can listen passively, or casually, and get a general impression of what is going on. But when the communication matters, you should switch to active or conscious listening. Active listening requires much more effort, so only do it when necessary.

The purpose of active listening is to understand all that someone says, without being influenced by what you want to hear. You must purposely cut out subjective impressions, especially since you—like everyone else—tend to hear only what you want to hear. Listening, in fact, is most difficult when you strongly disagree with what people say. Your mind will probably be busy preparing your opinion and has no time to listen.

Often, it is important to listen between the lines, determining whether a speaker avoids an obvious topic, masks a real subject by something else, changes the subject before completing its discussion,

The following advice on listening is from [166]:

- Decide that you want to listen, and for what purpose.
- Decide how actively you want to listen.
- Decide whether you want to listen for facts or for ideas. Facts are easier to understand, but more difficult to remember. Ideas are often buried in facts, requiring analysis while you are listening.

Listening becomes easier once you have decided to listen and you know what to listen for. If you take notes, write down key words or short key phrases. Also number your notes (for example, 1a, 1b, and 1c) or indent them. This forces you to think about their structure and makes it easier to recall the information.

In military life, people acknowledge orders by repeating them. In civil life, you acknowledge that you heard by nodding, asking questions, stating your understanding of it, and stating your actions. You acknowledge important matters in writing, for example, a meeting report (Appendix G).

APPENDIX E
Having a Productive Meeting

Developers and users must attend many meetings to discuss plans, issues, and trade-offs in developing and using information systems. Productive meetings require preparation, and you cannot just sit with others and hope that something useful will come about.

To assure that meetings are productive, first plan and control meetings. Distribute an agenda beforehand to all invited, with points for discussion and the expected result—making it a self-fulfilling prophecy.

Establish and enforce the ground rules of the meeting. Rules can be formal or informal, depending upon the occasion. Make sure that goals and time limits for each point are clear from the agenda. Also make certain that all needed people are at the meeting, and no more. Delay a point if a key person cannot attend. Have someone take minutes of the meeting to record decisions.

There are many subtle ways to wreck a meeting, and the leader or the other participants may not understand the cause or have the ability to correct it. Quiet participants must be encouraged, while the most outspoken ones controlled, so that everyone feels like a contributor. Avoid situations in which people blame each other, find scapegoats, or justify themselves; such behavior blocks progress and serves no purpose. If a group meets regularly but not very effectively, it can be useful to discuss effectiveness in a separate meeting with an outside professional.

When discussing a controversial or complex subject, it is a good idea to outline it on a flipchart. Making a point visible acknowledges it and gives other people a chance to add to it; visualization also serves to achieve a common understanding. Use a work plan that shows dependencies and relationships for dealing with matters that require several meetings.

If there is no one to introduce a subject, use this technique to start the discussion: First, invite all participants to give key words for the subject. Write them on flipchart paper without comments. Group the key words that belong together, again without comments. A meaningful discussion can then start on what is and is not important in each group of concepts. London devotes [116] Chapter 11 to meetings. Use the following checklist to evaluate meetings.

MEETING CHECKLIST

Study beforehand any rules or procedures for conducting the meeting. Evaluate the meeting on the following points:

- How well was the meeting prepared by the leader? Consider these items:
  - Agenda and goals
  - Actions to be taken before the meeting
  - Supplied background and reference material
  - Suggested time constraints
  - Participants and whether all needed ones were invited and present
- How well did participants prepare for the meeting?
- What did you think of the leader's opening and preamble?
- How well were minutes or decisions of the previous meeting discussed?
- Note for each point on the agenda:
  - How well was the point introduced?
  - How was the flow of discussion?
    Exploratory → procedural → factual → decisive?
  - How disciplined was the discussion? Did the leader have to intervene? Why? Was everyone encouraged to say something?
  - Did the leader summarize after each point?
- How was the meeting wrapped up? Were decisions repeated? Was work to be done summarized?
- Did the meeting end on time?
- Were rules and procedures adhered to? Refer to Robert's Rules of Order when there are no other rules.
- Did all participants properly understand what happened at the meeting?
  - Did all participants feel that they contributed?

  - Did participants intervene on procedural issues?
- How well were the minutes or decisions recorded afterward?

APPENDIX F
Daydreaming and Brainstorming to Generate Ideas

Daydreaming stimulates our imagination. It is a way we speak to ourselves when we are awake. While daydreaming, we imagine things and situations. As Einstein observed, "Imagination is even more important than knowledge, for knowledge is limited, whereas imagination embraces the entire world." If you need much creativity to develop and use information systems, you need even more imagination. Without imagination, you cannot perform or even plan an activity.

As children, we heard fairy tales and other stories that brought us in contact with things and situations that we could not possibly experience otherwise. They stimulated our imagination. Although many people do not value daydreaming and imagining as skills for adults, they are the basis for all creative activities. Several books to stimulate your imagination are Ackoff [1], Adams [2], Halpern [81], von Oech [153], and Perkins [159].

Like daydreaming, brainstorming is a special technique to generate many creative ideas in a short time. In brainstorming, a group of people meet to generate many possible and impossible solutions with one person's imagination triggering another's. This technique is valuable when analytical thinking has provided a few solutions but has not produced the desired solution.

In order for brainstorming to be effective, however, you must plan and control the technique. First, there must be a clear reason for it, such as a problem for which no solution seems possible. Second, there must be a leader to guide the process. Third, there must be a group of up to fifteen people from as many different areas as possible.

The rules in a brainstorming session are that everyone must express his or her wildest thoughts, that each must use the wildest thoughts of others to come up with even wilder thoughts, and that every idea must be welcomed. It is very important to avoid any discussion or judgment of ideas. As the leader, you must strictly enforce these rules.

There are typically six phases in a brainstorming session:

1. Explain the rules of brainstorming.
2. State the original problem and discuss it.
3. Restate the problem in the form of one or more questions. Write the questions on a chart in the form of "How can we. . .?"
4. Brainstorm these questions, with the leader noting all ideas on charts and putting them up on the wall.
5. Select ideas from those shown to generate new combinations.
6. Conclude with a statement of how and when the evaluation will take place and how participants will be told the result.

Brainstorming sessions should not last more than a few hours because they are tiring due to the intense concentration needed. It is important that all ideas are visible to participants during brainstorming so they can help to generate new ideas. After the brainstorming, type all ideas, send a copy to all participants, and let insiders evaluate the ideas in a systematic way (Rawlinson [170]).

APPENDIX G
Writing a Meeting or Activity Report

When you attend a presentation (Appendix D) or meeting (Appendix E), it is a good idea to write a report about it, especially if you attended as representative of a group or an organization. You may also report on an activity you've performed. The report serves to inform other people of what happened and to clear your mind.

To make a report, you must know the answer to three key questions: Who is audience for the report? What must they understand? What attention will they pay to your report? The answers to these three questions will tell you what report to make, if any.

It obviously serves little purpose to prepare a fifty-page report if receivers only read the first page. In any case, put what you want to convey on the first page and let the necessary details follow. Attach a meeting's agenda to your report and use its structure for the details on decisions reached. Add who was present at the meeting and what important things they said. Also add a distribution list so receivers will know who has a copy.

Reporting on an activity to peers can be easier than reporting to management. Peers often take an interest in technical detail and argumentation. Managers are often busy and spend most of their time talking to other people instead of reading reports. They often take correspondence home to read in the evening.

For all people, be brief and clear, and suggest actions that might follow from your report. Remember, your report must not return with a question on it.

CHECKLIST FOR MEETING OR ACTIVITY REPORTS

Check your meeting or activity report by asking the following questions:

- Is the report addressed to all people who must know and may take action on items reported? Are others who must know on the "Copy for Information" list?
- Does the report have a one-page summary noting important items?
- Will the report be clear, concise, complete, and correct in the eyes of the addressees? (If necessary, put details such as an agenda or a work description in an attachment.)
- Are the purpose, place, and date of the meeting or activity correctly identified?
- Are the parties and participants present at the meeting or taking part in the activity correctly identified?
- Does your report identify all important items raised at the meeting or arising from the meeting? Does it identify all items discovered or accomplished by an activity?
- Have you chosen an optimum structuring method for your report, considering the information you want to convey? For example,
    - For a meeting: same sequence as an agenda
    - For a discussion: in a logical order of importance
    - For an activity: by subject
- Does your report propose actions, if any are needed?
- Does your report anticipate all questions the addressees may have?
- Is your report fair to all concerned? In other words, would you feel embarrassed if (apart from trade secrets) someone other than the addressees would read a copy of it?

APPENDIX H
Conducting an Interview

Interviews are used extensively to plan a new application, especially with knowledge systems. Their vital purpose is for the interviewers to understand the user environment, how the application can fit into it, and what are the application requirements. Especially for knowledge systems, the knowledge in the minds of human experts must be discovered and made explicit. Interviews must often provide the sound basis for application development.

There are two main types of interview: structured and unstructured. In a structured interview, you prepare all questions beforehand. In an unstructured interview, you only define general topics and use ad hoc questions to discover facts and opinions (Weinberg [208]).

Information obtained during an interview must not be colored by the views of the interviewer. Don't use directive questions, such as "You like this great book, don't you?" Use neutral questions instead, such as "What do you think of this book?"

Rogers, the American psychologist, invented a powerful technique called *reflecting* (also called *mirroring*) to ask nondirective questions [176]. The technique is to start with a general question. From there, reflect every answer into another question, asking for further explanation or just repeating the statement and waiting. This is an efficient way to obtain neutral information; in fact, you can also use it in any human communication. (Weizenbaum implemented this technique in a program called ELIZA [210, 211], but remember that reflecting requires empathy—true understanding of the other person—to be useful [176].)

Nondirective interviewing is very important in information system development. You need it to understand existing organizations and procedures and to establish detailed processing requirements, avoiding subjective impressions.

Because interviews are relatively expensive, they should be well planned and conducted properly. Design an interview so that you can easily summarize its results afterward. Make interviews go right the first time because you will seldom get a second chance. Use trial interviews to test your procedures. London devotes [116] Chapter 5 to interviewing.

APPENDIX I
Talking Person to Person

Speaking one to one can have a concrete purpose to resolve issues within an organization. The initiator establishes the purpose of the talk, which may be to gather general information. The content and format of talks often depend on the roles participants have in the organization.

Because each person-to-person talk is different, I can only give some general recommendations:

1. For the talk to be efficient, the invited person may need to prepare and therefore must understand the purpose beforehand. Initiators should hold a surprise talk only when the surprise is pleasant. People invited should ask for a postponement if they feel threatened and need time to prepare for an effective discussion.

2. Stop a person-to-person talk when you realize your opening leads to nothing but frustration for both sides. Since it is often impossible to recover from an improper opening {2.12}, restart later with a proper opening.

3. Avoid negative emotions from either side. Confining yourself to facts and fact-supported views will keep the discussion orderly and effective.

4. In a directive talk, be clear in what you have to say and how you say it. Be happy when there is reason to be happy and serious when there is reason to be serious. Euphemisms, insincerity, and dressing serve no purpose. What needs to be said must be said.

5. In a nondirective talk, be neutral. Use the "reflecting" technique of asking nondirective questions (Appendix H).

6. Delaying a request—a form of denial—can be the least offensive, but it is also the hardest form of response to overcome. Conversely, don't ask a question if you cannot accept no for an answer.
7. Don't ask unnecessary questions, and don't give answers to questions not asked.
8. Avoid fear on either side; it is detrimental to effective communication.
9. Respect the other person; it is the only basis for effective and efficient person-to-person talks.

APPENDIX J
Negotiating for Agreement

Let us never negotiate out of fear.
But let us never fear to negotiate.
—John F. Kennedy

We negotiate in one form or another almost every time we speak, and we negotiate whenever we try to achieve something through someone else, often in the form of a suggestion. Negotiating is a form of role playing to reach an agreement. Many negotiations are necessary in organizations that develop and use information systems to reach agreements that are fair to all parties.

Negotiating is a form of role playing and communication involving a variety of strategies. In this appendix, I'll discuss the preferred strategy: In a win/win strategy, parties seek an agreement that is in the best interest of the organization they belong to.

In any strategy, as with any communication, a proper start is important. First get the attention of the person you want to negotiate with, by becoming interested in him or her. Active listening is a neutral way of having an interest and obtaining useful information for the later negotiation.

The second part of the introduction is to establish what you have in common and to clarify each other's role. If you have little in common, try paraphrasing what the other party said or did and ask whether your understanding is correct.

Negotiation also requires planning. Use the first three elements of the ISVIC procedure to do this (you must determine implementation at the negotiation table). Flexibility is the key to successful negotiation. Objective analysis makes you understand the three major factors that determine your negotiating strategy:

- *Information* about the negotiated subject, your needs and abilities, and those of the other parties. You must understand what is at stake and what strategy to use. You must also understand how other parties view the subject. You will be in a bad negotiating position if your basic assumptions contain subjective impressions and are proved wrong.
- *Time limits* that exist for you and other parties, and that will affect negotiations. Time is almost always a major factor in negotiations and you must understand it well.
- *Power* that you and others have affects what you consider a best agreement.

Here are some general observations on performing the actual negotiating process (Fisher and Ury [61]):

1. Talk about positions only to understand them, not to discuss their pros and cons. People often defend their views and ideas as if they were their children; avoid strong emotions.
2. Separate the people from the subject. People will react fiercely when they are attacked personally. Rationally consider the subject and the interests of all parties.
3. Consider all possibilities before reaching an agreement. Every party should end up feeling that all options were considered and that a best agreement was reached.
4. Discuss criteria for reaching an agreement. This will provide the objective rationale for the agreement.
5. Keep talking until everyone is satisfied that the agreement is best overall. Negotiating ends when you stop talking.
6. Be patient. Agreements are often reached at or beyond the deadline.

To summarize: Negotiating starts with an exploratory opening, with the purpose of understanding, not confrontation. A second phase can be diagnostic, in which you analyze the situation together. Collaboration is key in a win/win strategy; look at options in the same direction rather than from opposing directions. To continue good working relationships, it is a must that all parties get a fair deal from the negotiation. As in all forms of communication, negotiation builds on trust. Trust shows your willingness to negotiate and to play fair. Negotiations fail when there is no trust.

APPENDIX K
Elements of a Manual

Manuals are an important material evidence of software, often the only kind. Besides being pleasant to read, they should be well organized, so readers can find what they need. Here is a summary of the elements of a user manual:

- Front cover, stating the product's name and the type of manual
- Title page, which may include product details and a full address of the company
- Copyright page, containing details about the edition, copyrights, and trademarks
- Section on safety procedures to be followed when using the product
- Preface, stating the manual's purpose, the relation of its content to specific user groups, instructions on using the manual, and prerequisites to its use
- Guide to other manuals, indicating its relationship to other manuals for the product
- Table of contents, listing the part and chapter titles, section headings, and page numbers
- List of illustrations and tables, including captions and page numbers
- Summary of changes, listing any revisions made since the last version
- Definition of symbols
- Text, divided into parts, chapters, and sections (the introduction gives an overview of terminology and concepts; bars in the margin show changes since the last version)

- Appendices, containing overviews and details that would disturb the logical flow of the text; order the appendices with letters
- Glossary, explaining special terms and abbreviations used
- Bibliography, including details about other publications
- Index
- Reader's comment form, to give feedback to the writing group
- Back cover, stating the publication number and company information

Section 8.2 discusses writing a user manual. Designing and making an index follows in Appendix L.

APPENDIX L
Designing and Making an Index

Design an index so readers can easily find what they are looking for. It must have enough entry points to be comprehensive, but not so many that the index becomes unwieldy. To make a useful index, anticipate what readers, both novice and expert, will want to look up. Index all important items, but include only their relevant occurrences. Begin the index when the complete text is available and the page numbers will not change, unless you can mark index entries in your word processor. Then use the analysis part of ISVIC to design an index structure as follows:

1. *Investigating* to understand what your readers will be looking for. Gather all concepts, words, acronyms, author names, abbreviations, and anything else that a reader may look up.
2. *Structuring* entries in alphabetic order is a mechanical task. A workable technique is to write the entries on cards and manually sort them. If you put the entries in a database, the computer can sort them for you. Using a computer simplifies the making of design iterations after verifying a printout of the index structure.
3. *Verifying* is a visual check of the index structure to see whether all entries are in the right place and to check for duplications and omissions. When you are satisfied with the index design, you are ready to add page numbers.
4. *Implementing* by adding the page numbers on which relevant text for the entry is found. If you start your use of the entry word with a definition, the first page number always refers to that definition.
5. *Checking* the conciseness, completeness, and correctness is the very last activity. Remember that page numbers may change if text is added or deleted.

It is certainly possible to combine the two steps of designing and building an index for simple manuals. But if your readers really need an index to find things, you and your readers are better off with an index that is designed and then built. A good index is one of the most useful parts of a book. It takes time to make, but it can save readers much time for them to find what they need.

APPENDIX M

Keeping a Diary as an Aid to Memory

Keeping a diary and reviewing it regularly will help you become conscious of your activities and thereby achieve more with less effort and more satisfaction. A diary serves as an aid to memory. It only requires a notebook and some discipline.

Always have your notebook with you when talking with people, to record decisions and things to do. Use the right side to record facts while you talk. Use the left side to note goals, decisions, things to do, and assumptions that need checking, while you talk or review.

Review your diary regularly, adding new items on the left side that require attention and ticking off items dealt with. When reading your diary, reflect on how you work and how you can improve your role. Use a diary for your benefit, not to check up on other people.

Reflecting is a powerful way to become more successful in what you undertake. Make it a daily routine to take ten minutes to consider the results of the day's work and to plan tomorrow's work. On the following day, make your plan a self-fulfilling prophecy.

APPENDIX N
Nonverbal Communication

There are more things in heaven and earth, Horatio,
Than are dreamt of in your philosophy.
—W. Shakespeare, *Hamlet* [192]

Words are often the least important part of a message: We project an image and receive an impression of others. According to Mehrabian [130, 131], 55 percent of what people respond to in our messages is nonverbal, 38 percent is vocal tone, and only 7 percent is words. In case of a contradiction, nonverbal behavior will likely determine the impact. This is why nonverbal communication is so important in human communication and therefore in automation.

There are two unique personalities involved in communication: a sender and a receiver. They each give a personal touch to the communication in several ways:

- Emotions, opinions, values, motivations, and expectations "color" true meaning.
- The communication affects your self-respect and can either motivate you or make it difficult for you to understand the real message.
- The sender's and the recipient's respective roles affect the communication.
- Body language is often an important addition to the spoken words.

Nonverbal factors—the personal side of communication—are an expression of our uniqueness. This side uses another channel to communicate matters that words cannot readily express. Perhaps we overcome the ambiguities of natural language by making use of these nonverbal factors. We add our personal touches unconsciously and process the personal touches of others intuitively, possibly to check trustworthiness and intentions.

We can learn to control nonverbal communication in a practical training situation, and by watching other people. An awareness of them helps to improve our communication skills. Some people are born nonverbal communicators. In the extreme case, people control their nonverbal factors so well that they can deceive us.

Here are some recommendations on nonverbal communication to help you best get your message across:

- Use the proper undertone. Smile when the message is happy and don't smile when it is unhappy.
- Be positive. People like to hear what is the matter. They have little interest in what is not the matter.
- Be confident. Confidence is the best promoter in communication. Say what needs to be said without fear, because fear is the worst promoter.
- Respect other people. Everyone has the right to have emotions, feelings, and opinions; they make an individual unique. Consider them without trying to manipulate them.
- Avoid judging other people. If you must make a judgment, judge the behavior not the person. People can change their behavior only after understanding why it is improper in a given situation.
- Be specific in stating your goal. Help the other person easily understand what you really want.
- Be flexible in how to reach your goal. There are a thousand ways to get there. Let the other person choose the way.
- Use a helping orientation. Look at problems from the same viewpoint; avoid opposing views that may cause conflicts.
- Tell people what you are going to tell them and why, so they can place your message. And tell them what you told them, so they can verify correct understanding. The 3T formula can help you overcome nonverbal obstacles.
- Improve your understanding of the human world by exposing yourself to its many and varied aspects. Understanding will help you communicate to other people.

Implicit behavior is an expression of your intentions and attitudes. Instead of controlling your implicit behavior, it is much simpler to have the right attitude.

Glossary

Acceptance test. A test to determine whether a system fulfills specified criteria.

Activity. A task carried out in the life cycle of an information system during development or use.

Analysis. The systematic breakdown of a complex subject to structure it for design; precedes *synthesis.*

Application. An organizational process that is computerized; for example, airline reservations or on-line banking.

Architecture. The logical structure (or part) of an information system; the parts and their relationships.

Auditability. The capability of a system to be assessed of its effectiveness and efficiency of the investment in it; includes the provision for an audit trail of data manipulation, program execution, and access attempts.

Batch. An information processing mode in which jobs are started by the computer operator; contrast with *interactive.*

Brainstorming. A technique for generating many ideas in a seemingly unstructured meeting to produce the best solution to a problem.

Business model. A model of essential organizational processes.

Certification. A written guarantee that an information system complies with specified requirements.

Computer center. The central group that runs computer systems for other groups.

Computerization. The implementation of organizational processes by means of a computer system in concert with people.

Computer system. A combination of hardware and software, integrated for a specific purpose.

Conception. The act or power to conceive an idea in the mind, forming a mental model.

Conceptual model. A visual representation of an entity or concept, made to understand and check its validity.

Configuration management. Identification, definition, and verification of software components, to control changes to a particular version and those from version to version.

Data. A collection of characters that is interpreted by an information system to form information.

Database. A means to store and retrieve data.

Development documentation. Description of the architecture and design of the software for developers.

Documentation. Text and illustrations explaining the structure and use of something; see also *development documentation, phase documentation, user documentation.*

Effectiveness. Achieving a goal by doing the right things; that is, a high effectiveness requires less effort.

Efficiency. The ratio of result to effort required; that is, a high efficiency results from doing things the right way.

End user. The person who works at a computer terminal, often just called a *user.*

Ergonomics. A synonym for *human factors,* derived from the Greek words "ergon" (work) and "nomos" (laws of).

Feedback. A response showing the effect of an action; also called *reinforcement.*

Groupthink. "A deterioration of mental efficiency, reality testing, and moral judgment that results from in-group pressures" (Janis [102]).

Hardware. The material parts of a computer, including printers and terminals; supplements *software* and *otherware.*

Hidden agenda. Implicit assumptions that are not verified with other people; an addition to *groupthink.*

Hierarchy. A concept in which some elements are subordinate to another element in a tree structure.

Human factors. All factors that contribute to the efficiency, satisfaction, and well-being of end users doing their job at the physical, psychological, and social levels; see also *ergonomics.*

Information. The data, text, and graphics processed and thereby made meaningful to people by using known conventions.

Information center. A central group in a user organization to help end users work with large computer databases.

Information plan. A plan that describes how all information will be used in an organization; contains information models.

Information processing. Arranging data into meaningful information; four basic forms are transaction, output, decision, and informal information processing.

Information system. A system, consisting of *hardware, software,* and *otherware,* capable of collecting, processing, protecting, and distributing *information.*

Input. Data entered into a system or process.

Interactive. A mode that starts processing directly from a terminal; contrast with *batch.*

ISVIC. A procedure to investigate, structure, verify, implement, and check a situation, problem, or system from a human point of view.

Life cycle. A repetitive series of activities to keep an information system current; includes planning, development, and use.

Logical. As perceived, independent of an implementation technology; contrast with *physical.*

Maintenance. The final stage in information system development, to keep it current.

MBO. Management by objectives, a formalized procedure to plan and control human activities.

Mental model. A representation that people have in their head.

Mind. The spiritual power of the human being.

Mind set. The disposition of a person to think or act in a particular way; also called mental set or set.

Model. A representation of an entity or concept; a pattern; see also *conceptual model, mental model.*

Network. Interconnections between terminals and computers; informal connections between people.

Objectives. Description of the goals for a development project.

Off-line. Not connected to a computer; contrast with *on-line.*

On-line. An end user's ability to interact directly with a computer; contrast with *off-line.*

Operations. The group that enables, monitors, and controls the running of an information system.

Organization. A group of people and facilities structured to achieve certain goals; for example, an enterprise, a business, or an institution; the structure itself.

Otherware. All items other than hardware and software, necessary to operate an information system; includes all users.

Output. The result of an operation or process in a computer system.

Panel. The information displayed in a window on the screen of a terminal (VDT).

PC. Personal computer; a small computer originally intended for a single user.

Perception. The process by which we become aware through our five senses of things or changes.

Phase. A stage in the life cycle of an information system, which is completed with a review; may consist of part of an activity, a single activity, or multiple activities.

Phase documentation. Description of the status of a development project for review at the end of each development phase.

Phase process. The formalized procedure to develop and use an information system in stages.

Physical. Characteristic of a particular implementation technology; existing in reality; contrast with *logical.*

Pilot test. A first trial of using a developed system, typically at the user's site.

Power. The ability to influence other people.

Privacy. Freedom (as related to information processing) from having personal information on paper or contained in a database.

Process. A defined series of events achieved under given conditions.

Program. A set of instructions that a computer is capable of interpreting and executing; part of *software.*

Pygmalion effect. A synonym for the *self-fulfilling prophecy.* Pygmalion was a mythological king of Cyprus who carved a statue that came to life with the help of Aphrodite.

Quality assurance. The organizational process used to ensure desirable characteristics in software during its development.

Reinforcement. Another word for *feedback,* a response showing the effect or quality of an action.

Requirements. The capabilities needed by a user to perform an application.

Role. Expected behavior patterns attributed to a person.

Safety. Freedom from danger while using a computer.

Screen. The glass window of a VDT on which panels are displayed.

Security. The protection of hardware, software, and information from unauthorized access, modification, or destruction; includes prevention of malicious disclosure of information.

Self-actualization. The property of being self-aware, self-controlled, and self-competent.

Self-fulfilling prophecy. A statement, expression, or thought that causes itself to happen; also called *Pygmalion effect.*

Self-respect. Respect for one's own character, an important part of our self-image; also called self-esteem.

Senses. The special faculties of the body by which a person is conscious of things; the five senses are sight, hearing, smell, taste, and touch.

Software. The set of computer programs, procedures, and their associated documentation; supplements *hardware* and *otherware.*

Structure. The arrangement of the parts in a whole; also called *model* or view.

Support. The group or function that introduces and helps end users to interact with an information system.

Supporting materials. Manuals, guides, reference cards, training materials, and so on, made available with a computer system to aid in its use.

Synthesis. The building and combination of parts to form a new whole; follows *analysis.*

System test. A test carried out by the development group to check proper operation of the information system.

Technology. The means used to build hardware and software.

Terminal. The physical device, part of a workstation or network, used to communicate with an information system; also known as *VDT* or CRT.

Transaction. A means to transmit an action to an information system.

User. A person or the group using computer systems and their results in an organization; includes *end user(s).*

User documentation. Description of the operations of hardware and software for the user.

User representative. A person in the development organization who represents the interests of future users of a system under development.

VDT. Video display terminal; also improperly known as a cathode ray tube or CRT.

Win/win strategy. A negotiating strategy whereby all parties come to a mutually satisfactory agreement.

Window. Part of the screen of a VDT where a program communicates with an end user.

Workstation. A VDT, special furniture, and other means that make up the workplace for an end user.

Bibliography

[1] Ackoff, R.L. *The Art of Problem Solving.* New York: John Wiley & Sons, 1978.

[2] Adams, J.L. *Conceptual Blockbusting.* San Francisco: W.H. Freeman & Co., 1974.

[3] Alvesson, M. *Organization Theory and Technocratic Consciousness: Rationality, Ideology and Quality of Work.* Berlin: Walter de Gruyter & Co., 1987.

[4] Ansoff, H.I. *Strategic Management.* London: Macmillan, 1979.

[5] Argyris, C. *Interpersonal Competence and Organizational Effectiveness.* Homewood, Ill.: Richard D. Irwin, Inc., 1962.

[6] ________. *Integrating the Individual and the Organization.* New York: John Wiley & Sons, 1964.

[7] Aron, J.P. *The Program Development Process, Part I: The Individual Programmer.* Reading, Mass.: Addison-Wesley, 1974.

[8] ________. *The Program Development Process, Part II: The Programming Team.* Reading, Mass.: Addison-Wesley, 1983.

[9] Aronson, E. *The Social Animal.* San Francisco: W.H. Freeman & Co., 1976.

[10] Baddeley, A.D. *The Psychology of Memory.* New York: Harper & Row, 1976.

[11] ________. *Your Memory: A User's Guide.* New York: Basic Books, 1982.

[12] Barnes, L.B. "Managing the Paradox of Organizational Trust," *Harvard Business Review,* Vol. 59, No. 2 (March-April 1981), Reprint No. 81201, pp. 107-16.

[13] Becker, W.C., et al. *Teaching: A Course in Applied Psychology.* Chicago: Science Research Assoc., 1971.

[14] Blanchard, K., and S. Johnson. *The One Minute Manager.* New York: William Morrow & Co., 1982.

[15] Blanchard, K., and N.V. Peale. *Management and Ethics.* New York: William Morrow & Co., 1988.

[16] Block, J.H., ed. *Mastery Learning: Theory and Practice.* New York: Holt, Rinehart & Winston, 1971.

[17] Blokdijk, A., and P. Blokdijk. *Planning and Design of Information Systems.* London: Academic Press, 1987.

[18] Boehm, B.W. *Software Engineering Economics.* Englewood Cliffs, N.J.: Prentice-Hall, 1987.

[19] ________, and P.N. Papaccio. "Understanding and Controlling Software Costs," *IEEE Transactions on Software Engineering,* Vol. 14, No. 10 (October 1988), pp. 1462-77. Reprinted in T. DeMarco and T. Lister, eds. *Software State-of-the-Art: Selected Papers.* New York: Dorset House Publishing, 1990.

[20] Bolter, J.D. *Turing's Man.* Chapel Hill, N.C.: University of North Carolina Press, 1984.

[21] Booch, G. *Software Engineering With ADA.* Menlo Park, Calif.: Benjamin-Cummings Publishing Co., 1983.

[22] Boulding, K. *The Image: Knowledge in Life and Society.* Ann Arbor, Mich.: Ann Arbor Paperbacks, 1961.

[23] Bradshaw, P. *The Management of Self-Esteem.* Englewood Cliffs, N.J.: Prentice-Hall, 1982.

[24] Brooks, F.P., Jr. *The Mythical Man-Month.* Reading, Mass.: Addison-Wesley, 1982.

[25] ________. "No Silver Bullet," *Computer,* Vol. 20, No. 4 (April 1987), pp. 10-19. Reprinted in T. DeMarco and T. Lister, eds. *Software State-of-the-Art: Selected Papers.* New York: Dorset House Publishing, 1990.

[26] Burns, J.M. *Leadership.* New York: Harper & Row, 1978.

[27] Buzan, T. *Use Both Sides of Your Brain.* New York: E.P. Dutton, 1977.

[28] ________. *Speed Reading.* New York: E.P. Dutton, 1984.

[29] ________. *Use Your Perfect Memory.* New York: E.P. Dutton, 1984.

[30] Card, S.K., T.P. Moran, and A. Newell. *The Psychology of Human-Computer Interaction.* Hillsdale, N.J.: Analytic Press, 1980.

[31] Carroll, J.M. "The Adventure of Getting to Know a Computer," *Computer,* Vol. 15, No. 11 (November 1982), pp. 49-58.

[32] Carroll, L. *The Complete Illustrated Works.* London: Chancellor Press, 1982.

[33] Copland, A. *What to Listen for in Music.* New York: McGraw-Hill, 1939.

[34] Coren, S., and J.S. Girgus. *Seeing Is Deceiving: The Psychology of Visual Illusions.* Hillsdale, N.J.: Analytic Press, 1978.

[35] Craik, K.J.W. *The Nature of Explanation.* Cambridge, England: Cambridge University Press, 1943.

[36] Crosby, P.B. *Quality Is Free: The Art of Making Quality Certain.* New York: McGraw-Hill, 1979.

[37] Crystal, D. *The Cambridge Encyclopedia of Language.* Cambridge, England: Cambridge University Press, 1987.

[38] Curtis, B., ed. *Human Factors in Software Development.* Amsterdam: North-Holland, 1986.

[39] ________, et al. "A Field Study of the Software Design for Large Systems," *Communications of the ACM,* Vol. 31, No. 11 (November 1988), pp. 1268-87.

[40] Davies, I.K. *Objectives in Curriculum Design.* New York: McGraw-Hill, 1976.

[41] ________. *Instructional Technique.* New York: McGraw-Hill, 1981.

[42] Dean, M. "Using Experimental Psychology in Technical Writing," Pittsburgh: *Proceedings of the 28th International Technical Communication Conference* (May 1981).

[43] ________. "How a Computer Should Talk to People," *IBM Systems Journal,* Vol. 21, No. 4 (1982), pp. 424-53.

[44] DeMarco, T. *Structured Analysis and System Specification.* Englewood Cliffs, N.J.: Prentice-Hall, 1978.

[45] ________. *Controlling Software Projects: Management, Measurement & Estimation.* Englewood Cliffs, N.J.: Prentice-Hall, 1982.

[46] ________, and T. Lister. *Peopleware: Productive Projects and Teams.* New York: Dorset House Publishing, 1987.

[47] Dessler, G. *Organization Theory.* Englewood Cliffs, N.J.: Prentice-Hall, 1986.

[48] Dow, G. *Learning to Teach: Teaching to Learn.* London: Routledge & Kegan Paul, 1985.

[49] Dreyfus, H.L. *What Computers Can't Do.* New York: Harper & Row, 1972.

[50] ________, and S.E. Dreyfus. *Mind Over Machine.* New York: The Free Press, 1986.

[51] Drucker, P.F. *Management: Tasks, Responsibilities, Practices.* New York: Harper & Row, 1974.

[52] Dudley, G.A. *Increase Your Learning Power.* North Hollywood, Calif.: Wilshire Book Co., 1966.

[53] Dyer, W.W. *Your Erroneous Zones.* New York: Harper & Row, 1976.

[54] ________. *Pulling Your Own Strings.* New York: T.Y. Crowell, 1978.

[55] Ellis, A. *Executive Leadership: A Rational Approach.* New York: Citadel Books, 1982.

[56] ________, and R.A. Harper. *A New Guide to Rational Living.* North Hollywood, Calif.: Wilshire Book Co., 1975.

[57] *Ergonomics Handbook.* IBM Corp., IBM SV04-0224. Armonk, N.Y.: 1985.

[58] Fagan, M.E. "Design and Code Inspections to Reduce Errors in Program Development," *IBM Systems Journal,* Vol. 15, No. 3 (1976), pp. 182-211.

[59] Farnsworth, T. *Power Plays.* London: Arrow Books, 1988.

[60] Fielding, J.S. "What Do You Mean, You Don't Like My Style," *Harvard Business Review,* Vol. 60, No. 3 (May-June 1982), pp. 128-38.

[61] Fisher, R., and W. Ury. *Getting to YES: Negotiating Agreement Without Giving In.* Boston: Houghton Mifflin, 1981.

[62] Flesch, R. *The Art of Clear Thinking.* New York: Collier Books, 1971.

[63] ________. *How to Write, Speak, and Think More Effectively.* New York: Harper & Row, 1975.

[64] Flores, F.C., and T. Winograd. *Understanding Computers and Cognition.* Reading, Mass.: Addison-Wesley, 1987.

[65] Fowler, H.W. *A Dictionary of Modern English Usage.* Oxford: Oxford University Press, 1975.

[66] Furst, C. *Origins of the Mind.* Englewood Cliffs, N.J.: Prentice-Hall, 1979.

[67] Galbraith, J.R. *Organization Design.* Reading, Mass.: Addison-Wesley, 1977.

[68] Gane, C., and T. Sarson. *Structured Systems Analysis: Tools & Techniques.* Englewood Cliffs, N.J.: Prentice-Hall, 1979.

[69] Gardner, H. *Frames of Mind: The Theory of Multiple Intelligences.* New York: Basic Books, 1983. (Also London: Heinemann, 1983).

[70] Gause, D.C., and G.M. Weinberg. *Exploring Requirements: Quality Before Design.* New York: Dorset House Publishing, 1989.

[71] Gazda, G.M., et al. *Theories of Learning.* Itasca, Ill.: F.E. Peacock Publishers, 1980.

[72] Gentner, D., and A.L. Stevens. *Mental Models.* Hillsdale, N.J.: Analytic Press, 1983.

[73] Gilb, T. *Principles of Software Engineering Management.* Reading, Mass.: Addison-Wesley, 1988.

[74] Goldkind, S. *Machines and Intelligence.* Westport, Conn.: Greenwood Press, 1987.

[75] Goleman, D. *Vital Lies, Simple Truths: The Psychology of Self-Deception.* New York: Simon & Schuster, 1985.

[76] Goodman, P.S., et al. *Change in Organizations.* San Francisco: Jossey-Bass, 1982.

[77] Gregory, R.L., ed. *The Oxford Companion of the Mind.* Oxford: Oxford University Press, 1987.

[78] Gross, J. *The Oxford Book of Aphorisms.* Oxford: Oxford University Press, 1987.

[79] *A Guide to Using Color.* IBM Corp., IBM G320-6296. Armonk, N.Y.: 1985.

[80] Gyllenhamar, P.G. *People at Work.* Reading, Mass.: Addison-Wesley, 1977.

[81] Halpern, D.F. *Thought and Knowledge: An Introduction to Critical Thinking.* Hillsdale, N.J.: Analytic Press, 1984.

[82] Hambly, K. *How to Improve Your Confidence.* London: Sheldon Press, 1987.

[83] Handy, C. *Understanding Organizations.* Harmondsworth, England: Penguin, 1984.

[84] Harrison, R. "Understanding Your Organization's Character," *Harvard Business Review,* Vol. 50, No. 3 (May-June 1972), pp. 119-28.

[85] *Harvard Business Review.* "On Human Relations, Vol. 3" (PL 1337). New York: Harper & Row, 1986, pp. 119-28.

[86] Haugeland, J. *Artificial Intelligence: The Very Idea.* Cambridge, Mass.: MIT Press, 1985.

[87] Havel, V. *Living in Truth.* Amsterdam: Meulenhoff, 1986.

[88] Heider, J. *The Tao of Leadership.* New York: Bantam Books, 1986.

[89] Heinich, R., et al. *Instructional Media.* New York: John Wiley & Sons, 1985.

[90] Hersey, P., and K. Blanchard. *Management of Organizational Behavior.* Englewood Cliffs, N.J.: Prentice-Hall, 1982.

[91] Herzberg, F., et al. *The Motivation to Work.* New York: John Wiley & Sons, 1959.

[92] Hilgard, E.R., R.C. Atkinson, and R.L. Atkinson. *Introduction to Psychology.* New York: Harcourt Brace Jovanovich, 1975.

[93] Hughes, J.L. *Programmed Instruction for Schools and Industry.* Chicago: Science Research Assoc., 1962.

[94] Hunt, D.E., and E.V. Sullivan. *Between Psychology and Education.* Hinsdale, Ill.: Dryden Press, 1974.

[95] Hunt, M. *The Universe Within.* Brighton, England: Harvester Press, 1982.

[96] Huxley, J. *Man in the Modern World.* New York: Harper Brothers, 1948.

[97] *IEEE Software.* Vol. 4, No. 5 (September 1987). Special issue on Software Quality Assurance.

[98] *IEEE Software.* Vol. 5, No. 2 (March 1988). Special issue on Computer-Aided Software Engineering.

[99] *IFIP 1970 World Conference on Computer Education Proceedings.* Amsterdam: August 24-28, 1970.

[100] Jackson, M.A. *Principles of Program Design.* London: Academic Press, 1975.

[101] ________. *Systems Development.* Englewood Cliffs, N.J.: Prentice-Hall, 1983.

[102] Janis, I.L. *Victims of Groupthink.* Boston: Houghton Mifflin, 1972.

[103] Jensen, R.W., and C.C. Tonies. *Software Engineering.* Englewood Cliffs, N.J.: Prentice-Hall, 1979.

[104] Juran, J.M. *Quality Planning and Analysis.* New York: McGraw-Hill, 1970.

[105] ________. *Quality Control Handbook.* New York: McGraw-Hill, 1974.

[106] Katz, D., and R.L. Kahn. *The Social Psychology of Organization.* New York: John Wiley & Sons, 1966.

[107] Kearsly, G., ed. *Artificial Intelligence and Instruction.* Reading, Mass.: Addison-Wesley, 1987.

[108] Kepner, C., and B.B. Tregoe. *The Rational Manager.* New York: McGraw-Hill, 1965.

[109] Kidder, T. *The Soul of a New Machine.* Boston: Little, Brown and Co., 1981.

[110] Kitto, H.D.F. *The Greeks.* Harmondsworth, England: Penguin, 1957.

[111] Knight, D. *Ordering the World.* London: Burnett Books, 1981.

[112] Korda, M. *Power! How to Get It, How to Use It.* New York: Random House, 1975.

[113] Laing, R.D. *Wisdom, Madness & Folly.* London: Macmillan, 1985.

[114] Lammers, S. *Programmers at Work.* Redmond, Wash.: Microsoft Press, 1986.

[115] Lindsay, P.H., and D.A. Norman. *An Introduction to Psychology.* New York: Academic Press, 1977.

[116] London, K. *The People Side of Systems.* London: John Wiley & Sons, 1976.

[117] Machiavelli, N. *The Prince.* Harmondsworth, England: Penguin, 1986.

[118] Maier, N.R.F. *The Appraisal Interview.* New York: John Wiley & Sons, 1966.

[119] Mann, N.R. *The Keys to Excellence.* Santa Monica, Calif.: Prestwick Books, 1987.

[120] *A Manual of Style,* 12th ed. rev. Chicago: University of Chicago Press, 1969.

[121] Marder, D. *The Craft of Technical Writing.* New York: Macmillan, 1960.

[122] Martin, J. *Application Development Without Programmers.* Englewood Cliffs, N.J.: Prentice-Hall, 1982.

[123] ________. *Strategic Data Planning Methodologies.* Englewood Cliffs, N.J.: Prentice-Hall, 1982.

[124] Maslow, A.H. *Toward a Psychology of Being.* New York: Van Nostrand Reinhold, 1968.

[125] ________. *Motivation and Personality.* New York: Harper & Row, 1970.

[126] McCormick, E.J. *Human Factors in Engineering and Design.* New York: McGraw-Hill, 1976.

[127] McGregor, D. *The Human Side of Enterprise.* New York: McGraw-Hill, 1960.

[128] ________. "An Uneasy Look at Performance Appraisal," *Harvard Business Review,* Vol. 50, No. 5 (reprinted September-October 1972), pp. 133-38.

[129] McMenamin, S.M., and J.F. Palmer. *Essential Systems Analysis.* Englewood Cliffs, N.J.: Prentice-Hall, 1984.

[130] Mehrabian, A. *Silent Messages.* Belmont, Calif.: Wadsworth Publishing, 1971.

[131] ________. *Nonverbal Communication.* Chicago: Aldine Atherton, 1972.

[132] Metzger, P.W. *Managing a Programming Project.* Englewood Cliffs, N.J.: Prentice-Hall, 1973.

[133] ________. *Managing Programming People: A Personal View.* Englewood Cliffs, N.J.: Prentice-Hall, 1987.

[134] Miller, D.W., and M.K. Starr. *Executive Decisions and Operations Research.* Englewood Cliffs, N.J.: Prentice-Hall, 1969.

[135] Miller, G.A. "The Magical Number Seven, Plus or Minus Two: Some Limits on Our Capacity for Processing Information," *The Psychological Review,* Vol. 63, No. 2 (March 1956), pp. 81-97.

[136] Miller, R.B. "Response Time in Man-Computer Conversational Transactions," Montvale, N.J.: *Proceedings of the 1977 AFIPS National Computer Conference,* pp. 409-21.

[137] Mills, J.A. "A Pragmatic View of the System Architect," *Communications of the ACM,* Vol. 28, No. 7 (July 1985), pp. 708-17.

[138] Mintzberg, H. *The Nature of Managerial Work.* New York: Harper & Row, 1973.

[139] ________. *The Structuring of Organizations.* Englewood Cliffs, N.J.: Prentice-Hall, 1979.

[140] ________. *Structure in Fives: Designing Effective Organizations.* Englewood Cliffs, N.J.: Prentice-Hall, 1983.

[141] Morse, J.J., and J.W. Lorsch. "Beyond Theory Y," *Harvard Business Review,* Vol. 48, No. 3 (May-June 1970), pp. 61-68.

[142] Mowrer, O.H. *Psychology of Language and Learning.* New York: Plenum Press, 1980.

[143] Mumford, E. *Designing Human Systems.* Manchester, England: Manchester Business School, 1983.

[144] Murphy, J. *Secrets of the I Ching.* West Nyack, N.Y.: Parker Publishing Co., 1970.

[145] Naisbitt, J. *Megatrends.* New York: Warner Books, 1982. (Also London: MacDonald & Co. Publishers Ltd., 1984).

[146] Newell, A., and H.A. Simon. *Human Problem Solving.* Englewood Cliffs, N.J.: Prentice-Hall, 1972.

[147] Nichelson, J., and M. Lucas. *All in the Mind.* London: Methuen, 1984.

[148] Nichelson, N., and T.D. Wall. *Theory and Practice of Organizational Psychology.* New York: Academic Press, 1982.

[149] Nickerson, R.S., et al. *The Teaching of Thinking.* Hillsdale, N.J.: Analytic Press, 1985.

[150] Nolan, R.L. *Managing the Data Resource Function.* St. Paul, Minn.: West Publishing, 1982.

[151] Norman, D.A. *The Psychology of Everyday Things.* New York: Basic Books, 1988.

[152] ________, and S.W. Draper. *User Centered Systems Design.* Hillsdale, N.J.: Analytic Press, 1986.

[153] Oech, R. von. *A Whack on the Side of the Head.* New York: Warner Books, 1983.

[154] Oncken, W., Jr., and D.L. Wass. "Management Time: Who's Got the Monkey?" *Harvard Business Review,* Vol. 52, No. 6 (November-December 1974), pp. 75-80.

[155] Ouchi, W.G. *Theory Z.* Reading, Mass.: Addison-Wesley, 1981.

[156] Paivio, A., and I. Begg. *Psychology of Language.* Englewood Cliffs, N.J.: Prentice-Hall, 1981.

[157] Pascale, R.T., and A.G. Athos. *The Art of Japanese Management.* Harmondsworth, England: Penguin, 1982.

[158] Payer, L. *Medicine and Culture.* New York: Henry Holt, 1988.

[159] Perkins, D.N. *The Mind's Best Work.* Cambridge, Mass.: Harvard University Press, 1981.

[160] Peter, L.J., and R. Hull. *The Peter Principle.* New York: William Morrow & Co., 1969.

[161] Peters, T.J. *Thriving on Chaos.* New York: Alfred A. Knopf, 1988. (Also London: Pan Books, 1989.)

[162] ________, and R.H. Waterman. *In Search of Excellence.* New York: Harper & Row, 1982.

[163] Pirsig, R.M. *Zen and the Art of Motorcycle Maintenance.* New York: Bantam Books, 1974.

[164] Plato. *The Republic,* trans. A.D. Lindsay. London: J.M. Dent, 1976.

[165] Price, J. *How to Write a Computer Manual.* Menlo Park, Calif.: Benjamin-Cummings Publishing Co., 1984.

[166] *Principles of Selective Listening.* New York: Argyle Publishing Corp., 1968.

[167] *Prisma-Citatenboek.* Utrecht: Het Spectrum, around 1950.

[168] *Quality System and Management Standards.* International Standards Organization, ISO 9000-9004. Geneva: 1987.

[169] Ragan, T.J. "The Oldest Medium," *Educational Technology* (May 1982), pp. 28-29.

[170] Rawlinson, J.G. *Creative Thinking and Brainstorming.* Farnborough, England: Gower Publishing, 1981.

[171] Reddin, W.J. *Managerial Effectiveness.* New York: McGraw-Hill, 1970.

[172] ________. *Effective Management by Objectives: The 3-D Method of MBO.* New York: McGraw-Hill, 1971.

[173] Robbins, S.P. *Organizational Behavior.* Englewood Cliffs, N.J.: Prentice-Hall, 1986.

[174] ________. *Organization Theory.* Englewood Cliffs, N.J.: Prentice-Hall, 1987.

[175] Rogers, C.R. *On Becoming a Person.* Boston: Houghton Mifflin, 1961.

[176] ________. *A Way of Being.* Boston: Houghton Mifflin, 1980.

[177] ________, and B. Stevens. *Person to Person: The Problem of Being Human.* Lafayette, Ind.: Real People Press, 1967.

[178] Rosenthal, R., and L. Jacobson. *Pygmalion in the Classroom.* New York: Holt, Rinehart & Winston, 1968.

[179] Rottenberg, A.T. *Elements of Argument.* New York: St. Martin's Press, 1985.

[180] Rule, J.B., et al. *The Politics of Privacy.* New York: New American Library, 1980.

[181] Russell, B. *The Analysis of Mind.* London: Allen & Unwin, 1921.

[182] ________. *The Conquest of Happiness.* London: Allen & Unwin, 1930.

[183] ________. *A History of Western Philosophy.* New York: Simon and Schuster, 1945.

[184] Russell, P. *The Brain Book.* New York: Hawthorn Books, 1979.

[185] Ryle, G. *The Concept of Mind.* Harmondsworth, England: Penguin, 1963.

[186] Sacks, O. *The Man Who Mistook His Wife for a Hat.* London: Gerald Duckworth & Co., 1985.

[187] St. Aubyn, G. *The Art of Argument.* New York: Taplinger Publishing, 1985.

[188] Sauter, S.L., et al. "Job and Health Implications for VDT Users," *Communications of the ACM,* Vol. 26, No. 4 (April 1983), pp. 284-94.

[189] Schank, R.C., and R.P. Abelson. *Scripts, Plan, Goals and Understanding.* Hillsdale, N.J.: Analytic Press, 1977.

[190] Schneider, M.L., and J.C. Thomas. *Human Factors in Computer Systems.* Norwood, N.J.: Ablex Publishing, 1984.

[191] Scott, W.G., et al. *Organization Theory: A Structural and Behavioral Analysis.* Homewood, Ill.: R.D. Irwin, 1981.

[192] Shakespeare, W. *The Illustrated Stratford Shakespeare.* London: Chancellor Press, 1982.

[193] Shneiderman, B. *Software Psychology: Human Factors in Designing the User Interface.* Boston: Little, Brown and Co., 1980.

[194] Smith, A. *The Body.* New York: Viking Press, 1968. (Also Harmondsworth, England: Penguin, 1985.)

[195] ________. *The Mind.* New York: Viking Press, 1984. (Also Harmondsworth, England: Penguin, 1985.)

[196] Smith, M.J. *When I Say No, I Feel Guilty.* New York: Dial Press, 1975.

[197] Snyder, C.R., and H.L. Fromkin. *Uniqueness.* New York: Plenum Press, 1980.

[198] Sternberg, R.J., and D.K. Detterman, eds. *What Is Intelligence?* Norwood, N.J.: Ablex Publishing, 1986.

[199] Stoner, J.A.F., and C. Wankel. *Management.* Englewood Cliffs, N.J.: Prentice-Hall, 1986.

[200] Strunk, W., and E.B. White. *Elements of Style.* New York: Macmillan, 1979.

[201] *System Application Architecture Common User Access: Basic Interface Design Guide* (IBM SC26-4583) and *Advanced Interface Design Guide* (IBM SC26-4582). IBM Corp. Armonk, N.Y.: 1989.

[202] Toffler, A. *Future Shock.* New York: Random House, 1970.

[203] Turner, W.S., et al. *Systems Development Methodology.* Amsterdam: North-Holland, 1987.

[204] Watson, T.J., Jr. *A Business and Its Beliefs.* New York: McGraw-Hill, 1963.

[205] *Webster Encyclopedic Dictionary of the English Language.* New York: Avenel Books, 1980 edition.

[206] Weinberg, G.M. *The Secrets of Consulting.* New York: Dorset House Publishing, 1985.

[207] ________. *Becoming a Technical Leader.* New York: Dorset House Publishing, 1986.

[208] ________. *Rethinking Systems Analysis & Design.* New York: Dorset House Publishing, 1988.

[209] ________. *Understanding the Professional Programmer.* New York: Dorset House Publishing, 1988.

[210] Weizenbaum, J. "ELIZA," *Communications of the ACM,* Vol. 9, No. 1 (January 1965), pp. 36-45.

[211] ________. *Computer Power and Human Reason.* San Francisco: W.H. Freeman & Co., 1976.

[212] Winograd, T. *Language as a Cognitive Process: Syntax.* Reading, Mass.: Addison-Wesley, 1983.

[213] Woodson, W.E. *Human Factors Design Handbook.* New York: McGraw-Hill, 1981.

[214] Yates, J.E. *Managing Stress.* New York: American Management Association, 1979.

[215] Yourdon, E. *Techniques of Program Structure and Design.* Englewood Cliffs, N.J.: Prentice-Hall, 1975.

[216] ________. *Managing the System Life Cycle.* Englewood Cliffs, N.J.: Prentice-Hall, 1982.

[217] ________, and L. Constantine. *Structured Design.* Englewood Cliffs, N.J.: Prentice-Hall, 1975.

Author Index

Subject Index